PLANNING AND IMPLEMENTING TECHNICAL SERVICES WORKSTATIONS

Michael Kaplan
Editor

AMERICAN LIBRARY ASSOCIATION
CHICAGO AND LONDON 1997

While extensive effort has gone into ensuring the reliability of information appearing in this book, the publisher makes no warranty, express or implied, as to the accuracy or reliability of the information, and does not assume and hereby disclaims any liability to any person for any loss or damage caused by errors or omissions in this publication.

Trademarked names appear in the text of this book. Rather than identify or insert a trademark symbol at the appearance of each name, the authors and the American Library Association state that the names are used for editorial purposes exclusively, to the ultimate benefit of the owners of the trademarks. There is absolutely no intention of infringement on the rights of the trademark owners.

Project editor: Joan A. Grygel

Text design and composition: Connie Richardson, the dotted i

Composed in Stone Sans and Stone Serif in QuarkXPress 3.32

Printed on 50-pound Finch Opaque Smooth, a pH-neutral stock, and bound in 10-point coated stock by Data Reproductions Corp.

The paper used in this publication meets the minimum requirements of American National Standard for Information Sciences—Permanence of Paper for Printed Library Materials, ANSI Z39.48-1992. ∞

Library of Congress Cataloging-in-Publication Data

Planning and implementing technical services workstations / Michael
    Kaplan, editor.
        p.   cm.
    Includes bibliographical references and index.
    ISBN 0-8389-0698-2 (alk. paper)
    1. Processing (Libraries)—United States—Data processing—
Planning.   2. Microcomputer workstations—United States—Planning.
I. Kaplan, Michael (Michael Steven)
Z699.355.U6P57   1997
025′.02—dc21   97-6204

Printed in the United States of America.

01 00 99 98 97   5 4 3 2 1

Contents

Figures   vii

Preface   ix

Acknowledgments   xiii

Introduction   xv

    What Is a TSW and Where Do You Find One?   xvi
    The Future of TSWs   xvii

▼
PART I
Background and Planning

Chapter 1

Hardware and Network Considerations   3

    Michael Kaplan

        Hardware   4
        Keyboards and Mice   6
        Monitors   7
        Local Area Networks   11
        The Internet   12
        Appendix: Games on the Computer   15

Chapter 2

Software Considerations 16

Michael Kaplan

Winsock Compatibility	18
Why a Windows Workstation?	18
The ALA Character Set	21
Macros and Macro Packages	22

Chapter 3

A Developer's Point of View 39

Mark Wilson

Basic Considerations	40
Target Audience	40
Problem Domain	42
Hardware Issues	42
Systems and Language Issues	43
Application Issues	46
Functionality	47
The Librarian-Developer Link	51

Chapter 4

National Cooperative Programs 53

Michael Kaplan

Origin of the Program for Cooperative Cataloging	54
Cooperative Cataloging Council	56
Cooperative Cataloging Council Automation Task Group	58
Appendix: CCC Strategic Plan Automation Recommendations	63

▼

PART II
Online Documentation and Online Tools

Chapter 5

Online Documentation First Steps: Cataloger's Desktop 67

Bruce Chr. Johnson

Origins	68
How Cataloger's Desktop Works	71
Machine Requirements	77
The Future	78

Chapter 6

Library of Congress Classification: SuperLCCS
and Classification Plus   81

Anaclare Frost Evans

SuperLCCS CD   83
Classification Plus   92
Appendix: System and Network Requirements for
    SuperLCCS CD and Classification Plus   101

Chapter 7

Dewey for Windows   103

Diane Vizine-Goetz and Mark Bendig

Editorial Support System   104
Classification Record Enhancements   105
DDC Hierarchies   107
Library of Congress Subject Headings   108
Sample Bibliographic Records Showing DDC/*LCSH*   108
The DDC Database   110
Indexes   110
Dewey for Windows System Design   111

▼
PART III
Productivity Enhancers
Macros and Programmatic Approaches

Chapter 8

Northwestern University's Toolkit   123

Gary L. Strawn

Development and Distribution   125
Automated Creation of Authority Records   135
Assistance with Call Numbers   136
Conflict Resolution   141
Next Steps   142
Appendix: Specifications for Machine-Generated
    Authority Records   146

Chapter 9

Custom Applications: The Library of Congress Experience   153

David Williamson

On the MARC   154
National Library of Medicine CIP   159
ClipSearch   162

▼
PART IV
Ergonomic and Training Issues for the Desktop Environment

Chapter 10

Ergonomics and Design   173

Bruce Trumble

A Workplace Ergonomics Program   174
Defining the Problem   175
Designing an Ergonomics Program   179
Ergonomics Policy Statements   188
Appendix: Resources for Ergonomics Research   190

Chapter 11

Training   193

Julia C. Blixrud

What Constitutes Training?   193
Why Train?   194
Trends in Training   195
Training Investments   195
Current Sources for Library Technical Training   197
Development of a Technical Services Workstation
  Training Program   199
Training Obstacles   205
Elements for Successful Training Programs   206

▼
PART V
The Symbiotic Future
Technical Services Workstations, the Internet, and the World Wide Web

Chapter 12

The TSW and Emerging Technologies:
A Researcher's Perspective   211

Diane Vizine-Goetz

Scorpion   212
The Challenge   214

Bibliography   217

Index   221

Contributors   235

Figures

2.1   NewKey Main Menu   27
2.2   Set of NewKey Macros   27
2.3   NewKey Copy Macro   28
2.4   Cataloging Copy Macro   29
2.5   Bibliographic Record before and after Cataloging   30
2.6   Harvard Depository Project Record before and after Changes   32
2.7   TCP3270 Quick-Keys   34
2.8   TCP3270 Basic Editor   34
2.9   HOLLIS and OCLC under Passport for Windows   36

5.1   Cataloger's Desktop List of Tools   72
5.2   CONSER Cataloging Manual's Opening Screen   72
5.3   Cataloger's Desktop LCRI Table of Contents   73
5.4   Cataloger's Desktop Query Templates   75
5.5   Cataloger's Desktop Implicit Links   77

6.1   SuperLCCS Table of Contents   84
6.2   SuperLCCS Link to a See Reference   85
6.3   SuperLCCS "Hits"/Detailed View/Hot Links   85
6.4   SuperLCCS with Added Gale Note   86
6.5   SuperLCCS Links to Tables   86
6.6   SuperLCCS Linked Table   87
6.7   SuperLCCS Detailed View of LC Classification   88
6.8   SuperLCCS Search Box   88
6.9   SuperLCCS Search Results for "Diabetes" in "H"   89

6.10 SuperLCCS Search Results for "Diabetes Mellitus" in "R"   89
6.11 Classification Plus List of Infobases   94
6.12 Classification Plus Search Results for "Statistics" in "HA"   95
6.13 Classification Plus Link to a Table   96
6.14 Classification Plus Linked Table   96
6.15 Classification Plus View of LCSH with Links   97
6.16 Classification Plus Hypertext Link from LCSH to RC658.5   98

7.1 Creating the Electronic Dewey System   104
7.2 ESS Record for 025.04, "Information Storage and
       Retrieval Systems"   106
7.3 Hierarchy Information for DDC 005.71   107
7.4 DDC Database Indexes   111
7.5 Dewey for Windows System Design   112
7.6 Dewey for Windows with Index, Hierarchy, Search, and DDC
       Number Windows   113
7.7 Dewey for Windows Browse View   114
7.8 Dewey for Windows Search View with Open LCSH Window   115
7.9 Dewey for Windows Custom Display View Example   115
7.10 Dewey for Windows Browse View with Open Note
        List Window   117
7.11 Dewey for Windows Summary View with
        Open Past Searches Window   118

8.1 CLAR Toolkit Buttons Used at Northwestern   128
8.2 CLARR Toolkit Buttons Used at Other Institutions   128
8.3 Toolkit Bibliographic Verification Report   132
8.4 Toolkit Bibliographic Validation Report   134
8.5 Toolkit Simple Personal Name Authority Record   136
8.6 Toolkit Series Authority Record   137
8.7 Toolkit Classification Number Summary for a Topical Heading   139

9.1 On the MARC Bibliographic Record Creation   155
9.2 On the MARC Name Authority Record Creation   157
9.3 TCEC Version of NLM CIP Record   160
9.4 Initial LC Version of NLM Record   160
9.5 Completed NLM/LC Record   161
9.6 Initial View of ClipSearch   163
9.7 ClipSearch Search Box   164
9.8 LC Bibliographic Record Used for ClipSearch Searching   165
9.9 ClipSearch Types of MARC Codes   167
9.10 ClipSearch Lists Feature   168

12.1 Scorpion Classification Page   213
12.2 Scorpion Electronic Table of Contents   214
12.3 Scorpion Proposed Classification   215

Preface

During 1995 the subject of technical services workstations (TSWs) began to attract national attention in the library technical services community. Two national organizations can claim a major share of the credit for this: the Program for Cooperative Cataloging (PCC) and the American Library Association's Association for Library Collections & Technical Services (ALCTS). On November 14, 1994, PCC's predecessor, the Cooperative Cataloging Council (CCC) and its Automation Task Group sponsored a meeting with library service vendors at the Library of Congress to make contact with a diverse group of library automation vendors and to introduce them to CCC and its automation goals. High on the automation wish list of CCC was the development of powerful workstations customized specifically for the technical services community. Such technical services workstations already existed, largely as locally developed extensions of a basic computer workstation. In 1994 it was not possible for an institution to simply order a fully functional TSW directly from a vendor. In 1996 we began to see the fruits of that 1994 meeting as vendors rolled out the first real generation of workstations and accompanying software packages developed specifically with technical services functions in mind.

As chair of CCC's Automation Task Group, and later as chair of PCC's Standing Committee on Automation, I had already commenced discussions with ALCTS about sponsoring a series of ALCTS Institutes on technical service workstations: "The State of the Art of Cataloging." (I should note that the seed for these institutes grew out of Robocat '94, a workshop sponsored by NELINET in May 1994.) ALCTS was keenly interested and moved expeditiously to schedule four institutes in the spring and fall of 1995. These institutes were held in Atlanta, Georgia; Dallas, Texas; Pomona, California; and Minneapolis, Minnesota. Two more were added later, in New York, New York (1995), and in Washington, D.C. (1996). So high was the interest that at least two other Online Computer Library Center, Inc., OCLC regional networks have inquired about hosting similar institutes, and two different, revised versions of the original institute were proposed and accepted as preconferences for the Library and Information Technology Association/Library Administration and Management Association (LITA/LAMA) national conference in Pittsburgh in October 1996 and for the Association of College and Research Libraries (ACRL) eighth national conference in Nashville in April 1997.

The presenters at the original set of institutes (Janet McCue, Mann Library, Cornell University; Matthew Beacom, Yale University; Bruce Chr. Johnson and Julianne Beall, Library of Congress [LC]; Mark Bendig, OCLC; and myself) represented different aspects of the spectrum of planning and developing TSWs and TSW applications:

- ▶ planning TSWs and processing electronic resources in a TSW environment (McCue)
- ▶ installing TSWs and training staff in their use (Beacom)
- ▶ electronic documentation in the form of LC's Cataloger's Desktop and Classification Plus (Johnson)
- ▶ Electronic Dewey and Dewey for Windows (Beall and Bendig)
- ▶ DOS and Windows interfaces/clients and the application of macro-driven processing to technical services (Kaplan)

Discussion of this major new trend in technical services comes at a crucial time in the continuing evolution of technical services in general. It is not too far-fetched to say that the technical services profession is under attack from a variety of fronts, from those advocating total outsourcing of technical services to those demanding that technical services reform itself from within.[1] Certainly no other definable event has so crystallized the debate about the future of technical services as concretely as the Wright State decision to outsource its technical services operations and the subsequent OCLC-sponsored symposium, The Future Is Now: The Changing Face of Technical Services.[2] Technical services does have its passionate defenders, of course, but the debate is now about more than just the purity and intellectual integrity of the catalog.[3] It is about the application of business practices and techniques to technical services, and it is about the bottom-line mentality that is now irrevocably a part of library, indeed institutional, life in the 1990s and beyond. If technical services can be said to have a soul, then surely it is the very salvation or transformation of that soul that is at stake.

Notes

1. Ellen J. Waite, "Reinvent Catalogers," *Library Journal* 120, no. 18 (Nov. 1, 1995): 36–7. Waite wrote her article in response to the Gorman article in *LJ* noted below. Dorothy Gregor and Carol A. Mandel, "Cataloging Must Change!" *Library Journal* 116, no. 6 (Apr. 1, 1991): 42–7.

2. Arnold Hirshon, "The Lobster Quadrille: The Future of Technical Services in a Re-Engineering World," in *The Future Is Now: The Changing Face of Technical Services: Proceedings of the OCLC Symposium, ALA Midwinter Conference, February 4, 1994* (Dublin, Ohio: OCLC, 1994), 14–20.

3. Michael Gorman, "Innocent Pleasures," in *The Future Is Now: The Changing Face of Technical Services: Proceedings of the OCLC Symposium, ALA Midwinter Conference, February 4, 1994* (Dublin, Ohio: OCLC, 1994), 39–42. See also his article "The Corruption of Cataloging," *Library Journal* 120, no. 20 (Sept. 15, 1995): 32–3.

Acknowledgments

▼ I am indebted to many colleagues for their time and collaboration as I have refined my thoughts on TSWs. I cannot name them all individually, but chief among them are those who graciously agreed to contribute the chapters to this book. I also want to thank my companions in the ALCTS institutes (and all those who attended and gave us the fruit of their experiences) and colleagues in the LITA/ALCTS Microcomputers for Technical Services Interest Group, now the LITA/ALCTS Technical Services Workstation Interest Group (especially Matthew Beacom and David Williamson), the Cooperative Cataloging Council, its six task groups and CCC Automation Task Group, the Program for Cooperative Cataloging Executive Council and the PCC Standing Committee on Automation, the New England TSW/NOTIS discussion group (Cornell, Columbia, Harvard, MIT, Princeton, and Yale universities), many friends in the Library of Congress's Cataloging Directorate (Robert August, Richard Thaxter, and David Williamson), and all my colleagues (too numerous to name individually) in the Harvard College Library's Cataloging Services Department.

I do, however, have to thank by name Jane Ouderkirk, head of the Cataloging Services Department at Harvard, and my wife and my daughter, Maureen and Jessica Kaplan, all of whom have had to put up with frequent absences from office and home as I have attempted to serve partly as a traveling salesman and partly as an evangelist in spreading this new gospel of the technical services workstation around North America during 1995 and 1996.

Introduction

▼ The technical service workstation (TSW) has emerged as a major new weapon in the arsenal of those advocating evolutionary change within collection development, acquisitions, and cataloging. What started out as a cataloger's workstation has now metamorphosed into a TSW capable of enhancing and transforming the entire range of technical services functions, procedures, and workflows.[1]

Where is the proof that these TSWs are capable of exerting a positive impact on the profession and can counter the arguments advanced by the outsourcing crowd? Here are some statements about productivity from the 1994 TSW survey conducted by the CCC Automation Task Group:

Cornell University's Mann Library: acquisitions time cut in half

Harvard College Library's Cataloging Services Department: production up 63 percent despite an 18 percent reduction in hours

Library of Congress: productivity for certain phases up by as much as 25 percent

New York Public Library: significant increase in throughput with fewer staff

Pennsylvania State University: productivity [for the most experienced and capable TSW users] in original cataloging increased on the order of 200 percent to 300 percent

UCLA: total output increased while number of staff decreased

University of Nevada, Las Vegas: 10 percent less time required to catalog LC copy; 25 percent less time for member copy

University of North Texas: backlogs (including long-term backlogs) have disappeared[2]

Moreover, technical service workstations are no longer just for the members of the Association of Research Libraries (ARL) of the world. The economics of personnel costs (constantly rising) versus computer and telecommunications costs (constantly declining) are driving management everywhere to realize that the smart *business* decision is to maximize the productivity of their staff members by providing them the best tools available to do their jobs.[3]

What Is a TSW and Where Do You Find One?

Where does one go then to purchase a Technical Services Workstation? This is an easy question, but it does not yet admit of an easy answer. The TSW is best compared to a stereo system. A stereo system comprises a receiver (or amplifier and tuner), a CD player, a tape deck, and speakers—plus a selection of CDs, tapes, and radio stations. In technical services terms, CDs and tapes would be the software or the local bibliographic resources; radio stations would be remote resources. The TSW's hardware components include the system unit made up of the motherboard and CPU, memory, disk drive, display adapter, and network card and perhaps a CD-ROM drive and bar-code reader; monitor; keyboard; and mouse. (The printer is not part of this configuration.) But it is the TSW equivalent of the CDs, tapes, and radio stations that differentiates the technical services workstation from just another administrative computer. Their TSW counterparts include (but are not limited to) the following:

fully functional, ALA-character-set enabled software used in technical services sessions with the local system (itself a local resource)

Telnet software (to connect to remote resources)

Web browser software

Z39.50 client software for search/retrieval from remote locations

macro (productivity) software

local or remote sources of documentation

connections to resource files (locally mounted LC files; local or remote vendor files)

connections (dedicated, dialup, or Internet) to bibliographic utilities (additional remote resources)

Purchasing the basic hardware components of the technical services workstation is now a relatively uncomplicated matter. The only real decisions to make pertain to the vendor from whom to buy them and the precise system configuration to purchase. Accept the fact that this configuration is a moving target and will constantly escalate and evolve as new developments make new demands on our systems. (The 1995 survey commissioned by the PCC Standing Committee on Automation and now published as an ARL SPEC Kit, *Technical Services Workstations,* is a good starting place for researching more about the equipment and current trends, and I have used it liberally in my discussions of hardware and software in this book.) **It is, however, the choice of the software components and the ability to network that will determine whether the computer makes the evolutionary leap and becomes a true technical services workstation.**

While those institutions that responded to the 1994 TSW survey conducted by the CCC Automation Task Group and the 1995 survey conducted by the PCC Standing Committee on Automation have developed their own workstation configurations, vendors are now beginning to bring the components of just such platforms to market. As the market for TSWs becomes more mature, more vendors will offer their own TSW versions. Certainly any institution that is in the process of acquiring a new local system should include a fully loaded, fully functional technical services workstation in its request for proposal.

In the following pages experts in a number of different areas have contributed chapters in an attempt to cover the range of issues that a well-rounded discussion of technical services workstations invokes: issues of implementation, configuration, workflow, development, documentation and classification, productivity, the World Wide Web, training, and ergonomics. Alert readers will discover one omission, and that is discussion of the Macintosh as a TSW platform. With all due apologies to Macintosh devotees, theirs is a small proportion of the TSW population and does not appear to be attracting substantial attention from those groups developing new tools for technical services. Results of the survey collected for the ARL SPEC Kit demonstrate that quite decisively and, where the Macintosh is continuing to demonstrate a presence, it is largely as a Power Macintosh where the Macintosh has the option of running the new commercially available software in a Windows session.

The Future of TSWs

And what of the TSW itself? If it is our future, what is its future? As libraries shift their online systems architecture from a mainframe environment to a client-server architecture, we will begin to see the technical services workstation itself incorporate the client end of the client-server equation. This evolution is already under way. Vendors and local systems developers are just now beginning to release the first generation of software packages that will put Z39.50 search/retrieval and even update capabilities on any properly equipped and connected TSW. The TSW is the modular platform upon which this evolution will unfold itself. The TSW is no passing phenomenon, but rather the key element in defining a bright new future for technical services.

Notes

1. See the interesting discussion of the semantic evolution of the technology that Roger Brisson has collected in his article, "The Cataloger's Workstation and the Continuing Transformation of Cataloging," *Cataloging and Classification Quarterly* 20, no. 1 (1995): 5–12.

2. The productivity citations come from unpublished materials collected during the 1994 TSW survey.

3. See the flyer (executive summary) that precedes *Technical Services Workstations*, ARL SPEC Kit 213 (Washington, D.C.: Association of Research Libraries, 1996).

PART

I

Background
and Planning

Hardware and Network Considerations

Michael Kaplan
Harvard College Library

▼ The technical services workstation (TSW) is an evolving technology. It exists within an organizational context—technical services—but as a physical object it also exists within a spatial location and includes the computer and its software as well as its surrounding environment. (The term *workstation* is often used to refer to the furniture, particularly modular furniture specifically designed for computers, but in this book we will restrict usage of the term to the computer [except in Bruce Trumble's discussion of ergonomics in chapter 10].) A full and detailed discussion of the TSW must consider all these aspects and how they are interrelated.

Just what is a technical services workstation? The terminology and the concept have changed over time as the technology has evolved.[1] In her presentations at the ALCTS institutes on technical services workstations, "The State of the Art of Cataloging," Janet McCue relies on Douglas Engelbart for a working definition of the generic workstation. Both define a workstation as a gateway into an augmented knowledge workshop where we find the data and the tools with which we work and where we collaborate with our colleagues who are similarly equipped.[2] If we use this definition of a generic workstation as the starting place for defining a technical services workstation, we can define the TSW as follows:

> The TSW is a networked microcomputer capable of advanced editing and inputting features, customized for technical services

use and able to access and manipulate data in online catalogs and other pertinent resource files, both local and remote, using software developed specifically for those purposes.

In recent years technical service professionals around the world have formed online communities by means of Internet discussion groups (listservs) and have increasingly created online resources accessible through the World Wide Web (WWW). Just as these professionals do not exist in an intellectual vacuum, but rather in a "collaboratory," so too the fully developed TSW exists only in a networked, Internetted context.

In the Automation Appendix to its 1994 Strategic Plan, the Cooperative Cataloging Council developed a wish list for development of advanced workstations. We can describe many of the items on that list summarily as the application of word processing technology to technical services.[3] In the early 1990s, when most of us were still using "dumb terminals," this seemed very advanced. As those dumb terminals have begun to give way to desktop workstations, we can now see this as a logical evolutionary change. Many developments have contributed to this change, among them the disappearance of manufacturers' hardware support (annual maintenance contracts) for terminals, the rapid decline in the cost of computers, and added pressure on technical services departments to increase throughput, often with fewer staff. The expense ratio of computers to staff has changed radically over time, and computers, which were once rationed in technical services departments due to the capital costs associated with them, are now the one logical means of stretching staff costs to the utmost.[4]

Hardware

The Cooperative Cataloging Council Automation Task Group's 1994 TSW survey found TSW configurations from the venerable 8088-based personal computer (PC) on up and showed relatively few Pentium installations.[5] In contrast the Program for Cooperative Cataloging Standing Committee on Automation's 1995 survey done in preparation for the ARL SPEC Kit showed that the majority of TSW installations were then based on 80486 and Pentium processors. As of September 1995, it was already clear that most new installations, in fact, were 75 MHz (and higher) Pentium-based machines with at least 8 megabytes of memory (and increasingly with 16 megabytes) and came with a hard disk that had an average size of 540 megabytes. With machines of this caliber, it was no surprise that most institutions were using graphical user interfaces (GUIs). For the most part that means Microsoft Windows, though there are a few IBM OS/2 installations (the Library of Congress being the prime example) and a few Macintosh institutions.

Libraries are now operating much more like for-profit businesses and have accepted the need to provide equipment accordingly. This penetration of the library marketplace is still in its early stages and has not yet spread entirely even through the ranks of the Association of Research Libraries.[6] In many cases smaller libraries actually have an easier task moving their technical services departments forward and incorporating new automation initiatives because they have the greater flexibility that is often inherent in smaller organizations.

Libraries purchasing computers would be wise to use this hardware description as a floor-level on which to base their purchasing decisions and to be aware that computer technology is advancing ever more rapidly. As time passes, the floor-level for new purchases should rise appropriately. By early 1996 it was already clear that 75 MHz Pentium processors were becoming increasingly "obsolete" as Intel was beginning to abandon that "low" end of the marketplace in favor of 133-MHz (and higher) Pentium processors and the new Pentium Pro chip line. So, too, the movement from 8 to 16 megabytes of memory is being driven by Microsoft Windows '95 and its memory requirements as well as the requirements of running new software applications, particularly if several applications are to be run simultaneously. Moreover, purchase of large quantities of memory became even more advantageous, at least in the spring and summer of 1996, when memory prices—which have always been volatile but which nonetheless had held stable for a number of years in the early to mid 1990s—suddenly fell precipitously in price and reached historic lows.

According to the ARL SPEC Kit, many libraries are purchasing their computer hardware from a number of different vendors, among them IBM, Compaq, and Dell. Dell was the brand most frequently mentioned in the survey. Local suppliers and local system integrators are also cited as sources for the hardware in the survey. Once the hardware is purchased, libraries still have the task of loading the software and configuring the TSW to suit their local needs. Library software providers and local systems vendors are beginning to market fully configured TSWs, but at this time most TSW installations are of the home-grown variety.

Computers have been in libraries long enough now, and in great enough numbers, that libraries are experiencing questions related to the upgrade curve. For many years we have handled the issue of "obsolete" computers by passing them down the computing hierarchy to those who do not need machines as powerful as those at the top of the hierarchy. Gradually those machines have either reached the bottom of the chain or have become so outdated that they are fading away from library usage. Is there a sensible strategy for dealing with the upgrade curve?

One means that will help alleviate upgrade shock is to set a threshold configuration and a threshold cost. As equipment prices drop, a library should hold to its original threshold price but adjust its equipment configuration upward and constantly escalate the computer configuration that it can purchase for the same price as the original computer. While that will unfortunately mean that a library and its automation staff will have to deal with and maintain a variety of computer configurations over time, it will help ensure that the institution will not be faced with having to engage in wholesale replacements of entire "fleets" of computers. It will help ensure that machines fade from usage as a result of gradual, evolutionary change rather than sudden, revolutionary upheaval. If the library directors or department heads so choose, they can still pass machines down from high-power users to those who need less power.

No library administrator should consider the capital expense in purchasing computers as a once-in-a-lifetime expense. That is a self-delusion that some organizations (not just libraries) accepted as they began the expensive task of outfitting everyone in the organization with an appropriate computing device. The life cycle of computers is growing ever shorter, and the demands of new generations of operating systems and applications software guarantee that this will continue to be the case. An established replacement program of no more than five years (three to four years, if possible) should be factored into an institution's purchasing decisions.

Perhaps it will help alleviate shock at the potential costs to put this into perspective: an IBM-compatible PC based on an 8088 processor, with 256 kilobytes of memory, two full-height floppy drives (no hard drive), and a monochrome, textual monitor that was the standard in 1984 (and was comparable to the OCLC M300 computer) cost approximately $4,000 (in 1984 dollars).[7] Had the cost of that same computer kept pace with the national Consumer Price Index, it would have cost approximately $5,660 in 1994.[8] Similarly, a 25-megabyte hard drive cost $3,860 all by itself in 1986, and an 80-megabyte hard drive cost $7,860![9] While it is dangerous to quote current prices because they change so radically and quickly, in early 1996, one could have purchased a 133 MHz Pentium with 16 megabytes of memory, a 540-megabyte hard drive, 2 megabytes of video memory, a 15-inch VGA (color) monitor, a keyboard and a mouse, a 3½-inch 1.44 megabyte floppy, an integrated Ethernet card, DOS/Windows, and a 3-year on-site warranty for $2,512 (including delivery). That same configuration with a 17-inch monitor would have cost $2,757.[10]

Keyboards and Mice

The days when we all had to settle for the standard 101-key keyboard are over. There are a variety of keyboards currently available at a reasonable price, and no one should have to suffer from repetitive strain injuries based on the unavailability of alternative keyboards. (See chapter 10 for a discussion of ergonomics issues.) As many of us can attest, an institution can make no mistake worse than simply plunking down a computer and a keyboard on a 1930s-era desk. That is a sure prescription for ergonomic disaster.

Another issue relates to software-driven customization of the keyboard itself. Most packages now on the market aimed at catalog access in technical services allow at least some degree of customization of the keyboard. This is minimally true of the Cornell University's DOS product, TN3270, but largely true of the current generation of Windows products, such as McGill University's TCP3270 and OCLC's Passport for Windows.

While it is useful to encourage that level of customization of the keyboard that reflects ownership of a computer and (foreign) language-specific needs, such as the need to create diacritics easily by assigning them to quick keystroke combinations, we must remember that not all computers are always assigned to specific individuals. Even those computers that are so assigned may occasionally be used by others (during vacations or by students or temporary workers). Keyboards that do not readily reflect the accepted local conventions due to individual customization pose problems for wider use. Furthermore, keyboard macro programs are based on certain keystrokes having a certain, assigned meaning, and customization outside the norm defeats the intent of these programs.

Separate keyboard mapping files that can be created and loaded may be worth considering. In other cases, libraries should be wary of allowing them since it can prove an administrative, managerial, and training problem.

The situation with a computer mouse is even more striking since there are so many styles and models currently on the market. As libraries and library software move into the GUI environment, the mouse will take on greater importance for technical services processing than previously. It is important, therefore, to be sure that staff have a style of mouse with which they are comfortable. This is particularly true for left-handed staffers, who should have a mouse designed for their predominant hand. Also, just as an articulated keyboard tray is crucial for the keyboard, a mouse tray should be provided for use with the mouse. The mouse should be used at the same, proper level as the keyboard, and not placed at a higher level or further back on the desk surface itself.

Monitors

Of all the physical components of the technical services workstation, the one component that is the most neglected in actual planning and purchasing decisions is the monitor. This is extremely unfortunate since the monitor, along with the keyboard and mouse, are the parts of the workstation with which the user primarily relates. While there are alternative keyboard models available and while we are beginning to take more notice of them as a potential remedy to repetitive strain injuries, these alternative keyboards are relatively inexpensive. Higher-end monitors, on the other hand, will represent a much greater portion of the overall cost of the workstation, particularly larger and higher-resolution monitors. What follows is a bit technical but necessary for an understanding of the role monitors play in the overall construction of a TSW.

There are four aspects to the monitor that need to be considered separately, though they are somewhat intertwined. These are size, resolution, dot pitch, and refresh rate. (The issue of low-frequency emissions from monitors is, on the other hand, a potential safety issue.) Size and resolution are closely related, and they are the two aspects that are of more immediate concern in the selection of an appropriate monitor for the TSW configuration.

Size and Resolution

The salient questions these days relate to the size and resolution of the monitor. The reasons for this are closely related to the growing movement toward acceptance of Windows (or other graphical user interfaces) for library as well as administrative applications. In the DOS world, where one views a single application on the screen at a time, a 14-inch or a 15-inch monitor might well suffice. When, however, a user is trying to view multiple applications in multiple windows simultaneously, there is a clear advantage to a larger monitor. In this case the monitor should be 17 inches.

There is more to this than just the size of the monitor by itself. First of all, a 17-inch monitor has almost one-third more square inches than a 15-inch monitor. (This assumes that the entire advertised, diagonal measure of the monitor is available for viewing, but, in fact, the frame of the monitor cuts down on that measurement. Manufacturers are now starting to state more accurately the viewing size of their monitors.) Second, the larger size of the monitor allows the user to configure Windows to run more comfortably at a higher resolution of 1024×768 pixels. Compared with a resolution of 800×600 pixels on a 15-inch monitor, the user gains a premium of almost two-thirds more viewing area. (Attempting to run a 14-inch or a 15-inch monitor at the higher 1024×768 resolution can be excruciatingly painful for the person staring at the screen for long periods of time—the fonts are far too small for ease of use.) If the user is attempting to run multiple applications or to view multiple catalog records simultaneously, this added real estate makes all the difference between a difficult viewing experience and one that is comfortable.

There is a financial penalty associated with the larger monitors, however. While most technology assessment officers would recommend the larger monitor in the absence of all budgetary pressures, the 17-inch monitor still demands a considerable price premium over its 15-inch cousins. Pricing a number of computer bundles from a number of national manufacturers in January 1996, it was apparent that to upgrade from a standard 15-inch to a standard 17-inch monitor carried with it an incremental price increase of $250 to $300. Purchased separately, 17-inch monitors have shown only marginal downward movement in price and still carry a price-tag that can vary from $600 to $1,400. Eventually we can expect these prices to drift slowly downward, but they will still carry a premium over the smaller monitors. Only when the economics of manufacturing move the 17-inch monitor into the mainstream and when the mass manufacturers of computers adopt it as their standard are we likely to see the 17-inch monitor gain strong footholds in price-conscious library settings.

Many libraries, such as Yale University's, that have made substantial commitments to TSWs and would have liked to invest in 17-inch monitors have felt that this is an area where they have had to economize to keep their overall price affordable. Nevertheless, it is worth noting that a few institutions—Johns Hopkins University's Eisenhower Library among them—are beginning to invest in 21-inch monitors, at least on an experimental basis.

Resolution can also be discussed from the point of the "graphics adapter": for example, CGA (Color Graphics Adapter), EGA (Enhanced Graphics Adapter), VGA (Video Graphics Adapter), SVGA (Super Video Graphics Adapter). Currently, the VGA and SVGA are standard. SVGA is to be preferred, although VGA is still more common. Associated with the issue of the display adapter is the amount of memory it contains. Adapters with 2 megabytes of video memory (VRAM) are to be preferred to those with but 1 megabyte of DRAM (still the more common on basic systems) since they will enable the system to paint a screen on the monitor more quickly.

Dot Pitch

We have reached a temporary plateau in the matter of the dot pitch. Dot pitch is defined as the distance between the centers of neighboring dots of the same color. The crucial point is that the smaller the dot pitch, the better the quality of the monitor. At this time most standard monitors have a dot pitch of .28 mm, and no one should consider purchasing a monitor with a dot pitch greater than that. Some more expensive monitors are now appearing with a dot pitch of .26 mm or less, but these are still in a minority.

Refresh Rate

The refresh rate deserves mention here because it is directly related to the resolution. The refresh rate, like the dot pitch, is another technical issue not easily comprehended, but it is simply the rate at which an entire screen is "redrawn," and it is measured in hertz (Hz). A 72-Hz monitor is "redrawn" 72 times per second. The higher the resolution, the more pixels to be rendered and the harder it is to maintain a high refresh rate. Monitors with inadequate refresh rates appear to flicker, a phenomenon that is hard on the user's eyes. Moreover, the larger the monitor, the more the flicker is noticeable. At this time a refresh rate of 70 Hz is the minimum anyone should accept, but 72 Hz to 75 Hz and up is preferable.

Another related technical issue is that of interlaced versus noninterlaced monitors. Interlaced monitors redraw every other line on each refresh cycle, but noninterlaced monitors render the entire screen at a single pass. Noninterlaced monitors are much easier on the user's eyes.

Implications

So, why are these factors relevant, and why should they be considered before buying? The answer relates directly to how we are beginning to use TSWs in the Windows environment and how we will be using them in the future. Given that the future will consist of technical services staff opening multiple applications (multitasking) and that staff will frequently open multiple online sessions, imagine the following scenarios:

> an acquisitions librarian has a notepad/word processor session open to compose a claim to a vendor while having a catalog session and a Telnet session with the vendor/subscription agent's database open while being in electronic contact with the institution's central payments system

a cataloger has two OCLC sessions open (one to a bibliographic record and a second to an authority record) plus a bibliographic search session as well as a catalog session open in the local OPAC in addition to a documentation source such as the WWW Tools for Serial Catalogers or a Cataloger's Desktop session open to the Library of Congress Rule Interpretations or MARC code lists— five sessions in all

the acquisitions librarian or cataloger is copying and pasting data between sessions and is verifying, comparing, and manipulating data between various records or even sessions as he or she creates this record from scratch

To accomplish all of this skillfully and efficiently, the user needs as much Windows real estate as possible, and that translates directly into a larger monitor, moreover, one that can run at a higher resolution. That is where the emerging environment is headed. The problem now is how to reconcile it with financial constraints. Those libraries that are more forward-thinking will invest in the future by purchasing monitors more attuned to the workflow of the future.

Color Schemes

In the days of monochrome monitors, screen-color choices were a bit like the days of the old Model T Ford, except that instead of allowing a choice of black, black, or black, buyers could choose green or amber (sometimes even blue). That is still generally the case with inexpensive dumb terminals, but computers now come standard with color monitors of varying sizes and power. Microsoft Windows and many library-specific programs that run under Windows allow users to design their own color schemes within various parameters. Where library-specific programs are concerned, these color schemes can be applied to different areas of the display. McGill University's TCP3270, for instance, allows the operator to assign different colors to protected and unprotected high- and low-intensity areas, the operator information area, etc. For OCLC's Passport for Windows, the operator can apply different colors to text, the screen background, etc.

Ideally, staff should be empowered to choose a color scheme that they find agreeable and that is easy on their eyes. Different individuals find different color schemes appealing for different reasons. However, the experience at Harvard College Library is that staff, for whateverreasons, may nonetheless choose color schemes that are unnecessarily harsh on their eyes and that increase the risk of eyestrain. It is generally true that blacks, grays, and blues will be easier on one's eyes, particularly where the alternative is combinations of oranges, reds, greens, and yellows.

In general follow these guidelines in choosing color schemes for prolonged use:

▶ Use as few colors as possible to avoid creating a confusing display.

▶ Avoid extremes of the color spectrum.

▶ Avoid color combinations that create three-dimensional effects.

▶ Maximize the color contrast between the text and the background.

▶ Provide differentiation between protected and unprotected areas of the screen display (fields).[11]

If a degree of flexibility is desired, however, the most important aspect to control is the background color of the screen, which should be dark and provide a basic level of contrast to the textual information of the technical services session. Be sure to keep in mind staff who suffer from colorblindness. Also consider the effect of glare screens on particular monitors or particular color combinations.

Local Area Networks

Once the exclusive sphere of large businesses, local area networks (LANs) are now making rapid headway in library settings as well. The vast majority (84 percent) of those libraries that responded to the ARL survey and have TSWs also have LANs. While there are a number of different types represented in the ARL SPEC Kit, the majority (58 percent) are Novell LANs. A LAN is not appropriate for every institution, of course, and some libraries have followed the lead of their universities in opting for a campuswide Transmission Control Protocol/Internet Protocol (TCP/IP) network rather than installing LANs. Some other libraries, such as the Columbia University Library, that originally depended entirely on their campus TCP/IP network have now chosen to install LANs.

The great advantage of a LAN is that it can serve as a repository of commonly used software packages (for example, word processing, spreadsheet, database, communications, etc.) that need to be installed only once on the server. This relieves library automation staff of the need to purchase individual copies of every program and to install them on every machine. Instead, the library purchases a single copy with an appropriate number of licenses, and users run the programs from the server. In large institutions with dozens or hundreds of users, this serves an essential function.

LANs can also be the means to deliver information stored on CD-ROMs and make them available to local communities of researchers as well. In fact, this is behind the decision of a number of large institutions to go the LAN route.

The LAN is not without its expense, of course. Not only is there the cost of the network server and the server software but a LAN of any size and complexity will require the professional oversight of a LAN administrator. Except for peer-to-peer LANs and LAN packages that support less-complex installations, this is not a job that can be easily delegated or managed by technical services staff as an adjunct to an existing job. Very large installations, moreover, will likely require an institution to devote multiple positions to LAN administration. The Harvard College Library currently has an administrative head (who is also the automation coordinator for the library), four staff members (of whom one is a UNIX specialist and three are involved with new installations and maintenance), plus a staff administrator involved in management of a net-work with an installed computer base in excess of 450 computers spread out over a number of buildings. As a general rule, allow one LAN techni-cian for every fifty computers in situations that demand a high level of attention and maintenance. Institutions that can monitor and service computer installations remotely and do not require such a high level of attention or maintenance may be able to reduce the ratio to one LAN technician for every 100 installed computers.[12] It is also possible to con-tract out the cost of overseeing the server to an outside service provider.

In discussions with technical services managers, it is apparent that library administrators often view their LANs as an administrative infra-structure to support administrative applications. While LAN administrators are generally expert in dealing with the packages used for administrative purposes and in handling them in a LAN environment, very few have more than passing knowledge of the emerging suites of technical ser-vices applications that are LAN compatible. Such applications include the Library of Congress's Cataloger's Desktop and Classification Plus, Gale Research's SuperLCCS CD, OCLC's Passport for Windows, RLIN's Terminal Software, McGill University's TCP3270 for Windows, and soft-ware packages from most library local systems vendors. This leads to an interesting situation that any library administrator considering a LAN should ponder seriously: How do you divide the responsibility for sup-porting these products both on the LAN proper as well as on the indi-vidual workstations between the LAN administrator and the technical services specialists? If done properly, turf wars and conflicts in areas of responsibility will not occur and technical services professionals will re-tain the maximum level of independence to pursue new, entrepreneur-ial ventures to enhance their level of productivity. It is clear that many of the most striking accomplishments in technical services automation in the early and middle 1990s resulted from technically literate individ-uals in cataloging departments rather than from their counterparts in departments devoted solely to automation. The institutions that fos-tered that atmosphere benefited greatly from their efforts.

A similar situation exists with training for using the workstations as generic computers versus using them as TSWs as well as using the generic administrative software versus the specifically technical-services-oriented packages. Training, indeed, is an issue that deserves more at-tention than it has typically received. It is no accident that two OCLC regional networks, CAPCON and NELINET, established director of train-ing positions or that a significant number of programs at the American Library Association Annual Meetings recently have been devoted to is-sues of technology training for catalogers. (See chapter 11 for further discussion of training issues.)

The Internet

The LAN is but one facet of the networking equation. From the LAN TSWs should clearly be linked to the Internet. Once a casually accepted part of the library environment chiefly noted for delivering E-mail and listserv communications, the Internet is now very much the thread that ties library technical services departments everywhere into a single large, networked community. Increasingly, technical services departments are placing both local- and national-level documentation on the Internet, chiefly by means of the World Wide Web. As commercialization of the Internet increases and as access to it grows exponentially, even the smallest libraries will need to be assured of access. Technical services without access to the Internet is inconceivable today.

In the 1994 TSW survey the CCC Automation Task Group measured the penetration of OCLC's Telecommunications Linking Project (TLP) and Research Libraries Group's (RLG) EtherTerm within libraries. TLP and EtherTerm are means for libraries to connect computers on their LAN or TCP/IP networks to the national bibliographic utilities. OCLC and RLG originally directed these products at large institutions or consortiums. The 1995 survey did not attempt to measure that degree of connectivity directly, though, because by 1995 both OCLC and Research Libraries Information Network (RLIN) were allowing direct access over the Internet to their databases for technical services use. Since 98 percent of libraries responding to the 1995 survey reported they had Telnet capability, at least theoretically 98 percent of the libraries had the capability of accessing OCLC or RLIN over the Internet in their technical services departments. It is true, however, that they have to install OCLC or RLIN software to operate with full functionality in technical services mode.

Two related developments in the software and local systems vendor sphere, moreover, are furthering this dependence on the Internet. It is clear that the majority of local systems vendors are developing their new generation of software for technical services with Z39.50 designed as an integral part of the architecture. Search-and-retrieval and even updating will depend on Z39.50 protocols. Second, developers are beginning to integrate Z39.50 with Web browsers, so that the front end of the next generation of library catalogs will likely be a Web front end, at least for the public. BookWhere?, a Z39.50 program aimed at the mass market, has already shown how easy it is to use it as a helper application with Web browsers.[13]

Summary

TSWs are making rapid headway among libraries of all sizes. For new purchases the basic platform in 1995 and early 1996 was an IBM-compatible computer with either an 80486 or a 75-MHz (or higher) Pentium processor, 16 megabytes of memory, a 540-megabyte hard drive, and a 15-inch monitor. Faster Pentiums quickly came to the fore, and by the middle of 1996 it was abundantly clear that 100-MHz or even 133-MHz Pentiums were the norm for new purchases. Larger, 17-inch monitors will eventually gain a stronger foothold in the market. These systems can come from a variety of national manufacturers or local systems integrators.

Most institutions, at least most large institutions, are choosing to connect these TSWs to a LAN and then to connect the LAN to the Internet. Most TSW installations to date have been locally developed, but vendors are now starting to recognize the importance of TSWs to the library marketplace.

Notes

1. See Roger Brisson, "The Cataloger's Workstation and the Continuing Transformation of Cataloging," *Cataloging and Classification Quarterly* 20, no. 1 (1995): 5–12.

2. Douglas Engelbart, "The Augmented Knowledge Workshop," in *A History of Personal Workstations,* ed. by Adele Goldbert (New York: ACM Press, 1988), 207.

3. See the Strategic Plan and the Automation Appendix in *Towards a New Beginning in Cooperative Cataloging: The History, Progress and Future of the Cooperative Cataloging Council,* comp. by David W. Reser (Washington, D.C.: Library of Congress, Cataloging Distribution Service, 1994), 16–29.

4. See the discussion in the flyer (executive summary) that accompanies *Technical Services Workstations,* ARL SPEC Kit 213 (Washington, D.C.: Association of Research Libraries, 1996).

5. Joe Kiegel compiled both survey documents: "Analysis of the Technical Services Workstation Survey," available at gopher://marvel.loc.gov:70/00/services/cataloging/coop/coop_cncl/tswanaly, and the "Summary of the Technical Services Workstation Survey," available at gopher://marvel.loc.gov:70/00/services/cataloging/coop/coop_cncl/tswsurv.

6. About one-half of the ARL institutions responded to the TSW survey. About 65 percent of those institutions have already installed TSWs, and another 25 percent are planning to do so.

7. This was the standard configuration recommended in 1984. See the Association of Research Libraries, *Microcomputers in ARL Libraries,* ARL SPEC Kit 104 (Washington, D.C.: Association of Research Libraries, 1984), 37.

8. See the Association of Research Libraries, *Technical Services Workstations,* flyer.

9. Anaclare Evans brought this to my attention (E-mail message, Jan. 26, 1996).

10. These prices are based on quotes received from Dell Computer Corp. on Feb. 20, 1996, and include a standard educational discount.

11. I am grateful to Joan Swanekamp, formerly of Columbia University Library, for sharing with me the recommendations of that library's Ergonomics Committee/Subcommittee on Screen Colors.

12. I base these figures on interviews with several LAN managers, and this is in accord with accepted norms for LAN management.

13. Noted in a Sea Change Corp. announcement (Jan. 19, 1996) about the release of BookWhere? 2.0, which can automatically configure itself as a helper application for Netscape or Mosaic. When BookWhere? 2.0 encounters a database record that includes a WWW link to a document, it can automatically launch the configured WWW browser.

APPENDIX
▼
Games on the Computer

A great controversy revolves around the place of games on computers in the workplace. That ubiquitous game Solitaire that comes with Microsoft Windows was really designed as a teaching tool to give new computer users experience and confidence in using a mouse. It is superb at teaching the concepts of drag-and-drop, movement, and the single and double mouse click. Once those skills have been mastered, however, the role of games in the workplace becomes questionable. Staff members all too easily can become "addicted" to playing these and other games.

There are two issues here. The first is, do the games interfere with the staff members' work? Even assuming that they are not playing games on work time—and let us assume they are not doing so—should staff members who by necessity spend an increasing percentage of their day sitting in front of a computer be subtly encouraged to spend their break time and their lunch hour doing more of the same? The second issue is the question of how personal E-mail and personal listserv messages fit into the workplace. This is a much harder issue since few of us are likely to deny staff the opportunity to use these resources. Should we not then recognize the importance of encouraging the staff to take a break *away* from the computer? Administrators and managers who consider this matter seriously may well conclude that mandated breaks away from the computer are a necessary part of the day. For many of us, the days when we can offer offline tasks to our staff are long gone, and we have to consider how that affects the shape of the new work environment.

During 1995 the issue of games attracted the interest of government and the press. In Virginia, Governor George Allen banned games from state computers out of concern about misuse of the computers, particularly on government time. Several writers of comic strips addressed the issue. Parody or not, there does exist a computer program called GameCop (marketed by Analytic Concepts) that can sound the alert if someone attempts to play a game. Pat O'Donnell in The *Wall Street Journal* ("The Biggest Loser at Solitaire—the Company," December 19, 1994) and Charles Krauthammer in *Time* ("Cyberaddict, Share My Cure," February 27, 1995) devoted articles to the subject. O'Donnell recommended purging games from workplace computers. Krauthammer revealed that he had been a Minesweeper addict (and discussed his personal technique for curing it). It is true that removing such games from workplace computers may appear high-handed and patronizing, but we owe it to ourselves and our staff members to deal with this issue honestly. Once these games have served their functional role in teaching a new user how to control the mouse, they should be removed from the computer.

Software Considerations

Michael Kaplan
Harvard College Library

▼ If it is true that "clothes make the man (or woman)," then there can be no doubt that it is software that makes a generic workstation into a technical services workstation. It is a particular configuration of software designed around specific technical services functions that enables this transformation to take place.

Certain components of this software suite serve to connect individual technical services departments to the broader universe of technical services professionals worldwide. These components are the tools that keep us in contact with one another and enable us to exchange information and files quickly and easily: E-mail, listservs, Telnet, gopher, Web browsers, and file transfer protocol (FTP). These are the individual links of which our professional chain is comprised. But there are other software applications that are specifically aimed at technical services: terminal emulators and clients. A terminal emulator is a software program that enables a personal computer to emulate a particular type of dumb terminal in communicating with a mainframe; that is, it can mimic a specific terminal and talk to its mainframe host in a format that the mainframe can understand. Different types of terminals or terminal emulators are associated with different types of mainframes. But dumb terminals have few capabilities other than communicating with the mainframe. A client, on the other hand, can share the processing responsibilities with its host mainframe, which in this case is called a server. Client software resides on personal computers and extends the range of capabilities that we associate with desktop hardware. These emulators and clients allow us to connect and manipulate our databases and catalogs worldwide.

As old and technologically obsolete as it is, the world of DOS software applications is still here, albeit not for much longer. Some venerable DOS applications have recently been "displaced" by their Windows successors—OCLC's Passport for Windows and RLIN's Terminal for Windows software, for example. But others are still with us (or at least were at the time of this writing)—OCLC's Cataloging MicroEnhancer Plus (CatME+), for example, which will probably be replaced with a Windows version in late 1997. In the Harvard College Library's cataloging services department we still rely on the venerable Cornell TN3270 emulator, largely because we are not yet ready to abandon our NewKey macro program (discussed later in this chapter). The transition, already long overdue, will probably take place in 1997 as we move fully into a Windows world.

In almost every imaginable way the DOS world is proving problematic. Consider the following problems with the Cornell TN3270 emulator:

▶ Since it is a DOS application, only a single session can be run at a time.

▶ Multiple, simultaneous Windows are impossible.

▶ It is a glutton for computer memory.[1]

▶ It supports only a few network adapters (cards) and does not support many of the most popular models out today.

▶ It poses keyboard conflicts with other applications, even when it has been terminated.

▶ It supports display and input of the ALA character set, but it does not support printing of it.

▶ It is not winsock-compatible and cannot be open if a winsock application is running (more on winsocks follows).

Similar problems beset the CatME+, whose appetite for memory makes it all but impossible to run in a networked environment or under Windows. As the developers at OCLC have remarked, it was written in an age when DOS allowed only one application to run at a time, so there was no reason not to use as much of DOS's basic 640 kilobytes of memory as was necessary. A Windows version of the CatME+ is urgently needed—indeed, it is long overdue—but has been kept on the back burner by the development of Passport for Windows, which will set the basic design for all future OCLC software products.

If we accept the stated goal that we are evolving toward a world in which multitasking and multiple sessions are the rule, then these are unacceptable constraints. The only acceptable alternative is to migrate as quickly as possible to a pure Windows environment. For a variety of reasons, a number of essential library software packages appeared in Windows versions only in 1995. Foremost among these were packages for RLIN (June 1995) and OCLC (December 1995). Keeping with industry patterns common for Windows applications, both were released later than had been originally projected. So, too, McGill University's TCP3270 version 3.0 was released almost an entire year after its first projected release date.

Now that these initial packages are released, what do we have? We have Windows terminal emulators that are Winsock-compatible and fully support the ALA character set for display, input, and printing.

Winsock Compatibility

Of all the technical terms that users of TSWs must contend with, probably *winsock* and *winsock compatibility* are the most common and the most crucial. A winsock is an application programmer's interface, or API, that allows Windows programs to operate over the Internet. One of the commonest examples of a winsock is Trumpet Software International's Trumpet Winsock, but there are many others. The key attribute of winsocks is that they are all written to the same specifications to provide a standard networking layer for Windows networking applications. It is a given that any new Windows application designed to work over a TCP/IP network—such as OCLC, RLIN, Netscape, Mosaic, BookWhere?, etc.—all rely on a winsock to enable them to operate in an Internetted environment.[2]

In a winsock environment, all applications can coexist and be open simultaneously (multitasking) without either incompatibilities or conflicts. The only practicable limits are those imposed by available memory. This memory is not DOS's 640 kilobytes but the overall memory available to Windows (for example, 4 or 8 or 16 megabytes).

Why a Windows Workstation?

DOS has been with us for so long, and Windows in its various versions has been here for so long, that it is good to remind ourselves why it is we should be so keen on migrating to a pure Windows environment. Among the important reasons are the following:

- ▶ consistent interface among various Windows applications
- ▶ easier and more intuitive training due to consistent presentation of applications, including both library and nonlibrary applications
- ▶ multitasking
- ▶ multiple sessions
- ▶ ease of operating in an environment that encourages cut (or copy) and paste
- ▶ growing and complete support (display, input, printing) for the full ALA character set via software solutions (Windows fonts)
- ▶ potential for both online help and context-sensitive help, including help for applications, *AACR2R,* and the *Library of Congress Rule Interpretations,* MARC formats, MARC code lists, local documentation, etc.

- ▶ links between applications, including hypertext linkages (http://) over the Internet
- ▶ potential for elaborate programmatic macros that can move and format data between various applications automatically (or with minimal intervention)

Although some of these have already been discussed and others are intuitively obvious once mentioned, this is a list that should serve as a basis for discussion with any TSW developer. A fully functional TSW should address all these issues. For example,

How well does a TSW package conform to all standard Windows conventions?

Do menus pull down and reveal the expected options?

Can the user cascade, tile, or arrange the internal Windows as expected?

How easy is it to set up new sessions and connect to new sources of data?

Does the application incorporate Z39.50 protocols for search/retrieval? Who maintains the list of Z39.50 hosts and their search conventions? How is it to be updated? Can a Z39.50 session be launched from within a catalog session without leaving that session?

What is the level of data validation? Can it be maintained locally or only by the TSW developer?

Are data/format templates available? Can they be individualized and stored both on the local PC and on a server, if available?

Can information about hotkeys or macros be individualized as well as be maintained on a group basis?

Is help available in the form of an online manual?

If the user clicks on a MARC field and pushes the <F1> key (the standard key for Help), does context-sensitive help present itself? Can such information (or at least sections of it) also be printed out, not just topic by topic, but as an entire user's manual? This is particularly important with complex topics that require study.[3]

Is there easy access to keymap information for help on inputting diacritics and special characters?

Can those diacritics that are frequently used be assigned to hotkeys?

Is it possible to address a query to the Library of Congress Cataloger's Desktop directly from within the application?

Bear in mind an important distinction here—namely between terminal emulators, Windows applications such as those released by OCLC or RLIN or McGill University, and clients, those released by GEAC or The Library Corporation. OCLC, RLIN, and McGill University have basically given us Windows terminal emulators. McGill, for instance, provides a TN3270 emulation; OCLC offers a variety of emulations. In all cases, however, the Windows functionality is somewhat circumscribed compared with that offered by products incorporating Z39.50 clients such as those in GeoCat or ITS for Windows. Consider: the three emulators (OCLC's, RLIN's, and McGill's) all provide such standard features as menus, Windows help, mouse control including highlighting and cut/paste, but it is not possible to click (highlight)/enter or double-click a selection (line) in an index or guide screen and by that action retrieve the underlying record. This is a feature offered by GEAC's GeoCat, The Library Corporation's ITS for Windows, and Sea Change's BookWhere? Increasingly, expect terminal emulators to give way to Z39.50 clients as a new generation of software is released. The movement toward incorporating Z39.50 with Web browsers as a Web helper application will only increase this tendency.

Recently, too, one of the technical difficulties with using the Web as the front end to a catalog has been overcome. That is the development of "state" within a Web context. The Web has been by its very nature a "stateless" entity. While a "stateful" connection maintains an open line between a server and a client, Web browsers have until recently connected to a server only to retrieve information and then have terminated that connection. That has complicated the task of conducting sessions where it has not been possible to refine searches based on result sets because the server did not keep track of the search history. Now, however, OCLC and others have given their Web servers awareness of "state" by creating a session identifier that associates a searcher with a connection and keeps track of ongoing searches.[4]

For users of applications such as the proposed FolioViews Web version of Cataloger's Desktop that might be mounted on a Web server for pay-by-the-search sessions, this poses a potential solution to the problem of searching, refining results, and re-searching the database based on the result sets. (See chapter 5 for further discussions.) Together with other, ongoing developments in Z39.50 and the Web, it promises to change the way technical services operates and to help the transformation of the TSW into the technical services client (TSC).

One other consideration to keep in mind when considering various TSW packages is their ability to be used in a variety of technical services environments. When the Cooperative Cataloging Council's Automation Task Group convened its meeting with library service vendors at the Library of Congress in 1994 (see chapter 4), a key proposal that we presented to vendors was the issue of open versus proprietary systems. Library systems that are "open," for example, would allow libraries to choose the best software for technical services or public services use. Users of such systems would not be locked into using the vendor's proprietary software package just because it comes from the vendor of their online system. There has been some movement in this area since that meeting. At least one vendor is in fact marketing its TSW software to other library system vendors with the goal of offering it as an alternative for technical services users of other systems.

The ALA Character Set

One reason that library-specific software has not moved into the mainstream and into the Windows world more quickly than it has is that ours is a small niche market in the multibillion dollar world of software companies. As library products become more standardized around Windows and as the commercial importance of information on the Internet enables library products and library data to take a central place in the emerging global information network, this may become less of a hindrance.

There is one central facet of library technical services that has set the library world apart from the mainstream, the ALA character set. The ALA character set is very much related to the evolutionary development of TSWs because it has had a major role in dictating the framework under which TSWs have evolved.

A surprising fact elicited by the PCC Standing Committee on Automation's survey of TSWs was the number of institutions that have had to compromise on support of the ALA character set.[5] While full support of it is a universal desire, at least in the absence of all other constraints, the ability to support it across the board under all library applications has not been a simple matter, largely because the ALA character set has not been part of mainstream product development, including both hardware and software.

In the precomputer era, support for the character set was limited to a few models of terminals, most recently models such as the IBM 3163. The IBM 3163 could be enabled to support the character set by means of a font cartridge. However, in public services departments or in public areas, the terminal of choice was frequently the IBM 3151 terminal. That was incapable of using the font cartridge, so it could not display the character set for the public.

In the years since the introduction of computer platforms to technical services the modes of supporting the ALA character set have changed dramatically. In 1984 the OCLC M300 depended on an onboard, specialized computer chip for display of the font. By the time OCLC had moved to the M310 computer, it was feasible to use newer graphics adapters and software solutions to support the font. For OCLC the dramatic moment came in 1987 with the release of Terminal Software version 5.1 (still in the pre-Passport era). This software release exploited the graphics capabilities of the EGA (enhanced graphics adapter) to make use of loadable fonts. In 1985 RLIN released its first computer workstation, and RLIN's approach was to require a specific set of components, including the CGA (color graphics adapter), to generate diacritics and other special characters. Both solutions, the 1985 CGA and the 1987 EGA, made use of software solutions built on the graphics capabilities of the computers and were infinitely preferable to requiring a nonstandard hardware solution.[6]

In the nonutility, OPAC world other solutions were developed. In the NOTIS environment two examples were Yale University's YTerm and Cornell University's TN3270 emulators. Both were capable of displaying and allowing input of the full character set, but both had their limitations and were essentially "orphan" products by the early 1990s. Furthermore, while both could be run under Windows, neither was a true Windows application.

The development of true Windows applications that use fonts written for Windows and that fully support the ALA character set is at the heart of the new generation of software packages. This will be crucial in launching the next stages in the evolution of the TSW. By writing to Windows standards and using True Type fonts, for instance, developers gain the advantage of instant support for printing the character set on any graphics printer that is itself supported by Windows. This is a tremendous advantage in that it relieves developers of the necessity to write their own printer drivers, allowing them to concentrate on the core requirements of their programs and to develop advanced functionality rather than devoting further attention to the basic infrastructure on which the font must rest. Soon we will be able to look back to the time when opting for support of the full ALA character set meant sacrificing other essential requirements or when it meant paying a significant financial cost as a bump in the evolutionary road leading toward the TSW. We have already reached the stage, moreover, when no one requesting proposals from developers should accept anything less than full support of the ALA character set.

Macros and Macro Packages

There is no programmatic aspect of the TSW that should be closer to a user's or administrator's heart than that of the macro capabilities of the workstation. By *macro*, I mean "the ability of the operator to accomplish multiple keystrokes or multiple operations with a single key (hotkey)." Macros have been called various names over time, and many OCLC users first came to know them as "user-defined function keys." Macros may also be familiar to users of such programs as WordPerfect or Lotus 1-2-3 or Excel, all of which offer the capability of creating macros. Indeed, users of current versions of these programs can create very powerful and sophisticated macros.

It is important to understand that the types of macros that I am alluding to go light-years beyond storage of mere text (for example, "Includes bibliographical references"). Macros in technical services operations can in fact be miniprograms and are capable of actual operations, such as manipulating text, interpreting screens or records, and accomplishing significant tasks.

Four crucial reasons that macros should be accorded significant consideration in designing a TSW are their potential for

▶ creating an enormous increase in productivity

▶ increasing accuracy

▶ decreasing instances of repetitive strain injuries associated with manual keying

▶ automating authority-record creation and contributing to programs such as the Name Authorities Cooperative Project (NACO)[7]

Macro Use and Productivity

Among the increases in productivity associated with the changeover to TSWs reported in the Cooperative Cataloging Council Automation Task Group's 1994 TSW survey, Harvard College Library attributes its startling increase in productivity in large measure to the macro programs put into place at the same time that TSWs were installed.[8] In that survey, the Cataloging Services Department reported a 63 percent increase in productivity despite an 18 percent decrease in staffing hours (fiscal year 1994). The essential elements in Harvard College Library's macro usage included the following:

> macros running at high speed, decreasing time associated with unit records

> elimination of an estimated 1.5 million keystrokes per year in copy cataloging alone (based on an average of 50 keystrokes per record over 30,000 records)

> staffing hours previously lost to repetitive stress injuries recaptured and put to productive use

> increased accuracy because copy macros replace manual keying

> fewer hours devoted to problem solving because increased accuracy means fewer problems to solve

> programmed pauses for bar code insertion mean catalogers cannot omit wanding bar codes and potentially lose inventory control of the book

In fact, even if the error rate associated with manual keying were kept to 0.1 percent, which would be an extremely low figure, an estimated 1,500 errors affecting 5 percent of the copy-cataloged titles will have been eliminated from the system.

Macros have been with us for some time and have been the object of much discussion in journals such as *OCLC Micro*. They have also existed in very limited degrees in the terminal environment. The IBM 3163 terminal, long a favorite of the NOTIS community, has the ability to store up to twenty-four macros on its <F1> through <F24> keys. The true constraint, however, is storage: each function key has a limited amount of storage capacity, and the overall limit for all twenty-four function keys is only 256 characters.[9] This is a paltry level, particularly as the technical services community has come in recent years to discover and appreciate the truly marvelous accomplishments that macros and major programmatic approaches to acquisitions and cataloging can deliver.

There are several levels on which to approach macros. In the terminal environment, macros are a function of hardware and memory. Terminals do not have independent hard drives or large reserves of memory. This is very different from personal computers, where hard disk storage for macro programs is vast. For TSWs, then, macros are really software packages that can be either integral or external to the software used to conduct the local catalog session. The software packages can also be DOS packages or Windows packages and can be configured to run in a variety of ways. Let's examine several and discuss some of their advantages and disadvantages.

Essential Elements of Macro Packages

A powerful macro package should conform to the following minimum requirements:

1. *True recorder.* It should be possible to create a macro by recording a series of keystrokes in an actual operation rather than by working out the complete details of the keystrokes beforehand.

2. *Easy-to-use editor.* Almost every complicated macro sequence will require some manual fine-tuning, such as inserting pauses during which the mainframe system can respond.

3. *Step-by-step debugger.* This feature is necessary to test the macro and discover the precise nature of any problems that are encountered.

4. *Ability to store multiple macro files.* The potential for macro development is almost endless, and project-, unit-, and function-specific macros may best be stored in separate files. The operator should be encouraged to experiment and create personal macros and store them separately from the standard macros.

5. *Hotkeys.* It should be possible to start macros by pressing combinations of hotkeys (for example, <Alt>1, <Ctrl>1, <Shift><F1>, etc.). Windows-based programs may combine that ability with the ability to pull down a macro menu, highlight a particular macro, and click a Run button.

6. *Pause-until-resume.* A pause-until-resume feature can be combined with dialog boxes to prompt the operator for variable amounts of input, after which the operator can signal the macro to resume its operation.

7. *Fixed-length pauses.* This feature is similar to the pause-until-resume feature but very useful for incorporating fixed-length data, such as bar codes whose lengths are predetermined. Following the wanding of the required number of alphanumeric keys, the macro should automatically resume operation.

8. *If then/if not.* The easier it is to build logic sequences into macros (if this is true, do this; if this is not true, do this; if this is true, do not do this; if this is not true, do not do this), the easier it is to build complex macros that can intelligently assess well-defined scenarios and act accordingly.

9. *Control codes and nested macros.* Control codes such as wait, wait-for-key, cut screen region, etc., vastly extend the range of macro capability. Similarly, macros should be capable of calling other macros as needed.

10. *Multiple clipboards.* Many of the most useful macros operate by collecting areas of the MARC record (for example, 100 $a-$d,

245 $a, 260 $c) and reassembling them in defined sequences. To do this, the macro needs to store the different pieces of text in multiple clipboards or vaults or buffers. There are a number of different ways a program can accomplish this.

11. *"MARC aware."* This is a corollary of the preceding attribute. A macro should have the ability to parse the MARC record and capture defined elements by field or subfield.

12. *Move cursor to given field or subfield.* Similar to number 11, but in this case the macro would pause to await operator input or correction to an existing record.

13. *Looping or defined recursion.* This is a powerful but potentially dangerous element. If a list of records with well-defined attributes all need similar treatment or correction, for instance, it should be possible to have the macro run in a loop, making the same change or conducting the same operation on each record in the list, until the entire list is exhausted and the macro ceases to operate. Obviously, any such operation needs careful scrutiny to ensure that a runaway chain reaction or a series of incorrect changes do not take place.

14. *Dialog boxes.* These are popup query boxes that prompt the operator for input and can offer a variety of options (yes/no, buttons, variable input, etc.) to which the operator can respond as needed.

Finally, the macro package needs to be powerful yet easy to use. Creating or editing macros in "English language" terms by easy scripting is preferable to complex languages that require real programming expertise. Accomplishing this is actually the most difficult of all the listed elements since a powerful language is normally expressed in complex terms. Yet most libraries will be hard put to fully exploit such a language, even with access to a recorder to automate creation of simple macros.

NewKey

The macro package that Harvard College Library's cataloging services department chose to install at the same time that TSWs were installed was NewKey.[10] NewKey is representative of a class of DOS programs called TSRs, or terminate and stay resident programs. (Other, similar programs exist, but Harvard College Library believes NewKey was and is the best DOS program available for its purposes.) These are programs that reside in the computer's memory from the time they are loaded until they are removed. As such, they become part of the software that controls the computer. NewKey "eavesdrops" on keystrokes entered from the keyboard and checks keystrokes that are entered against its list of assigned macro hotkeys. When it recognizes an incoming keystroke that is on its list, it responds by playing back the macro sequence associated with that key. The computer is lulled into treating the keystrokes it receives as if they were coming from the keyboard, though in fact it is NewKey that is providing the keystrokes.

It is possible to load NewKey in a variety of ways:

as part of the AUTOEXEC.BAT (startup file), in which case it is always memory-resident and its use can be extended across a single application. In this way, NewKey can exert itself across a local catalog session and OCLC, for example, and be used to transfer OCLC authority records from OCLC to an authority template in the OPAC.

as part of the startup file for a catalog session, in which case it can also be unloaded when the operator exits a catalog session. In this case NewKey's impact is strictly limited to the catalog session.

in Windows under a so-called DOS box, in which case it affects only the program with which it is associated. In many respects this is the safest way to handle TSR programs like NewKey since their influence is circumscribed by the barriers of the Windows DOS box.

NewKey, however, is emphatically *not* a Windows program. It cannot be associated with any program that is designed for Windows. As such, its lifetime and usefulness is clearly circumscribed and will remain viable only for those institutions that choose to continue operating on a DOS plane, although that DOS plane can be approached via a Windows DOS box.

When loaded, NewKey can be accessed by means of a hotkey. Its basic menu structure allows the operator to load or unload any file (set) of macros as well as to display and edit those macros individually. One of the first macros created during the initial stages of macro development at Harvard was a "simple" copy/paste macro. It seems simple in retrospect, but at the time it was revolutionary. Like most other NOTIS libraries that depended on IBM 3163 terminals for input and editing in the technical services module, Harvard libraries were lacking any means to copy text within or between records. When technical services staff were presented in 1992 with a NewKey-mediated means to copy text, it was seen as an immediate validation of the concept of a workstation and an associated macro program versus a simple, dumb terminal. Figures 2.1 and 2.2 show the NewKey main menu and its set of macros. Figure 2.3 shows the copy macro.

NewKey presents a copy option on its main menu, but at Harvard we found it more expeditious to embed that function in a macro of its own. That macro in turn was embedded (nested) in many other macros. As such, it was the basic building block for our macro development. What follows are two examples of macro use at Harvard, one in copy cataloging and one as part of a backlog reduction project.

NewKey in the Copy-Cataloging Workflow

Like most libraries, Harvard College Library's Western Language technical services departments depend on copy cataloging for the bulk of their processing. That copy comes from either a locally maintained Library of Congress resource file, which consists of between four and five years' worth of LC monograph records accessible to everyone in

Figure 2.1 NewKey Main Menu

```
                        DIRECTORY
Macro      Status  Description
<altj>             Save HOLLIS #
<altk>             Recall HOLLIS #
<altl>             Search copied text
<ctrl=>            AOA5103
<ctrldn>           De l'<Γ>egalit<Γ>e des deux sexes. <Ç>l German
<ctrlend>          "Die Gleichheit der Geschlechter"
<ctrlg>            100:20: <Ç>a Poulain de La Barre, Fran<≡>cois, <Ç>d 1647
<ctrlnum/>         SAR for unnumbered series
<ctrlp>            Cut/paste
<ctrlpgd>          8c: <Ç>i wid <Ç>b Arc 207.5
<ctrlsdel>         SAR for srnk with copy/paste
<ctrlsend>         Author-title/Author u.t. ref.
<ctrlshom>         SAR with copy/paste for analytic series
<ctrlsins>         SAR (non-srnk) with copy/paste
<ctrlspgd>         Personal NAR (a.e.) with copy/paste
<ctrlspgu>         Personal NAR (m.e.) with copy/paste

 Scroll: [↑ ↓ PGUI                    :←┘] Escape: [F1] Exit: [ESC]
```

Figure 2.2 Set of NewKey Macros

technical services throughout the university, or from OCLC or RLIN. The university's office for information systems developed a program that compares key numbers (LCCNs or ISBNs) on provisional (acquisitions-level) records in the OPAC with the key numbers in the LC resource file

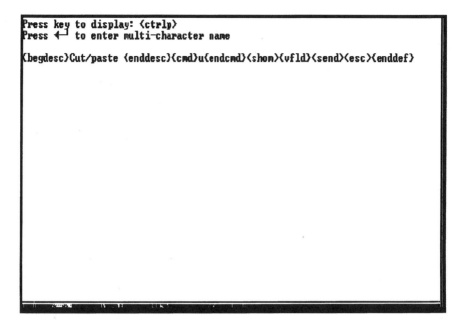

```
Press key to display: <ctrlp>
Press ←┘ to enter multi-character name

<begdesc>Cut/paste <enddesc><cmd>u<endcmd><shom><vfld><send><esc><enddef>
```

Figure 2.3   NewKey Copy Macro

on a weekly basis. When a match is found and it passes verification routines, the LC record is automatically moved from the resource file and replaces the bibliographic information in the provisional record. A report is generated alerting technical services staff to retrieve the book, finish its bibliographic processing, and forward it to end-processing and binding.

It is in the intermediate step involving the technical services staff that NewKey is of greatest help in standard copy-cataloging operations. Because a large variety of local call number schemes remain in use among Harvard University's almost 100 libraries, it is not feasible to automatically embed the LC call number in our LOC (holdings field). So, before the introduction of TSWs and NewKey, the copy cataloger did the following to catalog a book destined for storage at the Harvard depository (HD):

1. Transferred the LC call number from the 050 field to the LOC. Generally the 050 field and the LOC were on different screens, with the 050 field on screen 1 and the LOC on screen 2. It was necessary to copy the call number to the book, and then transcribe it back to the LOC. This was a common source of operator error since it involved two opportunities to commit a typographical error, and the screen 1/screen 2 situation did not allow the copy cataloger to easily compare the number he or she had keyed with the number provided by LC.

2. Keyed "$c Harvard Depository" prior to the call number, thus indicating the book's remote location. To judge by the hun-

dreds of variant spellings recently corrected in our online catalog, this was another source of frequent error.

3. Keyed a coded note, "$k HDI," used for inventory purposes.

4. Keyed a public note, "$n Consult Circ. Desk for [bar code]"—the
bar code number is wanded—so that the patrons can request the
book from the depository, where it is shelved by bar code.

5. Created an item record and wanded the bar code into the item
record.

6. Filed the item record, retrieved the catalog record, and issued a
"tape" command to transmit our holdings via file transfer protocol to OCLC so that they could be added to OCLC's WorldCat.

With TSWs and NewKey that same process has now been reduced
to the following three minimal steps:

1. Call up the record and start the macro with a hotkey.

2. Highlight the call number with the cursor key (the macro places
the cursor in the correct position to start) and press <Enter>.

3. Wand the bar code (just once; NewKey will remember it and insert it the second time).

All manual keying has been eliminated, and with it all opportunity for error. No step or note can be forgotten, the cataloger cannot
forget to issue the "tape" command, and the time required to catalog
the book is reduced to less than a minute. See figures 2.4–2.5.

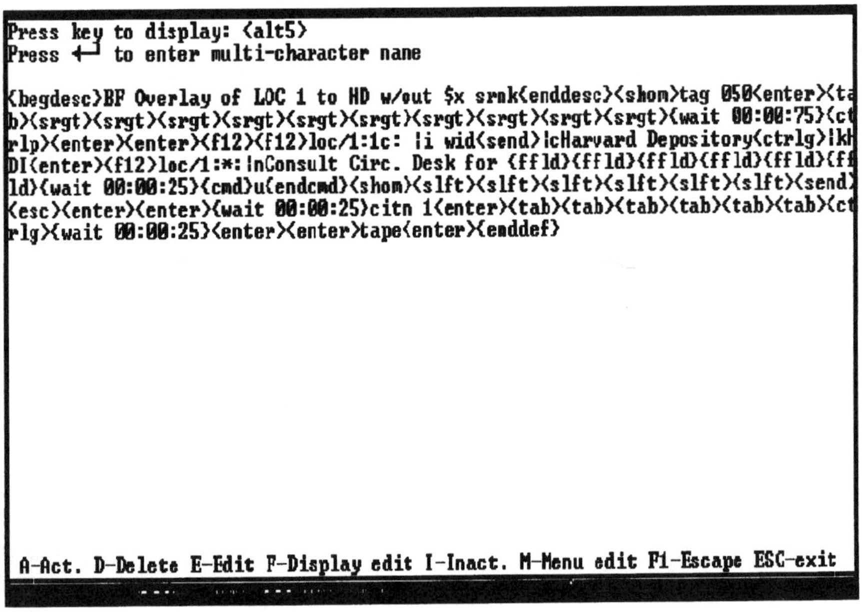

```
Press key to display: <alt5>
Press ←┘ to enter multi-character name

<begdesc>BF Overlay of LOC 1 to HD w/out $x srmk<enddesc><shom>tag 050<enter><t
b><srgt><srgt><srgt><srgt><srgt><srgt><srgt><srgt><srgt><wait 00:00:75><ct
rlp><enter><enter><f12><f12>loc/1:1c: |i wid<send>|cHarvard Depository<ctrlg>|kH
DI<enter><f12>loc/1:*: |nConsult Circ. Desk for <ffld><ffld><ffld><ffld><ffld><ff
ld><wait 00:00:25><cmd>u<endcmd><shom><slft><slft><slft><slft><slft><slft><send>
<esc><enter><enter><wait 00:00:25>citn 1<enter><tab><tab><tab><tab><tab><tab><ct
rlg><wait 00:00:25><enter><enter>tape<enter><enddef>




A-Act. D-Delete E-Edit F-Display edit I-Inact. M-Menu edit F1-Escape ESC-exit
```

Figure 2.4 Cataloging Copy Macro

```
010:    :  ‡a    93219737
020/1:    :  ‡a 3880426198
040:    :  ‡a DLC ‡c DLC
043:    :  ‡a e-pl---
050/1:00: ‡a DK4800.J45 ‡b B33 1992
082/1:00: ‡a 943.8/5 ‡2 20
100:1 :  ‡a Bach, Erle.
245:14: ‡a Das alte Hirschberg zwischen Handel und Poesie : ‡b eine 700
jāhrige Stadt im Herzen Europas im Spiegel ihrer Geschichte / ‡c Erle Bach.
260:    :  ‡a Husum : ‡b Husum Druck- und Verlagsgesellschaft, ‡c c1992.
300/1:    :  ‡a 227 p. : ‡b ill. ; ‡c 24 cm.
651/1:  0: ‡a Jelenia Góra (Poland) ‡x History.
LOC/1: p: ‡i wid
```
```
                                                                    ch.
    260:    :  ‡a Husum : ‡b Husum Druck- und Verlagsgesellschaft, ‡c c1992.
    300:    :  ‡a 227 p. : ‡b ill. ; ‡c 24 cm.
    651/1:  0: ‡a Jelenia Góra (Poland) ‡x History.
    LOC/1:1c: ‡i wid ‡c Harvard Depository ‡a DK4800.J45 ‡b B33 1992 ‡k HDI ‡n
    Consult Circ. Desk for HWU52U
```

Figure 2.5   Bibliographic Record before and after Cataloging

NewKey and Backlog Reduction

No area of cataloging has benefited from macro capabilities more than database management. Imagine long lists of incorrect headings routinely corrected by looping macros that have the authorized form embedded in them, or imagine a long list of complex series headings that need correction and that require only manual intervention to insert individual series numbers in the records. These are the sorts of macro capabilities that drive database management.

A more impressive example is a backlog-reduction project that Harvard College Library's database management team undertook between 1993 and 1995. Due to a change in policy regarding books stored in the Harvard depository, database management accepted the challenge to process and catalog some 172,000 books in HD that only had provisional records. The process as eventually configured made use of

▶ a Paradox database of the provisional records

▶ the OCLC Cataloging MicroEnhancer Plus (CatME+)

▶ three programs written in the C++ language designed to

extract information from the CatME+

feed information to NewKey and via NewKey to HOLLIS (Harvard's online catalog) for searching (ISBN or LCCN) and to insert information (the OCLC control number) to link the incoming utility record with our provisional record

set the OCLC holding codes in the CatME+ en masse

▶ NewKey is designed to

perform sequential searches of HOLLIS

manipulate the HOLLIS records

insert OCLC control numbers as links between the OCLC record and HOLLIS

This was quite an ambitious program, and it proceeded in two distinct phases. First, 92,000 HD provisional records that contained either

LCCNs or ISBNs were extracted from the Paradox database. These LCCNs or ISBNs were exported as ASCII files in groups of 470 records each. The files were named OCLCKEYS.DAT, which is the file that serves the OCLC CatME+ as an input file for searching. Once each file was searched, it was printed out using the CatME+'s automatic printout function. A cataloger compared the printout to HOLLIS to be sure that the "hit" was actually a "match" (about 0.7 percent were mismatches) and to note needed corrections to the OCLC record.

Prior to the verification stage, one of the C++ programs extracted from the CatME+ data file (LOCFILE.DAT) two parallel columns of key numbers: the OCLC control number and the search key that had been used for input (LCCN or ISBN). That file was used as input to a second C++ program, which extracted the LCCN or ISBN from the file one search key at a time. The program fed it to NewKey to retrieve the matching HOLLIS record and to input the OCLC control number into the HOLLIS record for matching (targeting) purposes. The third C++ program in a single operation changed the text in all OCLC 049 fields in the file LOCFILE.DAT from their default (HLSS) to the code used for HD books (HWS9). This eliminated the need for us to change the code in each record individually.

We then constructed the entire process as follows:

1. Cataloger starts recursive NewKey macro.
2. Macro "shells" to DOS (exits from the catalog session to a DOS prompt) and runs C++ program to extract LCCN/ISBN and OCLC control number.
3. NewKey captures the two numbers in two separate copy buffers.
4. NewKey returns to HOLLIS session and searches for matching HOLLIS record with LCCN/ISBN.
5. NewKey pauses for cataloger to verify that the record is a match. Cataloger presses <Enter> if it is, aborts the macro for that particular record if it is not.
6. If the record is a match, NewKey inserts OCLC control number into HOLLIS record for linking purposes, reformats LOC field (see figure 2.6) with public note, pauses for cataloger to wand bar code, creates an item record, and inserts bar code (that it has already copied) into the item record.[11]
7. NewKey pauses for cataloger to verify that the item record was successfully created and then loops back to step 2.

By means of this combination of programs, database management was able to search 92,000 records and provide cataloging copy for 55,000 titles in 14 months with the equivalent of one full-time equivalent (FTE) cataloger. Since Phase 1 ended in February 1995, database management has used similar techniques to manipulate the LOCs in 37,000 OCLC no-hits in addition to 80,000 records lacking LCCNs or ISBNs in preparation for further computer-to-computer searching. It is our firm belief that the job we did and the results we achieved were a conclusive argument in favor of the advantages of TSWs and macro programs. Furthermore,

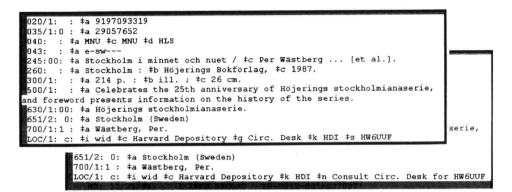

Figure 2.6   Harvard Depository Project Record before and after Changes

we did it more expeditiously and at a lesser cost than we could have achieved by using any existing outsourcing vendor, while at the same time adding value to our local database as well as to OCLC (enhances, duplicate reports). We believe that this is ample testament to the power and advantages of developing and implementing this type of technology.

Macros in the Windows Environment

It is clear that the future of the TSW is firmly rooted in a Windows environment. Only such an environment will provide the multitasking, the multiple sessions, the winsock-compatibility, and the copy/paste between sessions that are the basic building blocks of the Windows TSW. Harvard College Library has, therefore, been actively searching for a Windows-based successor to NewKey.[12] The results to date have not been overwhelmingly positive, at least as compared with what NewKey has offered us. The programs fall into three major categories:

  stand-alone commercial programs that can be "attached" to other Windows programs

  Microsoft Visual Basic (VB) and other such programs, such as Borland's Delphi or IBM's Visual REXX (for OS/2 users)

  library-specific programs, such as OCLC's Passport for Windows and McGill University's TCP3270 version 3.0, which incorporate Visual Basic-like macro languages

Harvard College Library tested two commercial Windows packages, CE Software's ProKey version 1.5 for Windows and Softblox's SmartPad for Windows version 3.0. ProKey is the Windows release of a previous DOS product.[13] It has a number of useful features, such as a recorder, pauses (both fixed and variable), multiple copy buffers (called "vaults"), an editor, and a debugger, but it was not found to be acceptable in actual use. Because the program allows only a limited number of controls over its operation and because it does not allow the user direct access to them except by means of running a macro through the debugger, it proved difficult to exercise detailed and precise control over its functioning. The debugger, for example, broke down at crucial places.

SmartPad offers a different functionality, part of which is a macro facility. SmartPad aims to allow the user to build "toolbars," those arrays of icons that fit beneath the menu bar or along the margins of a Windows program. With that and SmartPad's macro recorder/editor, it is possible to create macros and place them on any number of toolbars and even to embed toolbars within toolbars. Here again, however, precise control over the inner workings of the macros proved elusive. The editor was cumbersome and frustrating, and there was no step-by-step debugger. On the other hand, SmartPad allows for building of visually oriented toolbars in a highly aesthetic manner and allows for clever groupings of macros on toolbars that can lead to either drop-down menus or subsidiary toolbars.

What we can learn from these two programs is that a "canned" approach to macro development is unacceptable in actual use. A sophisticated and powerful program needs to offer the user direct access to the code that controls the macros. For Windows users, only Visual Basic and its cousins or derivatives seem to offer that level of control. It is no surprise, therefore, that Gary Strawn of Northwestern University chose Visual Basic as the foundation for his Cataloger's Toolkit (see chapter 8), that OCLC has chosen a variation of Visual Basic for its OCLC Macro Language (OML), or that the OS/2 practitioners at the Library of Congress have looked to OS/2's Visual REXX for creation of macros for their bibliographic workstations (see chapter 9). At Harvard University we have been experimenting with the OML that is embedded in Passport for Windows and the very similar implementation of Visual Basic contained in TCP3270 version 3.0.[14]

McGill's product is a 3270 terminal emulator, and as such, it is intended for users of IBM mainframes. As a 3270 terminal emulator, this software package enables the personal computer to communicate with the IBM mainframe just as though it were the dumb terminal that the mainframe expects. In the library community that translates, for example, to NOTIS users. TCP3270 is a complete package, and version 3.0, which appeared in November 1995, is a major upgrade, particularly in its programmatic capabilities. Previous versions of TCP3270 offered users the ability to create only rudimentary macros by hand. That ability still exists in version 3.0 of TCP3270 and is now known as Quick-Keys to distinguish it from the new macro facility in the program. (See figures 2.7 and 2.8.) It is likely that NOTIS institutions, perhaps cooperating under the aegis of NUGM (NOTIS Users' Group Meeting) can build a support group for creating complex macro programs that will enhance the productivity levels of the core functionalities of "generic" NOTIS libraries. (In January 1997, McGill Systems sold the rights to TCP3270, which has since been renamed HostExplorer, to Hummingbird Communications, Ltd.) Harvard's implementation of NOTIS is not generic, however, so it appears that it will be up to the individual libraries at Harvard to devise their own macro programs. In the case of both the generic and the nongeneric flavors of NOTIS, moreover, it is

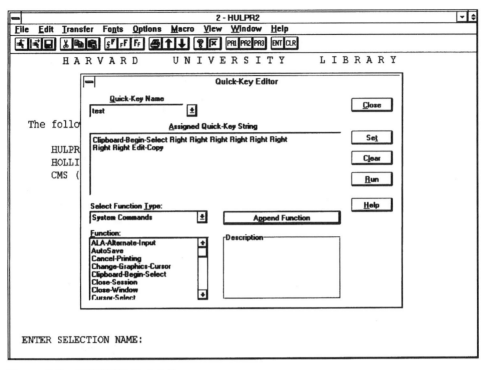

Figure 2.7   TCP3270 Quick-Keys

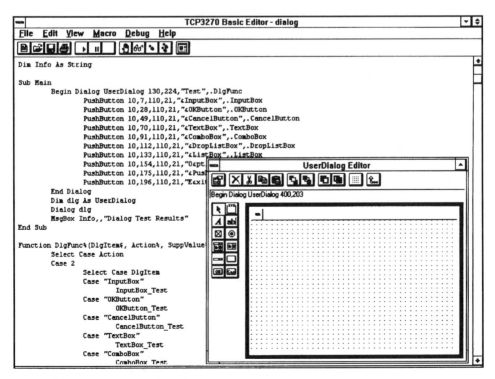

Figure 2.8   TCP3270 Basic Editor

fairly certain that exploiting the McGill TCP3270 macro language to its fullest will require true programming expertise.

OCLC obviously intends OML to offer a very high level of functionality. It will be integral to all new OCLC software products, including Windows rewrites of the Cataloging and ILL MicroEnhancers. The function keys in Passport for Windows (<F1> to <F12>, with <Alt>, <Ctrl>, and <Shift> combinations of <F1> to <F12> as well) that OCLC users have long used have been rewritten in OML. Other macros have been written, and OCLC has created a site for users to contribute macros for sharing on the OCLC product services menu. For those institutions that actually edit online in OCLC, OML promises to be a tremendous benefit, particularly since this is a series of very large communities with many pockets of programming talent. The implications of OML for national programs such as NACO are profound and may well prove decisive as institutions consider NACO membership. It certainly puts an entirely different perspective on how and where NACO records should be created, at least where OCLC members are concerned.

Most units at Harvard no longer edit records directly on OCLC but rather simply claim them online and then use their TSWs to edit the claimed records within the HOLLIS environment. (CONSER [Cooperative Online Serials Program] and CJK catalogers remain exceptions.) This drastically curtailed online telecommunications costs to OCLC at the same time as we leveraged our investments in workstation technology.

On the other hand, the cataloging services department experimented with using Passport for Windows to access HOLLIS in technical services mode and successfully created a keymap that allowed displaying, editing, and printing the full ALA character set. OCLC and HOLLIS could be run in separate sessions under Passport for Windows (see figure 2.9). Besides presenting an opportunity to consolidate training under a single software package, we hoped that Passport for Windows and OML could be exploited to move data back and forth seamlessly between OCLC and HOLLIS. But because Passport for Windows does not support a true TN3270 emulation, it was necessary to rely on a different emulation, an IBM 3163, and that appears to have been sufficient to cause problems in fully applying OML to a "foreign" environment.

Despite our preference for operating in our local environment, we are still discovering ways to use OML: for instance, creating dialog boxes for input of OCLC holding codes and HOLLIS control numbers. OML can be used to extract a control number from a HOLLIS session open under Passport for Windows and automatically format and insert it into an OCLC record also open under Passport for Windows. And the same OML macro can add the OCLC holding code or ask the operator via a dialog box what it should be.

In late 1996, Harvard College Library's cataloging services department received permission to move in a new direction, adapting a nonlibrary TN3270 emulation package (Reflection) from a commercial software developer, WRQ, for use with HOLLIS. To enable this package to work in the library's environment, the first prerequisite was to mesh it with a usable ALA font. Since that time, work has continued in creating the high-volume, macro-driven process that has prevailed under

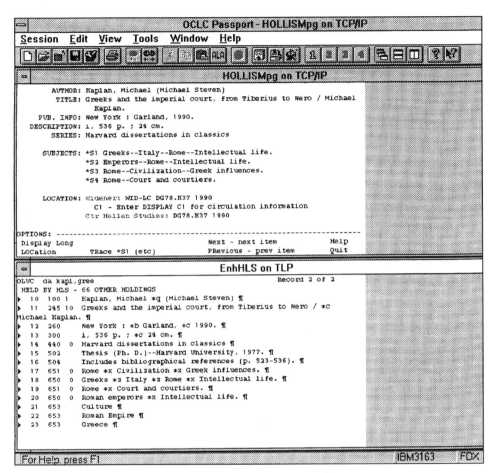

Figure 2.9 HOLLIS and OCLC under Passport for Windows

HOLLIS with NewKey. While still in its early stages and while many facets of technical services are yet to be fleshed out in detail, there are high expectations that this package will enable the Harvard College Library's technical services departments to move forward on a secure, stable, and creative platform.

The Future of Macro Programs

As more institutions become aware of the power of macros to increase their productivity, to ensure a higher level of quality-control by replacing manual copying with programmed copy/paste, and to reduce injuries associated with manual keying, we should expect to see more administrative and systems support for the programming efforts needed to create high-level macros. Particularly where there exist natural constituencies, such as those of OCLC or NOTIS users, we can hope to see the rise of cooperative efforts. A few model demonstration projects, such as the NACO authorities macro, will pave the way for major developments in cataloging and other technical services activities with TSWs as their platforms.

Notes

1. Programs such as Cornell's TN3270 and the OCLC CatME+ tend to need as much of the basic 640 kilobytes of "low" DOS memory as possible. If you are trying to run them on networked machines, that can pose major problems. After you have loaded all the network drivers and other device drivers, it is very difficult to find enough memory remaining below that 640 kilobytes limit to still run the CatME+. Without recourse to a memory manager, in fact, it is virtually impossible.

2. See my discussion, "Technical Services Workstations: A Review of the State of the Art," *Library Resources & Technical Services* 40, no. 2 (Apr. 1996): 174.

3. One of the more frustrating aspects of Passport for Windows is the absence of a printed manual and the user's inability to print one out locally except topic by topic. For the section on the OCLC macro language, which has well over 100 individual command topics, this is unacceptable. McGill University's TCP3270 version 3.0, on the other hand, incorporates the user manual as an Adobe Acrobat document.

4. Work on OCLC's WebZ server is reported in "ALA Annual 1995," in *OCLC Systems & Services* 11, no. 3 (1995): 10.

5. The elusiveness, but at the same time the importance, of the ALA character set was covered in the two TSW surveys. See Joe Kiegel, "Analysis of the Technical Services Workstation Survey," available on gopher://marvel.loc.gov:70/00/services/cataloging/coop/coop_cncl/tswanaly, and the "Summary of the Technical Services Workstation Survey," available on gopher://marvel.loc.gov:70/00/services/cataloging/coop/coop_cncl/tswsurv, as well as *Technical Services Workstations,* ARL SPEC Kit 213 (Washington, D.C.: Association of Research Libraries, 1996). See also Kaplan, "Technical Services Workstations," 172–4.

6. See Kaplan, "Technical Services Workstations," 172–3, and Howard Curtis, "The Scholar's Workstation: Networking on Campus," *Wilson Library Bulletin* 63, no. 2 (Oct. 1988): 47.

7. For a discussion on the PCC and NACO see both the discussion of OCLC's OCLC Macro Language later in this chapter and the separate discussion of the PCC in chapter 4.

8. See the two documents compiled by Joe Kiegel, the "Analysis" and the "Survey."

9. Belinda Chiang, "Expediting NOTIS Operations with Programmed Function Keys: a Comprehensive Guide," *Library Software Review* 13 (3): 212–23, is a good discussion of one institution's attempts at macro development using a terminal as its platform.

10. NewKey, "a keyboard enhancer for the IBM Personal Computer," version 5.4, ©1984-1992, by Frank A. Bell, is available from FAB Software, P.O.Box 336, Wayland, MA 01778. NewKey is shareware and can be found on many computer bulletin boards that maintain repositories of shareware.

11. The existing formatting of the LOC field posed a particular challenge. The LOC was initially constructed with a cataloging status indicator of "c," which meant the piece was considered cataloged, and with a "$g Circ. Desk $s [bar code]," which translated in the public catalog to "Consult Circ. Desk for [bar code]." No item record was created, however. As it happens, the cataloging status indicator "c" prevents a call number from being inserted into the LOC during processing of an incoming OCLC record. If database management sim-

ply changed the "c" to a "p" (for provisional), an incoming OCLC record with a call number would have caused the "$g Circ. Desk" to disappear, and without the "$g Circ. Desk" the "$s [bar code]" would not display, thus effectively depriving the patron of information about the book's shelving location. All the subsequent manipulations of the data that database management engaged in were designed to remedy these problems.

12. An excellent review of a number of macro languages can be found in Paul Bonner, "Cross-Application Macro Languages," *PC Magazine* (Feb. 8, 1994): 203–42.

13. ProKey is reviewed by Bonner, "Cross-Application Macro Languages," 214.

14. OCLC licensed its implementation of OML from Softbridge Basic Language, Inc. TCP3270's Visual Basic language is the WinWrap Basic Language from Polar Engineering and Consulting.

A Developer's Point of View

Mark Wilson
The Library Corporation

▼ Many librarians have displayed great ingenuity in "rolling their own" TSWs to simplify and ease technical services workflow, usually by employing off-the-shelf software intended for a nonlibrary environment. Success for these constructed packages is usually measured in terms of immediate utility rather than long-term benefits. Any awkwardness in using a home-grown TSW or any holes in its functionality are often tolerated since even a small, incremental increase in efficiency or productivity is better than continued reliance on the status quo.

The criteria for success in a commercially developed and supported TSW differ substantially from those tacitly accepted for locally created platforms. Developers must strive for completeness and face a series of decisions that constrain the final design, functionality, and deployment of the TSW. Developers cannot and should not expect to be forgiven shortcomings tolerated in a do-it-yourself workstation.

Dylan Thomas could have been describing the arcane and secretive world of software developers rather than the work of poets when he wrote, "In my craft or sullen art, practiced by owllight." The focus here is on providing some insight to librarians into the "craft or sullen art" of software development. Knowing the issues related to the design and implementation of library software in general and the TSW in particular will aid librarians in specifying their needs to developers and in evaluating newly released software products. This knowledge will help librarians challenge vendors to cooperate and outperform each other. The position of any competent developer should be that libraries will receive the greatest benefit through active and aggressive competition in the creation of new library software and by receiving from all vendors a warrant that these new products will be cooperatively synergetic.

The following is based on the experience of one particular library systems vendor, but its thrust and conclusions should be equally applicable to a variety of local systems developers and their products. The essential principles here can be construed as a generic evaluation of the TSW development process and the relationship between librarians and developers.

Basic Considerations

The Library Corporation's technical services MS-DOS product, BiblioFile Cataloging, deployed over the past decade in thousands of libraries, did not qualify as a true TSW because it addressed only the issues of MARC record editing and management. Various forums have made clear that MARC record editing and management were not enough and that technical services departments required a fully functional TSW to carry out their missions. Therefore, in late 1994, The Library Corporation elected to initiate a TSW project by developing a new product with broader functionality, ITS for Windows (*Integrated Technical Services*).

Just as for libraries, the first concern for a software developer is cost. Typical development expenditures for a stand-alone module can exceed $250,000. For a developer to risk so much capital, there must be some assurance of a positive return on the investment. Developers may choose from two possible courses to ensure realizing a profit: either to sell the product at a very high cost to a few libraries or to distribute the product at a lower cost to the broadest possible audience. The battlefield of library software development is littered with the corpses of firms that failed to do either.

Before committing to a project, a developer must first address certain fundamentals: the definition of the target audience of users, the problem domain of the software solution, the selection of a hardware platform and software vehicles, and the choice of an implementable subset of functionalities from within the problem domain of all possible functionalities. Other issues, such as the application's interface, its scale or scope, its impact on current practice, and user empowerment are of equal importance.

For the commercial developer the definition of a target user group actually resolves many of the other issues. If the product is to succeed, the target group must find the hardware platform and software vehicles attractive, the problem domain of interest, and the functionality implemented within the problem domain must meet or (better yet) exceed the user's minimal expectations.

Target Audience

Although some large libraries found the BiblioFile Cataloging MS-DOS product useful, it was deployed chiefly among medium- and small-sized libraries. Tiny libraries tended to use less-sophisticated tools or no tools at all, and the larger libraries usually relied upon and were constrained by the functionality provided by their local library automation package or their bibliographic utility. In defining the target audience for this new project, The Library Corporation could have elected to serve only its current client libraries, to expand its client base by targeting only libraries not using its MS-DOS product, or, as was eventually decided, to construct an application that could be tailored to the needs of libraries of all sizes and configurations.

At this point, librarians should raise the question, "How can a software product be designed so that it can be useful over such a wide range of constituencies?" Obviously, developers cannot limit their product's functionality to the lowest common denominator or impose other limits unacceptable to large segments of their target audience.

Our response was to begin design of a vertically functional component software package. What does this mean?

Vertical functionality focuses utility upon a specific problem domain: No attempt is made to support services beyond the immediate interest of the problem domain community. In other words, the problem domain of the TSW is support for all technical services activities, but other library functions lie outside the problem domain.

The term *component software* promises the ability to connect to a wide range of configurations and suggests a commitment to work with other vendors to provide a technique for attaching the developer's component software to their systems. For instance, while BiblioFile Cataloging used only The Library Corporation's CD-ROM databases, the ITS for Windows TSW product, in addition to being able to use its own CD-ROM databases, provides access to all of the bibliographic utilities and other large MARC databases via its built-in Z39.50 interface. In fact, a user of ITS for Windows need not even subscribe to or use The Library Corporation's CD-ROM databases.

Many request for information (RFI) documents that have been directed to local library systems and software developers in the past have defined and demanded monolithic systems. Libraries expressed a strong interest in a single vendor automation solution designed to provide integrated support for all library activities. Historically, this demand for integrated solutions has forced three constraints upon libraries. First, libraries could only request enhancements to an integrated system from the source vendor. Second, if the vendor failed to provide needed enhancements or provided enhancements at a marginal cost-benefit level for libraries, the only options left for libraries were to do without the needed enhancement or to replace the entire automated system, usually with another monolithically integrated system. Finally, while large libraries could afford full-featured integrated systems, smaller libraries could afford only integrated systems with limited functionality.

The current interest in the TSW and tools such as the "Scholar's Workstation" has been generated by the library community's experience with large integrated systems. The fact that most of the demand for TSWs comes from large libraries serviced by monolithic automation systems is especially revealing. It is clear that interest in the TSW itself predicts a major shift in the writing of the library automation RFI.

The forward-looking vendor must expect RFIs to change in focus over the next few years. The coming generation of RFIs will include requests for specifically defined and explicitly supported but limited activities: vertically functional (problem-domain oriented) component software. These RFIs will also dictate a shift in the specification of hardware platforms. Movement away from mainframe and mini installations toward the personal workstation linked to other workstations via a LAN (local area network) or WAN (wide area network) has already occurred. Finally, libraries will begin to demand interconnectivity between modules developed by competing vendors. In fact, by generating RFIs of this nature, librarians themselves can take control of the broader aspects of library automation development. Since vendors must respond to RFIs to remain viable, requests for vertically functional component software can shape the direction of future library automation development.

Problem Domain

The problem domain chosen for ITS for Windows was support of automated library technical services. Technical services are being redefined. Some experts advocate eliminating a library's technical services department as a problem domain of local interest and propose ways to deal with technical services issues externally. While these arguments carry weight in certain areas, the effects of removing a library's immediate control of technical services parallel the historical dependence upon monolithic integrated systems. As stated earlier, relinquishing local control of technical services limits a library's ability to respond quickly to locally defined problems.

On the other hand, other authorities see an expanding role for technical services. As more libraries find their constituencies broadened via Internet access, they sense a need for finer bibliographic control, broader support for the methods of collection evaluation and development, and improved resource allocation. In fact, the exciting and ongoing dialog about implementing a TSW lends support to this second view. The Library Corporation supports this second view and believes that there is a market for a well-designed and broadly implemented TSW.

Hardware Issues

While component software could be written to run on mainframes and minis, electing to do so would severely limit the target audience to very large libraries. The Library Corporation's decision to define a broad target audience dictated the selection of the hardware platform for ITS for Windows. Minis and mainframes were out; our target audience mandated the choice of a personal computer (PC) platform for ITS for Windows.

Even within the narrower range of the PC, developers really have only two courses they may follow in terms of hardware: to develop for a single PC hardware platform or to develop multiplatform PC applications. While a single application can be written to run on multiple PC platforms, doing so either potentially raises development costs or limits the application's functionality to that which is common to all of the hardware. If a vendor chooses to develop independent versions of the application in order not to constrict functionality and to exploit the unique advantages of each PC environment, both development and maintenance costs skyrocket. On the other hand, a developer's writing for a single PC automatically limits the application's target audience.

This situation presents a serious problem for librarians and developers. When libraries mandate a hardware platform in their RFIs for whatever reasons (affection, familiarity, or installed hardware base), the ability of many vendors to respond in a cost-effective manner is obviously limited. If developers mandate the installation of a new or unfamiliar hardware base in libraries as a requirement of using their applications, libraries face a double loss as their investment in and experience with an installed platform evaporates.

While some libraries own Apple and Macintosh personal computers and the larger, more affluent libraries even have Sun Workstations, the majority appear to use the ubiquitous Intel-based PC. However, even Intel-based PC hardware differs greatly from installation to installation. In terms of the microprocessor alone, an informal survey of libraries conducted before the development of ITS for Windows revealed that the Intel hardware currently in use in libraries ranged from the nearly extinct XT to the, at that time, newly released Pentium.

The Library Corporation intended to market ITS for Windows in both turnkey and software-only forms. Since XTs were impossible to obtain as new computers and Intel 286 microprocessors nearly so, they were eliminated as supportable platforms. Although scheduled production of Intel 386 machines ended in 1994, the survey indicated most libraries had recently upgraded or were in the process of upgrading to an Intel 386 or higher configuration. Luckily for developers, Intel processors beyond the Intel 386 could efficiently support software written for the Intel 386. As a hedge, it was decided that no Intel 386-specific code would be included in ITS for Windows. Thus, at a future date, the software could be upgraded to run even more efficiently on a higher level microprocessor without undergoing an expensive rewrite.

Systems and Language Issues

Software vehicles, the operating systems and programming languages underlying the deployment of a software product, are an even more difficult issue for developers to face than the hardware platforms. Although the choice of a programming language is essentially hidden from end users, the operating system is blatantly exposed. If users express strong feelings about their attachment to a known or installed hardware platform, they can be positively fanatical about their operating system.

A user's attachment to an operating system stems from an investment in learning its idiosyncratic behaviors. Switching operating systems levies expenses beyond mere capital outlay. Workflow and the ability to perform simple tasks can be radically altered by introducing a new operating system into the library.

Most potential ITS for Windows users, our marketing survey revealed, were familiar with MS-DOS. While MS-DOS can be forced to perform many of the functions provided by the newer operating systems, the effort expended in forcing that performance can add significantly to development time and cost. By eliminating MS-DOS as a candidate, only three widely deployed operating systems remained: the Microsoft family, IBM's OS/2, and the various flavors of PC UNIX. (The Microsoft family consists of the Windows 3.1x and NT operating systems, as well as Windows '95.)

Each of these operating systems offered essentially the same functionality. UNIX, however, was uncommon in all but the largest libraries, and only two library users of OS/2 were found, leaving the Microsoft family as a reasonable choice for the target audience selected. Again, as with the choice of the Intel 386 platform, developers electing to write for Windows 3.1 can, by carefully selecting the implementation and expression of their programming language, create a product that will perform reasonably well on any of the three Microsoft operating systems. By being even more careful, developers can have some expectation that OS/2 would support programs written initially for the Microsoft family. The Library Corporation elected to optimize ITS for Windows for Windows 3.1, but at the same time to minimize code that would fail on Windows NT, Windows '95, and OS/2.

Most users are unaware of the programming language underlying a software product. This is rightly so, for no user should be expected to master a programming language simply to use a software package. But although the programming language remains hidden, librarians should not believe that the choice of programming language is unimportant. A vendor's selection of one programming language over another has far-reaching consequences, not only in the actual implementation of the software package but for issues such as functional extensibility, product maintenance, and investment in design and development time.

Of these issues, product maintenance is more than likely the most important to librarians. All software has bugs, although sometimes years are required to expose bugs in what seems to be a perfect product. The real issue is how quickly discovered bugs can be removed without introducing new bugs into unrelated parts of the program. In a small software package the importance of this issue is somewhat diminished, but in a large and complex program, maintenance becomes paramount.

Second in importance only to maintenance is functional extensibility: the capacity to enhance current features or add new ones to a package. When released, a product usually contains all of the functionality the developers were aware of and able to implement. Users, especially librarians, quickly discover in addressing the product to their unique workflow that the product would be better if it delivered this or that behavior under specific circumstances.

In fact, during the first few months following the release of ITS for Windows, The Library Corporation received and implemented dozens of suggested enhancements from librarians. Had ITS for Windows not been designed with functional extensibility in mind, implementing such changes would have been difficult, expensive, unreliable, and time consuming. In actuality, the development team was able quickly to deliver reliable implementations of these suggested enhancements without increasing the cost of the product. In the same vein, bugs (horror!) were discovered and repaired quickly. Using the principles described next, the average time required to repair a product defect was five minutes.

Several new principles have evolved over the years in various programming languages to address the issues of maintenance and extensibility. By far the most important new method, the one chosen in ITS for Windows, is OOP (Object-Oriented Programming). Thus, even before a programming language could be chosen, it was necessary to choose a programming method. Most readers, if not familiar with its intricacies, at least have heard of OOP. As a method, OOP was specifically designed to support development of software products that are characteristically easy to maintain and extend. To make this clear, it is important to understand the difference between old and new programming practices.

The Library Corporation's original MS-DOS products were written in the Assembler and C languages that permitted, as programmers put it, "writing down to the metal." That is, programmers can explicitly control the hardware platform and operating system to maximize performance. Unfortunately, "writing to the metal" can severely limit hardware and operating system selection as well as program maintainability and extensibility. Since the ITS for Windows design specifically designated multiple Intel hardware platforms, various operating systems, and an extensible, maintainable design, a different approach was needed. Thus, "writing down to the metal" was abandoned in favor of OOP.

The most widely used application programming languages are C, C++, PASCAL, and to a lesser extent various forms of structured BASIC. No one programming language enjoys a privileged status, and, in fact, each language provides a programmer with a broad palette of benefits and liabilities. While some developers might disagree, it could be said that in general, C is a "to the metal" language supporting absolute programming control, BASIC is fast to implement but limited in expression, and object-oriented PASCAL and C++ can be platform independent, maintainable, and extensible.

A developer's experience always influences the selection of a programming language for a product. A change in programming languages for a development team roughly parallels the issues faced by a library contemplating a change in classification systems. Neither should be approached unadvisedly, and both have far-reaching consequences.

C++ offered several immediate advantages over other languages: The ITS for Windows development team could leverage its long experience with C, C++ offered OOP encapsulation, and there were several C++ compilers on the market that supported multiple platforms and operating systems. In actuality, midway through the development of ITS for Windows, a newly released object-oriented PASCAL language proved to serve some programming needs better than C++. The team elected to incorporate that version of PASCAL when needed, but to write the major portion of ITS for Windows in C++.

Application Issues

Once the back room issues of problem domain, target audience, platform, and vehicle are out of the way, developers face a series of core implementation issues. The developer must solve design problems related to how the user will interact with the application: the product's interface, functionality, and most importantly, how the user will employ the functionality of the program. These issues define the surface of the program.

Developers use the term *metaphor* to discuss the representational surface of an application, that is, the parts of the program exposed by the view screen, the keyboard, and the mouse. The precise meaning of this term as developers use it will become more evident in the following discussion.

There are two basic surface metaphors available to developers: the menu and the desktop. Selection of a metaphor by the developer or its specification by a library in an RFI has a substantial impact on the implementation and use of the application.

The menu metaphor permits the developer to maintain absolute control of a user's interaction with the software. A menu is like a road map. From the developer's point of view, every potential user action must be discovered and a clear path for that action's performance mapped out. Essentially, in a menu-controlled program there should be exactly one route available for the user to accomplish any specific activity. The advantage of the menu metaphor is that nearly anyone can be taught to follow a precise path to accomplish a task. The disadvantage is that the burden of task performance is placed upon the user who must learn by rote every performance path.

The desktop metaphor, on the other hand, more closely resembles actual workplace practice by providing the user with the means to select events as opposed to an arbitrary hierarchical set of paths. Because most complex professional tasks are event driven rather than mapped, the desktop metaphor is the more promising interface for a library TSW. Instead of committing to memory a set of task performance paths, the librarian is able to select the necessary event to accomplish the task at hand. With the desktop metaphor the assumption is that the user understands what the TSW task at hand involves and should be able intuitively to map out the necessary actions to accomplish that task. Again, while Windows applications can be made menu driven, the more natural interface for that operating system is the desktop metaphor. As one final benefit, the desktop metaphor has a less negative impact than does the menu metaphor on existing workflow patterns because the user may mimic current workflow by starting anywhere on the desktop to reach any particular task destination.

For the software developer, dealing with a library's existing technical services workflow patterns presents the greatest challenge. Librarians have invested much time, energy, and ingenuity in establishing the sequence of activities and tasks involved between the acquisition of materials and making those materials accessible to their clients. Many of these workflow patterns were developed to overcome shortcomings in local automation systems or to deal with local physical or personnel limitations. Although library professionals in general agree on the scope of technical services workflow patterns, actual practice varies greatly from library to library. Changes to these practices can be costly in terms of staff retraining and in the high level of vigilance that is required to reduce the possibility of the introduction of new systematic errors.

The developer's task is to limit as much as possible any negative impact the software product might have on existing workflow patterns. Since it is impossible by definition to both introduce a new software product such as the TSW and maintain precisely the current workflow (unless the TSW is an implementation of exactly *that* library's workflow), what must be demonstrated to a potential user is that, while current practice will be altered, the underlying components that supported current practice are still available.

However, maintaining the status quo is not the objective of the TSW. In addition to not disrupting current practice, it must actually empower the user to perform those same tasks more efficiently, provide for the support of tasks the user was previously unable to perform, and reduce the user's involvement in workflow by automating certain labor-intensive or error-prone tasks.

Functionality

Functionality, then, is closely tied to the surface issues discussed. By adopting a desktop metaphor the developer exposes functionality as an event-driven process and permits the user to select the functionality required for the task at hand. What, then, should the functionality of a TSW include?

In the design specification of ITS for Windows, functionality was first divided into broad areas, then each functional area refined to include specific details. This is the technique employed by most developers. If this principle is kept in mind when creating an RFI or specification for a product, there is a high likelihood that the developer's response will be satisfactory.

A discussion about the implementation of functionality, from a developer's viewpoint, could consist of wandering through a wish list of features and raising strawman development issues. Since other chapters in this book review the desirable and possible functionality of a TSW, the focus here will be upon the actual problems, issues, and design solutions encountered in incorporating specific functionality into The Library Corporation's TSW, ITS for Windows. At the same time, every attempt is made to broaden this exploration of functionality into more-general development issues.

Backward Compatibility

The first functionality issue confronting a developer with the introduction of a new software product is backward compatibility. The users of a developer's current product cannot be abandoned. The developer must either provide at least the same functionality the earlier product supported or ease current users' migration to the new product. For ITS for Windows, although our new CD-ROM databases were in International Standards Organization (ISO) format, it was necessary to provide access through the application to our proprietary BiblioFile Cataloging CD-ROM databases to permit libraries to leverage their investment in that product.

In fact, it was in the area of backward compatibility that the team made a design error. They underestimated the importance of supporting backwardly compatible catalog card and label printing. The assumption was made that card printing (other than a paper shelflist card) was of reduced importance in today's technical services departments and that those users who did require card sets could print them easily using the MS-DOS card printing utilities provided with BiblioFile Cataloging. Users of the beta and prerelease versions of ITS for Windows quickly showed the design team the error of its ways, and card and label printing capabilities were added to the list of backwardly compatible functions to be included in the final product.

Access to MARC and Local Databases

Beyond backward compatibility, the design team believed that the TSW's functionality must include access to MARC records, the ability to easily create or edit a record, support for record and authority validation, ease of communication with other vendors' systems, and above all, immediate access to the national standards used in technical services.

In the past, most technical services automation products (there were no commercially developed TSWs) provided either no access to a source MARC record database or access to only one vendor's or bibliographic utility's database. The TSW requires more: Access to many different MARC databases is a prime requirement. A library must be able to quickly search its local database, online utilities, the databases of other libraries, and the proprietary source databases provided by various vendors.

To provide access to local databases, the design for ITS for Windows had to deal with two distinct possibilities. If a library did not have a local database, it was necessary to provide at least the option of building and maintaining one. If a library had a local database, some means had to be developed for either moving that database into ITS for Windows or for providing easy access to the local database.

For those libraries that need to build and maintain a local database, ITS for Windows has a built-in database engine. Users may add and remove records easily as well as search the database by using standard access points. Because maintaining a local database might require special access points, users may also conduct searches based upon locally defined access points.

Other libraries may already have software to support the building and maintenance of local databases. These libraries need not use the built-in database at all and are free to move records back and forth from the application to their local databases. ITS for Windows supports the import and export of MARC records in two file formats: USMARC and a backwardly compatible BiblioFile format. Users also have access to the GTO (Generic Transfer and Overlay) functionality of local systems, if that local system provides one.

Of course, in addition to local MARC databases, a well-developed TSW must also allow easy access to a source of MARC records for copy cataloging. In addition to providing access to the many Library Corporation CD-ROM databases, ITS for Windows supports access to other vendors' databases. While it is possible to develop special interfaces co-operatively with every database vendor, it is far more practical to use an international standard as an interface with a foreign database. For that purpose, ITS for Windows incorporates a Z39.50 client.

The dissemination and implementation of the Z39.50 standard, although typically directed in support of public-access functions, can have a major impact on the development of the TSW. Suddenly, technical services departments can share cataloging copy in a manner impossible or much more expensive before the advent of Z39.50. It takes little imagination to envision ad hoc regional bibliographic utilities and consortia springing up everywhere with MARC records freely available for local consumption and editing.

Editing Data

There are many metaphors available for editing data. By far the most intuitive is the word processing metaphor. The difficulty is that the MARC record is a data structure rather than a text document. What is required for a MARC "document" editor is an awareness on the part of the editor of the structure of the MARC record.

The Library Corporation expended much energy in the development of its MARC editor. Making a word processor-like MARC editor implied that the functionality of word processing be applied to the MARC structure in a manner transparent to the user. To this end, standard word processing commands were incorporated with commands uniquely MARC-aware. Just as a text word processor is aware of paragraphs and sentences, the ITS for Windows MARC "word" processor is aware of fields, subfields, and indicators. Cut and paste commands, for instance, are aware of both source and destination structures. One can paste data into a field, or a field into a record, or a set of fields from one record into another record but cannot mistakenly try to paste a field (complete with its tag number, indicators, and data) into another field.

Within the word processor-like MARC environment, some events must be restricted by the editor. The 008 field allows only certain codes and has a specified length. The MARC editor prevents the user from entering faulty codes or changing the length of such fields. The editor must be flexible, however, so ITS for Windows permits cataloging wizards who know when breaking a rule is necessary to put aside such controls.

Some fields, like the 005 field, are system controlled, and ITS for Windows prevents even the wizards from tampering with them.

Beyond MARC awareness, the MARC word editor must be able to deal with other MARC-specific issues. For instance, cataloging frequently requires characters not normally available in a word processor. The Library Corporation developed and included an ALA TrueType font to be used with ITS for Windows to handle diacritics and other MARC font issues.

Validation and Codes

Mere editing of a record is not enough. Users must be able to quickly and easily establish that the completed record conforms to standards. To this end ITS for Windows, as should any TSW worthy of the name, included record-validation functions as part of the editing interface. One validator examines the structure of the edited MARC record for compliance with, at the user's option, either USMARC or OCLC standards. Another validator supports authority control by checking name and subject authorities against the local database.

One of the difficulties catalogers face is the interruption of workflow when a specific rule or code must be researched before cataloging can continue. In the past, the cataloger had to pick up and leaf through a manual to find the appropriate information. The Library of Congress's Cataloger's Desktop significantly improved the situation, but it is still necessary to switch windows from the editor to the Cataloger's Desktop, then to search for the topic of interest in that application. The designers of ITS for Windows went one step farther by providing context-sensitive leaps from the MARC editor to the precise information required. For instance, to discover appropriate indicators, subfield codes and usage, or specific codes, the user of ITS for Windows need only place the MARC editor's caret on the part of the MARC record in question and press the <F1> (Help) function key to be taken directly to the page and paragraph in the required national documentation.

Greater Efficiency

As useful as context-sensitive help and validation are, they do little to reduce some labor intensive tasks. What is needed is a means to teach the TSW how to perform certain tasks on its own. ITS for Windows supports three methods for easing labor intensive, repetitive activities.

Two are quite simple and follow the word processor model. Just as most word processors provide templates for commonly used documents, ITS for Windows provides a stable of templates for MARC editing. Users also may create and use as many of their own templates as they desire. And, just as word processors permit the recording of keystrokes to perform rote editing, ITS for Windows can record its MARC-aware keystrokes and even report error conditions when such a macro is applied to a record.

Far more efficient than merely recording keystrokes is the Macro-Scripting language included with ITS for Windows. By entering and editing simple English commands, users can build a script that will perform very complex transformations to a MARC record. An extension to the command language permits the script to be applied to not just one record, but to a whole series of records without operator intervention. Like the keystroke recorder, a scripting language macro can be instructed to stop when an error condition is encountered.

Many features of the ITS for Windows TSW at the detail level have been ignored in this discussion. It is the broader areas of functionality that are important and useful when evaluating an already developed TSW or when specifying TSW requirements to a developer.

The Librarian-Developer Link

How does the librarian/user influence a developer? During conversations with a developer, the user who keeps in mind the issues previously described ensures that communication will take place at some level. But, in point of fact, the communication should extend far beyond those issues.

The design of ITS for Windows was based in part upon such conversations. Of more importance were the opportunities presented when librarians either complained about, praised, or suggested enhancements to current products.

Some information is gained through the stilted dialog RFIs allow, but an RFI is usually the product of a committee or a consultant and often looks backward or is constrained by parochial issues. Again, even the most open-ended RFI is time sensitive in terms of the vendor's response. It is an unfortunate truth that few RFIs express interest in influencing the development process.

Workflow Demonstration

Far more information is provided by exposing developers to the technical services workplace than by reading an RFI. As mentioned earlier, the greatest challenge presented to the developer is the encapsulation of workflow and current practice in the design of a new application. It is in this arena, most often, that librarians woefully report, "We asked for such and such and they gave us so and so." The only way to reduce occurrences of this sad scenario is to ensure that developers understand the reasons behind workflow practice. When providing a workflow demonstration for a developer, be sure to subject the developer to the same type of comprehensive examination a novice librarian would be given: Make sure the developer understands both *what* is done and *why* it is done.

Invite developers known to be interested in specific topics (or developers you wish to interest in specific topics) to conferences and meetings about those topics and ensure their participation in a meaningful manner. Insist that developers—not sales representatives—be there. Much good information can be had from sales representatives, but the function of sales is to deal with the present product: The developer must look forward.

This is not to say that sales representatives cannot influence development. Be assured that any salesperson worthy of the title will report your dissatisfaction, proposals, and praise to the development programmers. Take the time during a sales call to make suggestions for future products and to critique present ones. Above all, report to the salesperson any impediment to your purchase of the product.

Alpha or Beta Testing

Possibly the best way to influence the development process, outside of purchasing the product, is to offer to act as an alpha or beta test site. However, be advised by developers and by librarians who have undergone this ordeal by fire that it is not a role to be undertaken lightly.

To be productive, alpha testing demands much more than passive use or review of an application. The alpha tester is responsible for finding oversights and misunderstandings in the product design. (Remember the design problem with card-set printing!)

Beta testing, though as critical as alpha testing, moves the testers to a different set of responsibilities. When a product reaches the beta stage, the major questions to be answered are not about product design but about product reliability. By this time, the developer and the developer's immediate community have been exposed to the application for so long that it becomes easier and easier to overlook tests for functional failure. Although dependence upon the beta site for application testing is not absolute, real librarians doing real work are far more likely to uncover shortcomings than any artificial software test ever could.

If you like a product, tell the world. Publicity to a developer is what publication is to an academic: Paraphrasing the old saw, it's "publicity or perish" in the development world. Librarians would not believe how much attention is paid by developers to the comments made on Internet listservs. And, like everyone else, developers take personal pleasure when their creation excites someone to kind comments.

At one ALA meeting, a librarian wondered out loud if vendors ever made use of what was learned in picking her brains. This developer would have to answer that the task of developing ITS for Windows would have been impossible had not so many technical services librarians freely offered access to their advice and expended so much of their precious time in support of the effort.

National Cooperative Programs

Michael Kaplan
Harvard College Library

▼ Since it was first organized in 1992, the Cooperative Cataloging Council (now the Program for Cooperative Cataloging [PCC]) has had a strong influence on the development and the direction of development of technical services workstations (TSWs). This is partly due to the leadership of the Library of Congress (LC), which has stressed development of online tools such as its own Bibliographic Workstation (BWS) and the Cataloger's Desktop. LC uses these tools to create cataloging records (bibliographic and authority) more efficiently according to the dictum "more, better, faster, cheaper"—that is, with consistently more quality and at a lesser unit cost. It is also due to the realization that some of the earlier problems with national cooperative cataloging programs lay in their inherently inefficient, uncooperative nature. The symbiosis that should have always existed between the Library of Congress and its cooperating partners was more wish than reality.[1]

When LC began to develop its BWS and then expected its cooperating partners at that time to adopt it, a new strain arose in their relationship. Yet LC's vision for the BWS and the related tension—rooted in the cost of the BWS and its proprietary nature rather than its functionality—helped crystallize the thought processes of the directors of technical services of the large research libraries as they, too, began to consider how their institutions could adopt or adapt BWS-type technology. Neither the technology nor the concepts behind it were unknown territory to these individuals.

Exploring the genesis of the PCC and its impact on TSWs will cast much illumination on how and why TSWs are an essential part of the national productivity equation for libraries. At its core the PCC is more than just another cooperative program; it is a cooperative program arising at a time when a bottom-line mentality pervades both the for-profit and the nonprofit worlds. "Cui bono?" or "What's the benefit?" is a question never far from any administrator's mind in the 1990s.[2]

Origin of the Program for Cooperative Cataloging

The PCC is a joint venture of the Library of Congress and a large number of other national and institutional libraries. As the program grows, it is reaching out and is beginning to include smaller public or special libraries as well. OCLC Online Computer Library Center, Inc., and the Research Libraries Group (RLG) are also members of the program. At this time the PCC's membership includes approximately 200 libraries, but that number is growing.

The PCC encompasses a number of national cooperative cataloging programs that previously existed in their own right:

> National Coordinated Cataloging Program (NCCP), later known as the National Cooperative Cataloging Program, is now the bibliographic record component (BIBCO) of the PCC
>
> Name Authorities Cooperative Project (NACO)
>
> Subject Authorities Cooperative Project (SACO)
>
> CONSER, the national Cooperative Online Serials Program, which is merging with the PCC as its serials arm

National Coordinated Cataloging Program

The original NCCP began life in 1988 as a program envisioned and managed by the Library of Congress. In LC's original vision the eight participating libraries were to share the burden of creating national-level cataloging records for monographs, including creating all the authority records required by the bibliographic records on which they were dependent.

The initial costs of this program were partially underwritten by the Council on Library Resources (CLR), and in 1990 management decided to commission a study of the impacts of NCCP (including those components of NACO that were part and parcel of NCCP). This study, *The National Coordinated Cataloging Program: An Assessment of the Pilot Project,* exposed a number of problems and weaknesses in NCCP, but it pronounced the NCCP overall a cost-effective use of limited resources.[3] It also demonstrated that sufficient numbers of ARL libraries were reusing the NCCP records in copy cataloging such that the benefits of copy cataloging with national-level records outweighed the added costs borne by the participating libraries.

It was apparent, however, that problems existed. They were threefold:

> Participating institutions felt that LC was heavy-handed in its revision and acceptance of records. LC alone was empowered to define what "national level" meant. To be sure, this was a learning process on both sides. LC, on the one hand, and the libraries and catalogers in the field, on the other, were involved in a process of determining what it meant to be "remote clones" of LC. But the original name said it all: This program began as the National *Coordinated* Cataloging Program and only later evolved into the National *Cooperative* Cataloging Program.

> The few libraries participating in NCCP were restive. They were bearing a national burden for which few of them felt adequately equipped, and they were having a difficult time selling the burdens of their participation to their administrations and, in some cases, to their line catalogers. The mandate and the sense of mission were not clear and, therefore, could not be clearly articulated. While the benefits were enjoyed nationally, the burdens were felt locally. Furthermore, the participating libraries were all being heavily burdened by the continued monetary squeeze on higher education and a generalized national recession that made cost-cutting measures imperative.

> The third problem was technological. The system on which NCCP depended for input of records (Multiple-Use MARC System, or MUMS) was archaic and prone to problems. A full-fledged implementation of NCCP was predicated on development of the Linked Systems Project (LSP); this was to be the pathway for transmitting and exchanging records among the participating libraries, their utilities, and the Library of Congress. The bibliographic (as opposed to the authority) component of LSP, however, was never implemented. To participate in the bibliographic portion of NCCP—and it was the bibliographic component that differentiated NCCP from pure NACO—libraries had to obtain and install ComTerm terminals such as were in use at LC. These then had to be connected over telephone lines to the actual MUMS system at the Library of Congress.

It did not help matters that dealing with LC MUMS required learning another operating system and another set of search algorithms. In many cases this was either the third or the fourth such set of routines, coming after an institution's local catalog and OCLC and/or Research Libraries Information Network (RLIN). This represented a major training nightmare. Additionally, because of the way the program was constructed, it was not possible (until 1993) to take advantage of preexisting copy on either OCLC or RLIN or to use preexisting acquisitions-level records resident on the institution's own online catalog. No matter that a record might exist elsewhere in another system, the NCCP cataloger still had to key it from scratch directly into MUMS.

Of course, it was impossible at that time to catalog locally in one's own system and tape or use file transfer protocol—FTP did not yet exist in 1988—to transfer the records to the utilities or to LC for inclusion in the national database. None of the required protocols for that were in place. The ability to interlock local systems, utilities, and the national cooperative cataloging apparatus so that local systems and local, powerful workstations could be used in the cooperative processes was one of the most significant recommendations of the CCC Task Group 2, "Availability and Distribution."[4]

To compound matters, after NCCP had struggled on for two more years, new management at a number of institutions and continuing problems with NCCP, as then constituted, led to a summit meeting held November 4–6, 1992, at the Library of Congress to try to determine what direction NCCP should go. In a joint meeting between representatives of the CONSER community and the NCCP community, the NCCP representatives tried to ascertain what had made CONSER a successful program and why it was that NCCP, in contrast, was floundering. The final straw for NCCP in many institutions was the need to replace the ComTerm terminals with new, still proprietary, Library of Congress Bibliographic Workstations. While these BWSs were true workstations, and for many would have represented a first step in the introduction of technical services workstation capabilities into their processing environments, they came at a high price: The original LC BWS cost approximately $8,000 in 1992 and, while the cost dropped over time, it was still a very major capital investment. This was all the more true considering that the $8,000 was for hardware costs only and did not include telecommunications or other ongoing costs.

An alternative processing methodology became available at about this same time, namely input of national-level bibliographic records into OCLC. A few institutions new to NCCP opted to make use of that alternative. But, at the November 1992 summit, NCCP participants decided to take a step back and gain some perspective on where NCCP stood and where it was going. Harvard University, for instance, decided to enter a state of "hiatus" in its NCCP contributions, though continuing with CONSER and NACO, while this process unfolded and the new methodologies were assessed. From all these considerations arose the Cooperative Cataloging Council, a group of eight senior librarians at participating libraries and national utilities who pledged themselves to rethink the foundations on which cooperative cataloging was then being conducted.[5]

Cooperative Cataloging Council

The Cooperative Cataloging Council (still unofficially considered the CCC, despite the objections of those who hold rights to the use of trademark CCC) first met formally at the American Library Association's 1993 midwinter meeting in Denver. They decided to establish six task groups to consider specific aspects of transforming NCCP into a more vigorous and efficient program. The six task groups were

- ▶ Task Group 1, "More, Better, Faster, Cheaper"
- ▶ Task Group 2, "Availability and Distribution"
- ▶ Task Group 3, "Authorities"
- ▶ Task Group 4, "Standards"
- ▶ Task Group 5, "Cataloger Training"
- ▶ Task Group 6, "Foreign MARC"

In an interesting use of technology that was still somewhat new to the library community at the time, these six task groups met largely over the Internet in E-mail discussion groups and posted their surveys and requests for information on a variety of library listservs. All six reported their findings and recommendations at an open meeting at the Library of Congress on November 16, 1993. Throughout their reports ran a common thread of the need to adapt or develop newer and better means of harnessing technology and telecommunications to the requirements of creating and disseminating bibliographic and authority records in the national arena. The major automation recommendations in this regard bear directly on the issue of developing technical services workstations and connecting them into a national grid consisting of institutional libraries, national utilities, and national libraries. The Cooperative Cataloging Council issued its strategic plan in February 1994. The automation recommendations were collected into an appendix to the strategic plan. (See the appendix at the end of this chapter.) Chief among its recommendations were the following:

- ▶ encourage development of Z39.50
- ▶ encourage use of OCLC's Telecommunications Linking Project (TLP)/RLG's EtherTerm
- ▶ expedite development of online cataloging tools
- ▶ develop word processing-like capabilities within TSW platforms
- ▶ develop capability of windowing on TSWs
- ▶ develop customizable macros and macro packages

There is a direct line from the NCCP and its participants' complaints about multiple incompatible utilities and inputting platforms (OCLC or RLIN vs. LC MUMS vs. local systems) to the CCC's list of automation desires and the need to simplify the relationships of local systems and the national bibliographic utilities.

What did the CCC hope to accomplish with this particular list? It is clear first of all that the CCC was looking ahead to a technical services nirvana where it would be possible to launch a search from a desktop workstation placed on a campus network or LAN and go to the national utilities (TLP/EtherTerm) or anywhere else on the Internet (Z39.50). A seamless web would envelop catalogs and resource files and place the local OPAC squarely in that context. Once a record was retrieved, it would be easily edited and manipulated using all the tools commonly associated with word processing and user-defined macros. Furthermore, the cataloger would be able to do this while viewing a number of separate records simultaneously in separate windows to compare and verify all the requisite component parts of the finished record. Such a process was envisioned by the CCC Task Group 1, "More, Better, Faster, Cheaper," and it has been described by Roger Brisson.[6]

Cooperative Cataloging Council Automation Task Group

The Cooperative Cataloging Council was never intended to be more than a transitional body, and, indeed, it metamorphosed itself into the Program for Cooperative Cataloging's Executive Council at ALA's 1995 midwinter meeting in Philadelphia. During the interim period between the time the CCC issued its strategic plan and the time the PCC arose, however, the CCC constituted an Automation Task Group to begin advancing the CCC's automation goals.[7] That group, which became the Program for Cooperative Cataloging Standing Committee on Automation with the birth of the PCC, managed two major accomplishments during this interim period.[8] It conducted an Internet survey during the summer and fall of 1994 to collect information on TSWs, and it convened a meeting of library service vendors at the Library of Congress on November 18, 1994.[9]

TSW Survey

Let's consider the 1994 TSW survey first. A small number of institutions responded to it, but the number was still sufficient to glean important trends about this early phase (late first wave, early second wave) in the development of TSWs.[10]

The standard microcomputer reported in the survey was an IBM-compatible PC. Although Macintosh computers have strong adherents, it was clear that the emerging standard for technical services workstations should be based on the Intel family of central processing units (CPUs). (Of course, the Power Macintosh would now qualify.) Further evidence of this was the fact that several of the most important software developments directed toward the TSW, such as the Library of Congress's Cataloger's Desktop and Classification Plus, have PC versions only. The Cataloging Distribution Service found through its market research that the Macintosh market was simply too small to make the investment for the Macintosh platform recoverable.

The standard high-end microcomputer at the time of the survey had an equipment configuration that included

- ▶ 80486-class processor (minimum)
- ▶ 4 to 8 megabytes of memory
- ▶ 240-megabyte (and larger) hard drives (though LANs were starting to make the storage capacity of the desktop computer somewhat irrelevant)
- ▶ 15-inch VGA monitors
- ▶ Ethernet adapter and mouse

The standard software component configuration was

- ▶ Windows 3.1 or higher as the preferred graphical user interface
- ▶ OPAC software
- ▶ macro packages
- ▶ full range of administrative software including word processing, database, and spreadsheet programs
- ▶ Telnet, FTP, and E-mail software

The wish list included more memory, 17-inch monitors, and OPAC software capable of multiple, simultaneous sessions and full support of the ALA character set.

Meeting of Library Service Vendors

The timing of the survey was such that the Automation Task Group presented it publicly for the first time to the meeting of library service vendors. The intent of this meeting was to introduce the CCC/PCC to the vendor community and to enlist their help in advancing the goals of the strategic plan. Because TSWs to that point were largely the result of isolated institutional efforts, and because many of the most striking software developments were entirely grassroots efforts that frequently arose in cataloging departments rather than in library automation offices, it was no surprise that the vendor community knew little of these productivity-enhancing tools. At the meeting the Automation Task Group highlighted institutional programs that were indicative of those advocated by the strategic plan's automation appendix, among them:

macro-based cataloging routines at Harvard College Library's cataloging services department that increased productivity through macros, increased accuracy through use of copy/paste, and decreased instances of repetitive strain injury through reducing the need to manually key much of the required data (see chapter 2)

programmatic validation of bibliographic headings and automated creation of authority records through use of the Cataloger's Toolkit developed by Gary Strawn at Northwestern University (see chapter 8)

capture of data from electronically transmitted CIP galleys for use in LC's CIP program by simple markup of the text with ISBD punctuation and resulting in the creation of bibliographic and authority records as well as similar programs for use with records searched in remote locations via LC's host-based Z39.50 client (see chapter 9)

Cataloger's Desktop, an evolving source of electronic documentation (see Chapter 5)

LC classification online via the MARC Format for Classification Data, as implemented in the Minaret format (not the same as Classification Plus, which LC had not yet started to develop)

For many of those present, this was their first exposure to these productivity-enhancing tools. Except for those with solid institutional support, such as the Cataloger's Desktop at the Library of Congress, these developments were largely the results of resourceful catalogers working independently of their local library systems offices and trying to remedy problems and shortcomings they perceived in their local systems. The larger the institution, it seemed, the more the cataloging department needed to accomplish. The means to do this was to harness the power of the desktop microcomputer to overcome institutional and technological roadblocks posed by the mainframe and the mainframe development cycle.

Vendors left that meeting with a new understanding of the PCC and the goals of the national cooperative cataloging programs. Now, vendors are beginning to release actual workstation products or enhance those already under development, including Windows-based programs that support multiple sessions, embedded macro languages supporting online cataloging efforts, online documentation such as MARC code lists and more, and Z39.50 clients. All these are now being incorporated into packages much more powerful than those developed earlier.

One reservation the vendor community expressed at this meeting was the small sample size of the TSW survey. To remedy that, the PCC Standing Committee on Automation undertook a new survey in the form of an Association of Research Libraries SPEC Kit. Almost sixty institutions responded to this survey, and the results show the increasing penetration of technical services workstations into libraries in general and the workstations' increasing power. For instance, the new survey showed that Pentium-class processors are becoming more the norm in new purchases, as is 16 megabytes of memory.[11]

Expediting Bibliographic and Authority Records

There are two major developments under way that may well revolutionize the process of contributing BIBCO and NACO records. The first is OCLC's and RLG's expressed willingness and ability to batchload BIBCO records. For those libraries committed to editing in their local systems and yet wanting to contribute to BIBCO, this makes possible the use of local systems and local efficiencies (powerful workstations and preexisting acquisition records) while enabling the results to be used for the national programs. At the same time, it will be possible for libraries to use already existing utility records that they have brought into their local system to be the basis of these (transformed) national records, thereby avoiding the need to key or rekey a record that already resides elsewhere.

The second development is taking place at OCLC: Robert Bremer, of OCLC's database management department, has used the new OCLC Macro Language (OML) to write a program that automatically generates name authority records for personal or corporate main or added entries and that creates series authority records as well. While not as elaborate as Strawn's Cataloger's Toolkit, this macro program nevertheless serves a restricted, but vital purpose:[12] *They enable a cataloger to create NACO records with a single keystroke or at the push of a button.* While the result-ing authority record may not be perfect in all respects, the machine—and this does take place with the microcomputer's commanding and interacting with the remote system—is still capable of automatically generating the major part of the record, relieving the cataloger of much tedious work and providing a finished (or almost finished) authority record to edit or approve. As Bremer and others gain more experience with OML, we can expect catalogers to accomplish more and more au-tomatically, thereby reserving the cataloger's energies for the instances where human intellectual abilities are truly required.

Summary

We are approaching a watershed in technical services processing. Li-braries have now recognized the need to invest in suitably powerful computers to enable their technical services staff to accomplish their as-signed tasks in a productivity-conscious manner. New tools being devel-oped for these workstations will make a "small, small world" out of the multiplicity of technical services fiefdoms into which we now find our-selves placed. The Internet and the placing of library OPACs on the Internet, where they are universally accessible via Telnet software, was a first step. Now the World Wide Web and new electronic tools that were designed with easy networking in mind will prove great boons to the future of cooperative cataloging. The technical services workstation is the platform—the center stage—on which all of these events are transpiring.

Notes

1. Carol A. Mandel, "Cooperative Cataloging: Models, Issues, Prospects," *Advances in Librarianship* 16 (1992): 33–82.

2. The Library of Congress has released its "Audit of the Library's Coop-erative Programs" conducted by the Library's Inspector General's Office during fiscal year 1994. The audit found the cooperative programs cost-effective, result-ing in a direct net savings to LC of $300,000. See the article, "Audit of Coop-erative Cataloging Programs," *LC Cataloging Newsline* 4, no. 4 (Mar. 1996).

3. Council on Library Resources Bibliographic Services Study Committee, *National Coordinated Cataloging Program: An Assessment of the Pilot Project* (Washington, D.C.: Council on Library Resources, 1990).

4. The Final Report of Task Group 2 can be found in *Towards a New Beginning in Cooperative Cataloging: The History, Progress and Future of the Coop-erative Cataloging Council,* comp. by David W. Reser (Washington, D.C.: Library of Congress, Cataloging Distribution Service, 1994), 37–44.

5. The original members of the CCC were John Byrum (Library of Con-gress), Carol Mandel (Columbia University), Sue Phillips (University of Texas), Patricia Thomas (Stockton–San Joaquin County Public Library), Sarah Thomas (Library of Congress), Linda West (Harvard University), Liz Bishoff (OCLC), and Karen Smith-Yoshimura (Research Libraries Group). The history of the CCC is covered in *Towards a New Beginning in Cooperative Cataloging.*

6. See the Final Report of Task Group 1 in *Towards a New Beginning in Co-operative Cataloging,* 34–6. See also Roger Brisson, "The Cataloger's Workstation and the Continuing Transformation of Cataloging," *Cataloging and Classifica-tion Quarterly* 20, no. 1 (1995): 3–5, 18–22.

7. Members were Howard S. Harris (RMG Consultants, Inc.), Joe Kiegel (University of Washington), Michael Kaplan (Harvard University, chair), Sally McCallum (Library of Congress), and Sally Sinn (then at the National Library of Medicine, currently at the National Agricultural Library).

8. At that point Judy Brugger (Cornell University) joined the Committee.

9. Information on the meeting is contained in the Final Report of the CCC's Automation Task Group, which can be found on the PCC Home Page at gopher://marvel.loc.gov:70/00/services/cataloging/coop/coop_cncl/tgauto.

10. The two documents of the survey were compiled by Joe Kiegel. They are the "Analysis of the Technical Services Workstation Survey," available at gopher://marvel.loc.gov:70/00/services/cataloging/coop/coop_cncl/tswanaly, and the "Summary of the Technical Services Workstation Survey," available at gopher://marvel.loc.gov:70/00/services/cataloging/coop/coop_cncl/tswsurv.

11. Association of Research Libraries, *Technical Services Workstations*. SPEC Kit 213 (Washington, D.C.: Association of Research Libraries, 1996).

12. It seems inappropriate to refer to programs as elaborate as those that Bremer and Strawn have created as macros. They are really programmatic approaches to solving cataloging problems.

APPENDIX
▼
CCC Strategic Plan Automation Recommendations

I. Endorsed actions.

    A. Facilitate system interoperability.

        1. Encourage the standard use of USMARC (and/or UNIMARC).

        2. Align USMARC and CAN/MARC formats within the next 18 months.

        3. Adopt FTP as the preferred method of batch exchange of records.

        4. Encourage the development of Z39.50 client/server capacity by program participants.

        5. Encourage the development of TLP/EtherTerm capabilities.

    B. Automate as much of the cataloging process as possible, freeing catalogers to concentrate on the intellectual aspects of cataloging.

        1. Expedite the development of efficient, high-quality cataloger workstations that

            a. provide as many cataloging tools as possible (for example, AACR2-e, RI's, SCM, LCSH, code lists, LC classification schedules, Dewey) in as many automated forms as possible (for example, "pop-up" files, CD-ROM, gopher files, online files).

            b. have word processing capabilities (for example, cut/paste).

            c. are capable of windowing (for example, between authority and bibliographic records) and multitasking.

            d. provide access to multiple databases and resource files.

            e. are capable of cataloger-customized macros.

            f. provide templates or prompt screens with constant data.

        2. Automate creation of certain data elements in bibliographic records: for example, generate 5XX notes from fixed field values.

        3. Automate the generation of possible classification numbers from subject headings for selection and completion by the cataloger.

        4. Automate the creation of valid authority record (for example, 1XX generated from 245 $c; 670 generated from 245 $a and 260 $c) that the cataloger can subsequently enhance to add information and references as necessary.

II. Actions for further investigation.

    A. Link the bibliographic and authority databases to capitalize on machine validation and record creation capabilities.

B. Encourage, within the commercial and library sectors, more research and development of scanning and digitizing technologies. Possible uses include creation of preliminary descriptive cataloging records and enriching bibliographic records with table of contents data.

C. With commercial sector cooperation when possible, enhance bibliographic records to include table of contents data, additional subject headings, and multiple classification numbers.

D. Improve and expand online input and update capabilities for name and subject authority records so that contribution will be faster and easier.

E. Global change capabilities should be generic to all bibliographic database systems to facilitate database maintenance.

F. The following USMARC Authority Format elements need to be implemented by LC, utilities, and local systems:

1. Subfield 5 in all fields where currently defined.

2. Field elements and variable fields to support the creation of subject subdivision records (for example, 008/09, 18X, 48X, 58X fields).

3. Heading/subdivision linking fields (7XX) to allow links between headings in different authority files/thesauri.

4. Implement/develop capability to input authority records in non-Roman scripts.

G. Develop the ability to load additional files either as integrated or as separate files (for example, foreign authority records) along with providing the ability to interface the files, to perform cross-file/interfile searching, and to search the files as a single file.

PART

II

Online Documentation and Online Tools

Online Documentation First Steps

Cataloger's Desktop

Bruce Chr. Johnson
Library of Congress

▼ Imagine working in a cataloging department that provides the staff with an integrated library system that makes online cataloging easy. Every cataloger also has his or her own desktop personal computer (PC)–based workstation that makes it possible to catalog without carrying uncataloged books to shared workstations. You do not have to travel very many years back to remember when this situation was a wishful dream of the future.

This blissful picture of one-cataloger, one-technical services workstation (TSW) describes one facet of a technical services nirvana. It is a piece of our long-sought Holy Grail—except for one intellectual barrier: No matter how experienced the cataloger, there is no way that he or she can completely remember every iota of cataloging and USMARC documentation. Catalogers will always need to find the answer to "How do you do that?" or "What is the rule?" This need and the absence of an all-encompassing electronic documentation module has been a basic flaw in automating our desktop technical services systems.

The average original cataloger requires somewhere between three and nine shelf-feet of printed documentation. This documentation consumes much precious space both on the shelf and, more significantly, on the desk when it is being used. (One cataloger in British Columbia complained that he felt like a spectator at a tennis match, with the printed *USMARC Format* on one side of his workstation and the loose-leaf *Library of Congress Rule Interpretations [LCRIs]* on the other, looking first one way and then the other.)[1]

Moreover, cataloging documentation is expensive, assuming catalogers at each PC-based workstation have their own sets of references. And, after all, we are putting workstations on catalogers' desks to improve cataloger productivity, so should we not also be providing all the proper documentation to each cataloger so he or she can do the job efficiently?

There are two other complications worth noting at this point. First, print documentation is not always easy to use, particularly because each cataloging tool has its own editorial practice. Second, updating print documentation through replacement of looseleaf pages is a never-ending, arduous task.

With all of this in mind, concerned members of the cataloging profession felt that there had to be a practical solution for making comprehensive cataloging documentation available in a timely and cost-effective manner. To that end the Cataloging Distribution Service (CDS) of the Library of Congress (LC) has developed solutions to these problems in the Cataloger's Desktop.

Origins

The idea for these products began as an outgrowth of the 1980s' fascination with expert systems and artificial intelligence. As early as April 26, 1989, it was proposed that LC's CDS develop a product tentatively called "CD Descriptive Cataloging Expert System." This proposed CD-ROM product, as it was initially envisioned, would include the *Anglo-American Cataloguing Rules,* 2nd edition, Revised *(AACR2R)* and the *Library of Congress Rule Interpretations (LCRIs).* The intended audiences for this tool were users of CDS's CDMARC Bibliographic and The Library Corporation's BiblioFile CD-ROM products. In other words, it appeared that there might be interest in a windowed, online documentation tool for the (then) fairly narrow, completely stand-alone PC-based cataloger's workstation.

The 1980s saw the initial phases of development of information retrieval or, more properly, text retrieval. Product developers were trying to apply the idea of "artificial intelligence" to trace the decision-making process for highly repetitive tasks. A goal in this was the development of expert systems, an idea with much more promise than success in library applications, at least to date. Charles Fenly, in his monograph *Expert Systems, Concepts and Applications,* says that expert systems, by their very nature, are only successful if they attempt to replicate the decision-making process in an exceptionally "narrow, well-bounded and self-contained" domain.[2] Given the nature of expert systems (narrow and clear-cut) and cataloging (broad, with many divergent decision-making pathways), expert system technology did not lend itself to even narrow cataloging applications.

In part because of the unsuitability of expert systems and artificial intelligence for descriptive cataloging, the proposal for a "descriptive cataloging expert system" failed to move forward quickly. Another reason for the delay in committing to the product concept was that the commercially available software was long on promise and very short on delivery. Most packages provided rudimentary (chiefly Boolean) searching. Interfaces were primitive, and multitasking was only available in the most powerful computing environments, which were quite uncommon in technical services departments of the time. Right from the start, CDS believed that it would be better, cheaper, and quicker to use commercially available retrieval software than to build the software from scratch.

Concurrent with CDS's initial explorations of online text retrieval, several different groups were discussing the distribution of *AACR2R* in machine-readable form. In 1989 the board of directors of ALA's Resources and Technical Services Division (now the Association for Library Collections & Technical Services [ALCTS]) discussed the desirability of distributing *AACR2R* in an internationally recognized communications format.[3] (*AACR2R* already existed in machine-readable form in a proprietary typesetter's format.) While initial discussions focused on developing a MARC format for *AACR2R,* no immediate decision was made pending market research.

By April 1991, the project of CDS was beginning to take on the characteristics of the product as it was eventually released. That April it was recommended to CDS that the product should have the following functionality:

- ▶ IBM PC compatibility
- ▶ instant accessibility without leaving the cataloging application
- ▶ transparent hypertext linkages (not exact-text match dependent)
- ▶ full text keyword retrieval
- ▶ context-sensitive help
- ▶ full compatibility with Microsoft Windows and/or OS/2 operating system
- ▶ mouse compatible

It seemed clear that the following tools, plus an additional fifteen publications, should be included with a distributable, machine-readable *AACR2R* file:

- ▶ *Library of Congress Rule Interpretations*
- ▶ *Anglo-American Cataloguing Rules,* 2nd edition, Revised
- ▶ *USMARC Format for Bibliographic Data*
- ▶ *LC Classification Outline*
- ▶ *USMARC Format for Authority Data*
- ▶ USMARC code lists (various titles)
- ▶ LC's *Subject Cataloging Manual: Subject Headings*
- ▶ LC's *Free-floating Subdivisions: An Alphabetical Index*
- ▶ LC's *Subject Cataloging Manual: Shelflisting*
- ▶ *Cataloging Rules for the Description of Looseleaf Publications*
- ▶ *Graphic Materials: Rules for Describing Original Items and Historical Collections*

By this time it seemed apparent that this product would not be limited to users of CD-ROM products such as CDMARC Bibliographic and BiblioFile.

At about this time, there was an examination of "cataloging modifications" going on in the Library of Congress Collections Services service unit. In an August 1991 memo, Henriette Avram noted that

> Long the subject of heated debate, the *Library of Congress Rule Interpretations (LCRIs)* were recently examined to determine their importance in the cataloging process. It was determined that the *LCRIs* are crucial to an efficient cataloging operation not because they ensure consistency among catalogers at all costs, but because they successfully address the many questions that arise in the course of cataloging, thereby eliminating the cataloger's need to ponder excessively a difficult situation. The problems associated with the *LCRIs* can most likely be attributed to the lack of easy access to these and other cataloging tools. The bulky assemblage of rules and interpretations constitute a considerable obstacle, especially during the training process. *If the cataloging rules and the corresponding rule interpretations were pulled together in an online cataloger's workstation, some of the difficulties would be overcome.* [Emphasis added]

Tentative approval to develop a product came late in the fall of 1991, and a product description was complete in November. A major question remained regarding the operating system(s) the product should be developed for (MS-DOS, Windows, OS/2, or Macintosh), which titles should be included and in what order, and what user functionality was seen as most important. The platform that was eventually recommended was as follows:

IBM PC-compatible 386SX or higher

VGA monitor or higher to support display of all diacritics

DOS 5.0/Windows

32-bit technology (minimum 2 megabytes RAM, 4 megabytes preferred)

compatible with LANs (as many as twenty simultaneous users)

navigation by mouse

Features that were recommended included

frequent and timely updating

multitasking

keyword, keyword-in-context, Boolean, and proximity searches

ALA extended character set

user-input note files with user-assigned pointers to/from relevant text

linking *AACR2R* rule numbers with *LCRIs* and with related MARC tags

subsequent additions/changes to be flagged as such with release

ability to set defaults for files or material types to be searched

Software Selection

Of great concern to CDS was the operating system on which the product should be based. A survey group was asked which operating system they currently had and which one they expected to have in the future. Because they were not directly asked their opinion on which system they felt the product should be based, CDS did not get the definitive answer it desired. Nevertheless, the results definitely narrowed the choices to two: DOS and Windows. The survey also confirmed that Cataloger's Desktop had to be networkable.

CDS was convinced that there was a need to develop Cataloger's Desktop both as a DOS and Windows product simultaneously. Prototyping during late 1992 caused CDS to focus in on FolioViews from Folio Corporation. Finally, the decision was made to use the new version 3.0 for DOS when it was ready in mid-June 1993, because it combined the right features, would be available sooner than the alternatives, and would support a lower-end (640 kilobytes of memory) DOS platform. Folio also promised that infobases would be interchangeable in the DOS and Windows FolioViews products.

An event that altered the course of Cataloger's Desktop's development was new information received in fall 1993. Until that point, Folio Corporation had assured CDS that the DOS release of version 3.0 would run on a low-end DOS computer with 640 kilobytes of memory. By October 1993, Folio had revised its requirements for DOS machines, requiring the same 4 megabytes of memory as for the Windows software. With that piece of information in hand and the DOS software still in development, CDS decided that the initial product would be developed for Windows, with the DOS version deferred. This decision has never been reconsidered.

The first issue of Cataloger's Desktop was shown at the 1994 ALA annual meeting, and it shipped about a week after that. It included the *LCRIs, Subject Cataloging Manual: Subject Headings, Subject Cataloging Manual: Classification, USMARC Concise Formats, USMARC Format for Authority Data,* and the USMARC code lists. This list of nine tools (there are four USMARC code lists) has since expanded to more than thirty. The quarterly distribution cycle is timed to closely approximate distribution of *LCRI* updates.

How Cataloger's Desktop Works

When the user opens a Cataloger's Desktop session, he or she is immediately given direct links to the list of cataloging tools available, links to help topics, and a list of "What's New" in the issue. Executing the first link brings the user to a summarized list of tools (figure 5.1). (Originally this fit with all the tools listed singly on a single screen, but with the addition of so many tools, it has had to be compressed.) Double-clicking on any of the titles brings the user to the opening screen of that tool. In every instance, the tool has an abbreviated contents as a part of its opening screen. (See figure 5.2 for the opening screen for the CONSER

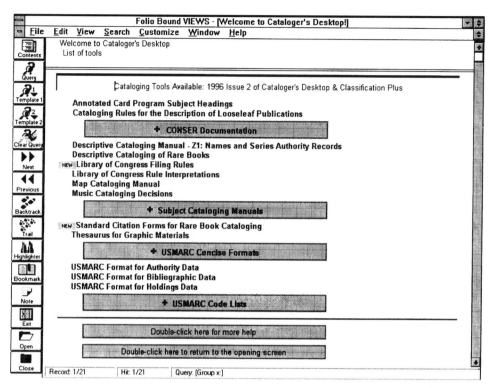

Figure 5.1   Cataloger's Desktop List of Tools

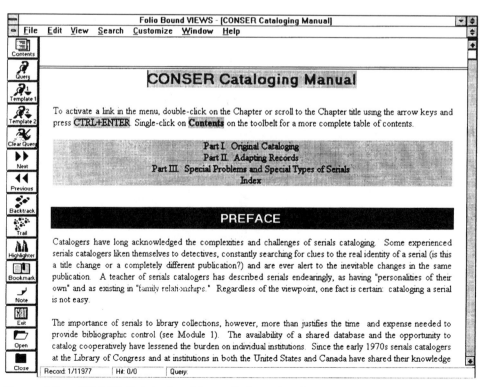

Figure 5.2   CONSER Cataloging Manual's Opening Screen

Manual.) If a user returns to the initial screen of the welcome infobase (initial greeting) and double-clicks for What's New, a list of the titles that have been added with this issue and the tools that have been updated appears. Double-clicking in turn on an updated title presents a list of what has been changed in the issue. The list of changes is hypertext linked to the changed sections within the tool.

Each infobase has a table of contents screen that gives an overview of the tool. Each chapter title can be expanded by double-clicking on the plus sign (+) to the left of the line (figure 5.3). Users advance to known sections by navigating through the infobase's table of contents. The table of contents is also a useful place for looking over the results of a query. In figure 5.3, the user has done a phrase search on *uniform title* (visible at the bottom right side of the screen) in the LCRI infobase. While there were 173 hits (indicated at the bottom of the screen), the user only wanted to look at the LCRIs in "Chapter 1, General Rules for Description." Not too surprisingly, the highest concentration of hits in "Chapter 1" (as noted to the left of the chapter or section numbers) is in "1.7, Note Area." Using the table of contents together with searching provides a very effective avenue for relevance ranking.[4]

Every title that has an index in its print publication also has one in the Cataloger's Desktop infobase. Most often, the infobase index is more precise than its print equivalent because the link is to the specific paragraph referenced in the index, not just the chapter or section. All

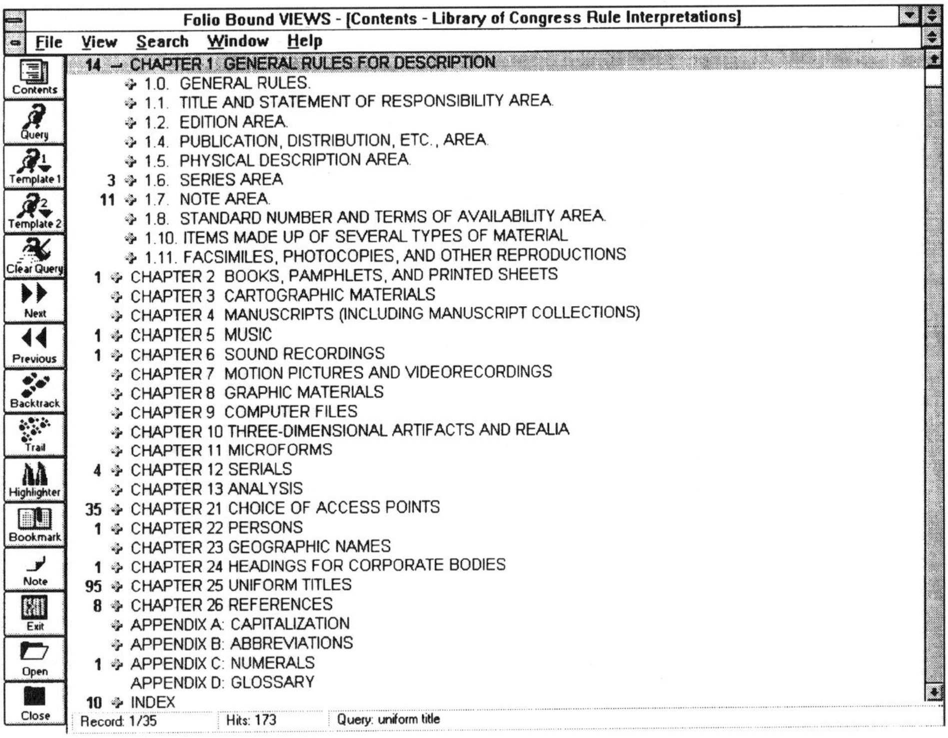

Figure 5.3 Cataloger's Desktop LCRI Table of Contents

infobases provide the capacity for limiting searches to just the index through query templates.

Catalogers frequently told CDS during the early development phases that Cataloger's Desktop had to include everything that was in the original print texts. The challenges included diacritical marks, non-Roman characters, and illustrations. The FolioViews 3.1 for Windows software handles all three types of challenges quite well. The software itself includes all of the commonly used West European diacritics. Non-Roman characters and illustrations are displayed in-line as graphic images. All illustrations (photos, prints, forms, diagrams, and charts) found in the original print texts are present in Cataloger's Desktop.

The FolioViews software allows users to do nearly every type of searching that technology permits, including Boolean, phrase, proximity, wildcard, thesaurus, and stem searching. Every word of every infobase is indexed. One challenge the Cataloger's Desktop development team had was finding a way to harness this powerful search-and-retrieval engine to make it simpler to use. A quick-reference card that summarizes the searching features accompanies the product, and searching tutorials and context-sensitive help are available.

The most useful enhancement to searching was the development of "query templates." These workforms allow users to do the most commonly executed searches by clicking the Template button on FolioViews' "toolbelt" and filling in the blank(s). For example, when using the *USMARC Code List for Geographic Areas* and searching for approved headings that include the word "German," simply click the Template button on the toolbelt and type in *german* (see figure 5.4, template 1). Only approved headings will be retrieved.

A more advanced use is to see whether text is present in very narrow sections of text. In figure 5.4, template 2, the searcher is working in the *Subject Cataloging Manual: Subject Headings* infobase. The word *wars* has been entered in the instruction sheet box, and the term *women* is entered in the search terms box. The first part of the search is attempting to find any instruction sheet (section) titles that included the word *wars*. The LC instruction sheet H1200 gives the instructions for subjects on wars. Entering *women* as a search term will determine whether the word is valid under *wars*. The result (one hit) indicates that it is a valid usage. The upper right quadrant of this template shows diagrammatically the results of the search. Had either part of the search yielded no hits, the searcher would have known it instantly. It is one of the virtues of the search engine that even the most-complex searches are executed very quickly.

Customization

Among the most frequently requested features was the need to customize the online tools. Catalogers have always added personal notes and observations, particularly in the *LCRIs* and the *Subject Cataloging Manual: Subject Headings*. Many institutions have also developed departmentwide policies about implementation (or nonimplementation) of

Template 1

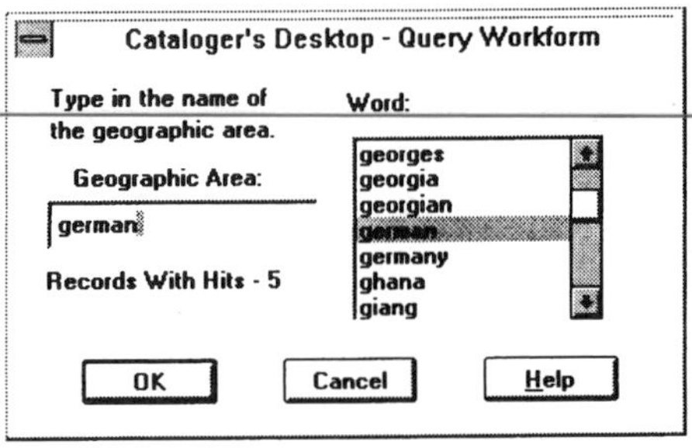

Cataloger's Desktop - Query Workform

Type in the name of the geographic area.

Word:

Geographic Area:

| germany |

georges
georgia
georgian
german
germany
ghana
giang

Records With Hits - 5

[OK]   [Cancel]   [Help]

Template 2

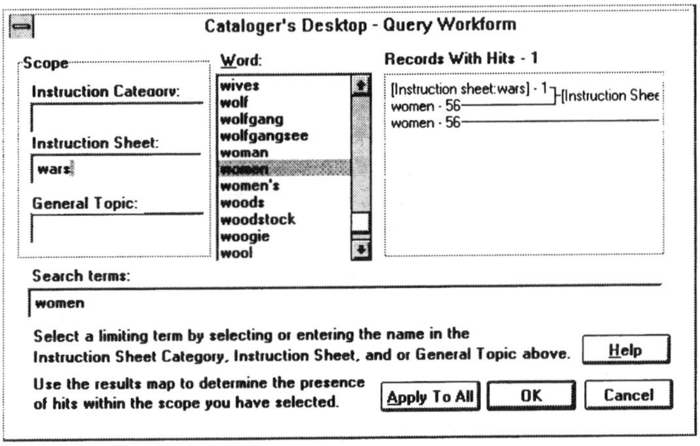

Cataloger's Desktop - Query Workform

Scope

Instruction Category:

Instruction Sheet:

| wars |

General Topic:

Word:

wives
wolf
wolfgang
wolfgangsee
woman
women
women's
woods
woodstock
woogie
wool

Records With Hits - 1

[Instruction sheet:wars] - 1 — [Instruction Shee
women - 56
women - 56 ————————[Instruction Shee

Search terms:

| women |

Select a limiting term by selecting or entering the name in the Instruction Sheet Category, Instruction Sheet, and or General Topic above.   [Help]

Use the results map to determine the presence of hits within the scope you have selected.   [Apply To All] [OK] [Cancel]

Figure 5.4   Cataloger's Desktop Query Templates

certain Library of Congress practices. Also requested was the need to highlight certain important passages as well as a means for quickly returning to frequently referenced topics. These capabilities and more are supported by Cataloger's Desktop and its underlying software, Folio-Views 3.1a. CDS had a broad range of choices of functionalities, including user-defined hypertext links within Cataloger's Desktop as well as to outside documents; defining and applying styles, fields, groups, and levels; and altering the infobase's appearance or structure, that would be made available to users of Cataloger's Desktop. However, CDS chose to emphasize three: notes, bookmarks, and highlighters.[5] The customization is accomplished through "shadow files." The cataloging tools come to the user on a Cataloger's Desktop CD-ROM and are frequently copied onto the network fileserver hard disk. The user cannot alter the contents of the master Cataloger's Desktop infobases since documentation ceases to be useful as documentation if it is not authoritative. Instead, notes, highlighters, and bookmarks are stored in a separate shadow file on the user's TSW hard disk or networked drive. The shadow file sits on top of the master infobase as a template and is empty (invisible) until the user puts something in it.

To see how this works, consider the note feature. A relatively common occurrence is that a cataloging department decides not to apply a particular LCRI or to apply it differently from the practice of the Library of Congress. To implement this feature, the user simply places the cursor at the beginning of a particular LCRI and clicks the Note button on the toolbelt. This opens a note window where the cataloger can type a comment, such as, "Our department does not apply this rule interpretation." When the cataloger is finished, the upper left-hand corner of the note window is double-clicked. A small note will now appear in the left margin. This note can be recalled by double-clicking on it. It is possible to use the Windows paste feature to insert information or examples from other applications into user-defined notes.

The bookmark feature is even easier to use. The user places the cursor at a spot that he or she would like to return to in the future and then clicks the Bookmark button on the toolbelt. A bookmark window opens, and the user is asked to name the bookmark. When done, the user clicks the OK button and that spot is saved. (It can be deleted in the future if it is no longer needed.)

The highlighter feature works in much the same way that a real highlighter works on the printed page. The user uses the mouse to block a section of text that needs to be emphasized and then clicks the Highlighter button on the toolbelt. A highlighter window opens, and the user double-clicks on the desired highlighter color. Now the text is highlighted for all future users of that shadow file.

Hypertext Links

Another important navigation feature is hypertext linking that allows the user to double-click on text or a button to jump from one place to another. In Cataloger's Desktop this takes on three forms: explicit links, implicit links, and conceptual links. A "web" of cataloging information is created through the application of all three types of hypertext linking.

Explicit links are made where the text tells the reader to consult another spot in the tool or a specific spot in another tool (that is, "cf. LCRI 21.30J"). Nearly all cataloging tools refer to other cataloging tools, such as from one section of the *CONSER Editing Guide* to another or from the *USMARC Format for Bibliographic Data* to the *USMARC Code List for Geographic Areas*. Because these jumps are precreated by the Cataloger's Desktop development team, the jumps can be very precise—to the specific spot that is referenced in the source document (as opposed to simply jumping to the other section or other document).

Implicit links are made where additional information is obviously available, but the user is not specifically referred to it. As an example, in LCRI 21.30J there is an explanation of tagging of titles and 246-derived titles along with USMARC tagged examples (figure 5.5). These examples, along with the explanations that they illustrate, have been hypertext linked to the appropriate passages in the *USMARC Format for Bibliographic Data*. Since the information is readily available and would

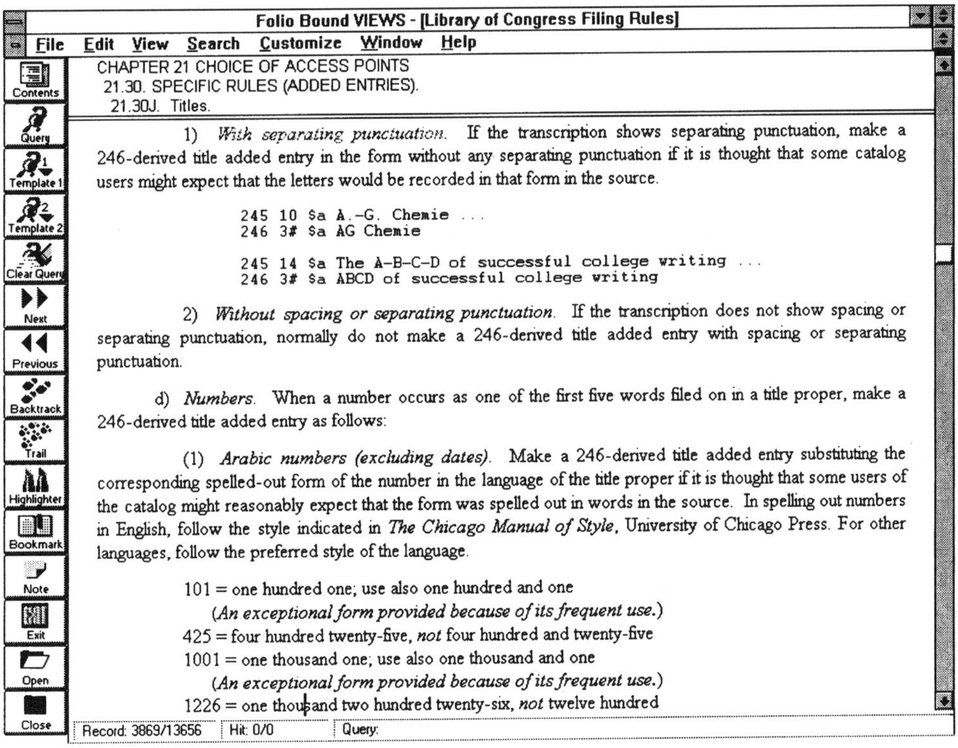
Folio Bound VIEWS - [Library of Congress Filing Rules]
File Edit View Search Customize Window Help
Contents
Query
Template 1
Template 2
Clear Query
Next
Previous
Backtrack
Trail
Highlighter
Bookmark
Note
Exit
Open
Close
CHAPTER 21 CHOICE OF ACCESS POINTS
21.30. SPECIFIC RULES (ADDED ENTRIES).
21.30J. Titles.
1) With separating punctuation. If the transcription shows separating punctuation, make a 246-derived title added entry in the form without any separating punctuation if it is thought that some catalog users might expect that the letters would be recorded in that form in the source.
245 10 $a A.-G. Chemie ...
246 3# $a AG Chemie
245 14 $a The A-B-C-D of successful college writing ...
246 3# $a ABCD of successful college writing
2) Without spacing or separating punctuation. If the transcription does not show spacing or separating punctuation, normally do not make a 246-derived title added entry with spacing or separating punctuation.
d) Numbers. When a number occurs as one of the first five words filed on in a title proper, make a 246-derived title added entry as follows:
(1) Arabic numbers (excluding dates). Make a 246-derived title added entry substituting the corresponding spelled-out form of the number in the language of the title proper if it is thought that some users of the catalog might reasonably expect that the form was spelled out in words in the source. In spelling out numbers in English, follow the style indicated in The Chicago Manual of Style, University of Chicago Press. For other languages, follow the preferred style of the language.
101 = one hundred one; use also one hundred and one
(An exceptional form provided because of its frequent use.)
425 = four hundred twenty-five, not four hundred and twenty-five
1001 = one thousand one; use also one thousand and one
(An exceptional form provided because of its frequent use.)
1226 = one thousand two hundred twenty-six, not twelve hundred
Record: 3869/13656
Hit: 0/0
Query:

Figure 5.5 Cataloger's Desktop Implicit Links

be useful to a cataloger trying to apply LCRI 21.30J, hypertext links help bring the user and the information together.

Finally, CDS has collaborated with cataloging policy specialists in the Library of Congress's cataloging policy and support office to build conceptual hypertext links. To understand just how important this involvement has been, look at the *Subject Cataloging Manual: Subject Headings* infobase. Many subdivisions in the "Free-Floating Subdivisions" section of the tool are related conceptually to separate instruction sheets. While the subdivision and its related instruction sheet may share no text (thereby suggesting one to the other), the user nevertheless needs the information found in the related instruction sheet to correctly apply the subdivision. This type of linking immensely improves the application accuracy of the cataloger, significantly improving productivity.

Machine Requirements

To successfully run Cataloger's Desktop, a computer system should meet or exceed the following specifications:

- Intel-compatible 80386 processor

- ▶ 4 megabytes of RAM (8 megabytes recommended); for OS/2 installations, at least 8 megabytes of RAM
- ▶ Microsoft Windows 3.1 or Windows '95 (must be installed)
- ▶ hard drive containing 2 megabytes of free space
- ▶ monitor and a graphics card capable of displaying Windows applications
- ▶ mouse or other Microsoft-compatible pointing device (highly recommended, though not required)

This configuration is exceeded by all TSWs commercially available now.

The Future

A number of enhancements to Cataloger's Desktop are forthcoming. Of particular interest to smaller libraries will be its availability over the World Wide Web (WWW). CDS has installed Folio Site Director, which will allow libraries to access Cataloger's Desktop through their Web browsers on a pay-as-you-go basis. While some features that many catalogers value (such as customized query templates and shadow files) will be missing from the Web products, Web access will provide cost-effective access to these products via their technical services workstations for libraries with smaller technical services budgets.

Cataloger's Desktop will continue to evolve over the coming years. CDS will migrate it to the new Folio 4.0 software. This software provides a number of enhancements to its functionality. Among them will be the ability to search any or all infobases without opening them first. The user will no longer need to know where to begin a search and can simply do the search and find all relevant references.

A closely related enhancement will be true relevance-ranked hit lists appearing in a separate window designed for that purpose. Users will also be able to frame queries in plain English ("natural language"), reflecting how they think and speak. Other improvements will include a soft interface that will make it possible for users to custom design the appearance and layout of what they see. Included with this will be a user-defined switch that will allow the cataloger to set the size of the display type. Display of tables should also be significantly improved.

All of these enhancements deal with improved searchability and display of cataloging documentation. The most significant documentation source still lacking in the Cataloger's Desktop is *AACR2R*, and its inclusion will represent a major milestone. It is anticipated that the three association copublishers of *AACR2R* will finally release it as an independent product on their own behalf and also make the SGML (Standard Generalized Markup Language) encoded file of the descriptive cataloging code available to cataloging documentation publishers for inclusion on their end-user products.[6] John Duke's thorough work in converting the copublishers' typesetting files into the SGML-encoded *AACR2R* file (usually referred to as AACR2-e) will finally enable documentation publishers such as CDS to fill the obvious gap in documentation with the descriptive cataloging rules. The copublishers are preparing licensing agreements to allow these various organizations the opportunity to develop products that will incorporate AACR2-e.

When the SGML AACR2-e file is added to Cataloger's Desktop, it will complete the web of links between *AACR2R* and the rest of the commonly used cataloging documentation publications. Library of Congress cataloging policy specialists, who have historically been intimately involved in the development of *AACR2R,* have been working for some time to prepare for this important linking project. Links between *AACR2R* and eight other cataloging documents have been identified and will be accessible by single-clicking on custom-built buttons.

Dr. Ben Shneiderman of the University of Maryland presented a discussion on measuring human-computer interactivity at a 1995 program at NASA's Goddard Space Flight Center. In the opening to his talk, Dr. Shneiderman noted that computer users *do not* want computers that are "user friendly." What they really want are computers that *empower* them to get the intended task done as quickly and simply as possible. The computer will seem easy if the user feels that the path to solving a problem or getting something done is visually intuitive.

Cataloger's Desktop is in many ways just the first step in what is likely to be a long, evolving process of online documentation development. The goal was to construct in these tools the fundamental infrastructure essential to a new paradigm in online documentation. If that goal has been met, then Cataloger's Desktop will provide catalogers with the means not just to search traditional cataloging tools better and more quickly but to use them in an entirely new knowledge framework.

In time, users will begin to look at these tools less as separate entities and more as part of a cataloging information "web." As a part of building the Cataloger's Desktop, the development team imposed editorial conventions intended to standardize the look and feel of all pieces of cataloging documentation. While one goal was to ease the transition from paper to online documentation, another was to integrate cataloging tools as tightly as possible.

It is inevitable that users will gradually lose track of which cataloging tool they are consulting as they search for answers to their questions. Each tool will look very similar and present information in a similar manner. This is good because we are not interested in the mechanics of searching or navigation but ultimately in finding the answers to questions.

Cataloger's Desktop is an important first step on the road to providing catalogers with online documentation and to advancing the goal of fully empowering catalogers to confront the electronic era.

Notes

1. J. McRee Elrod. autocat@ubvm.cc.buffalo.edu (Feb. 1994).

2. Charles Fenly, *Expert Systems, Concepts and Applications* (Washington, D.C.: Cataloging Distribution Service, Library of Congress, 1988), 24.

3. RTSD Board Document 89.22, Jan. 1989.

4. This is what Thomas K. Landauer (of Bellcore) refers to as "structured search feedback." A particularly interesting discussion of this can be found in his paper, "Helping People Get More Information out of Text," delivered at User Interface Strategies 1992 at the University of Maryland, Dec. 12, 1991.

5. Dr. Thomas Landauer ("Helping People") recommended that developers of online text retrieval products limit the range of choices that end users are given. By simplifying the display and focusing the user's attention on the very few most important functions, the product actually becomes easier to use and quicker to learn, thereby improving the user's productivity.

6. SGML is, in essence, NISO ANSI standard Z39.59-1988, *Electronic Manuscript Preparation and Markup* (Bethesda, Md.: NISO, 1988).

Library of Congress Classification

SuperLCCS and Classification Plus

Anaclare Frost Evans
Wayne State University

▼ For many years the visual image of a cataloger working at a desk is of an individual surrounded by piles of books, many of them open and being consulted as part of the process of subject analysis and classification. With the appearance of machine-readable versions of the *Library of Congress Subject Headings* some years ago, that image has changed a bit: The big red books are gone! But the cataloger was still surrounded by the many volumes of the Library of Congress Classification with its many updates and Adds and Changes. Catalogers have long wished that this were available in a more-compact, easier-to-use tool. As various other resources became available electronically, catalogers began to see various possibilities for the Library of Congress Classification. The development of the *USMARC Format for Classification Data* was one of the sparks that resulted in the Library of Congress Classification in electronic form.

As various institutions and forward-looking catalogers have developed the platform that we now know as the technical services workstation, one of the most wished-for components has been electronic classification tools, whether the Dewey Decimal Classification or the Library of Congress Classification. (Diane Vizine-Goetz and Mark Bendig discuss the Dewey Decimal Classification in chapter 7.) Even more than the *Library of Congress Subject Headings* or the various formats, this has been the long-sought goal of developers and technical services departments. The reasons, particularly for the Library of Congress Classification, are not difficult to detail:

▶ A complete set of the Library of Congress Classification, for instance, easily takes up three or four shelves.

▶ A complete set is horrendously expensive.

▶ It is difficult to keep up-to-date with regular Adds and Changes.

▶ It is difficult to consult, given lack of any complete or consistent indexing.

▶ Class-by-class terminology, captioning, and indexing is inconsistent both within an individual classification and among various classifications.

▶ Inconsistencies between the Library of Congress Classification and the *Library of Congress Subject Headings* are legion.

▶ There is a distinct lack of classification numbers embedded in corresponding subject headings.

Interest in this product went hand-in-hand with the development of the *USMARC Format for Classification Data* and the development of desktop computers and LANs powerful enough to support it. It is not particularly surprising, therefore, that two competing versions of the Library of Congress Classification appeared at about the same time. The cost of the printed products and the inability of most institutions to maintain adequate numbers of complete sets have made networked, electronic versions a necessity and an integral part of any serious technical services workstation configuration. What is interesting in comparing the two products is to observe that the groups behind the different versions have taken very different technical routes to develop their products.

Both versions of the Library of Congress Classification have now appeared as CD-ROM files. The first of these versions appeared during the summer of 1995. This was the beta test version of SuperLCCS CD from Gale Research. Shortly thereafter, the beta test version of Classification Plus became available from the Library of Congress. Both are single CD-ROM disks that contain the schedules and tables of the Library of Congress Classification. While the two sources provide access to the same data, the files and search engines are structured very differently. The beta test version of Classification Plus contained only a few schedules of Library of Congress Classification, so the overall performance of the two products cannot really be compared. The release versions of the products continue to be different, and the Library of Congress product will be incomplete for several releases. Only when all of the classification schedules are converted into the *USMARC Format for Classification Data*, have run the gamut of quality control, and are then released will Classification Plus be complete.

The goal here is to describe the two products sufficiently so that any librarian or institution that is considering the requisite components of a technical services workstation will have a clear picture of the place of online classification in the overall configuration. Enough specifics are supplied so that interested parties can make an informed decision about which electronic version of the Library of Congress Classification is best suited for their local environment.

SuperLCCS CD

The Gale Research SuperLCCS CD product contains all of the schedules and tables for the Library of Congress Classification. It incorporates the Adds and Changes to the schedules, and new data appears about one calendar quarter after it is issued by the Library of Congress. Gale Research will issue a completely updated version of the schedules with each quarterly release. The company has converted its printed versions of the Library of Congress Classification, also called *SuperLCCS*, into hypertext and made it searchable through the use of DynaText. This provides useful access to all of the schedules through a single search.

System and network requirements for SuperLCCS CD are listed in the appendix at the end of this chapter. It is worth observing that network installation for both these products allows for multiple-user access to a single copy of the CD-ROM without regard to CD-ROM drives in the individual workstations. It does not support access via dumb terminals.

Although the specifications state that SuperLCCS CD will run on 80386-based personal computers and attempts to install and use the software on an 80386 machine were successful, nonetheless, the software's operation in this configuration was too slow to be tolerable. On midrange 80486 machines, operational speed was acceptable with a double-speed CD-ROM drive and much better with the quad-speed drive. The best performance occurs if the entire CD-ROM can be loaded onto the hard drive.

The installation of SuperLCCS CD was quite easy. Following standard Microsoft Windows installation procedures, the process goes quite quickly with the files self-extracting and self-installing. All users really need to know are the letters that represent their hard drive and their CD-ROM drive. For the minimally Windows literate, simple and well-illustrated instructions are available to guide them through the installation process. Although network installation instructions are in the back of the manual and appear almost as easy to follow, there was no opportunity to test them.

The manual that accompanies SuperLCCS CD is clear and easy to use. At 140 pages, it is appropriate in length. The text is profusely illustrated with pictures of screens, and minitutorials are scattered through the text. The introductory pages of the manual contain a significant amount of material dealing with the use of Windows-based software so that users unfamiliar with Windows can get enough knowledge to use this package. There is a brief index and a detailed table of contents to aid the user. The manual does not deal with using the Library of Congress Classification as such, only with using the software.

Searching in SuperLCCS CD

From the main Windows Program Manager screen, users begin a SuperLCCS CD session by double-clicking on the SuperLCCS icon. The main body of the opening screen is divided into two parts: One is called "collection," and the other is called "title." At the bottom of the screen is a search box. A Help button is clearly indicated at the top of the screen as a very large button with a question mark on it. As with most applications that run under Windows, full on-screen help is available. It is also possible to change the arrangement of the panes of the window by indicating one's preference.

To open the schedules and begin a search, either click on the Title button or the Open button at the top of the screen. The resulting display is divided horizontally (see figure 6.1) into a table of contents in the upper window and the actual text, beginning with the Library of Congress Classification Schedule for "A" in the lower window. By moving the mouse pointer over the line separating the table of contents and the text until a double-pointed arrow appears, the size of the panes can be changed. This is easily accomplished by dragging the line to the desired position. Up and down arrows at the side of the screen allow the user to scroll forward and backward in the schedules. Hypertext links appear whenever there is a need for a link, for example, to link to a "see" reference, hot link, Gale note, or table (see figures 6.2–6.6). Double-clicking on the highlighted text takes the user to a table, to the preferred class number, or to related numbers that must be considered. This type of navigation is quite intuitive, and most staff who tested the product had no difficulty figuring out how to do this simple level of navigation.

The table of contents is the outline of the Library of Congress Classification itself. In front of each main class is a button with a plus

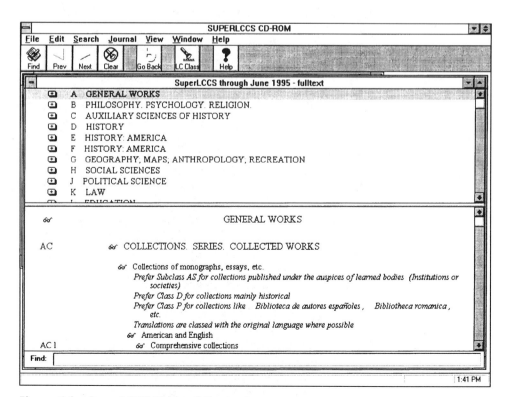

Figure 6.1   SuperLCCS Table of Contents

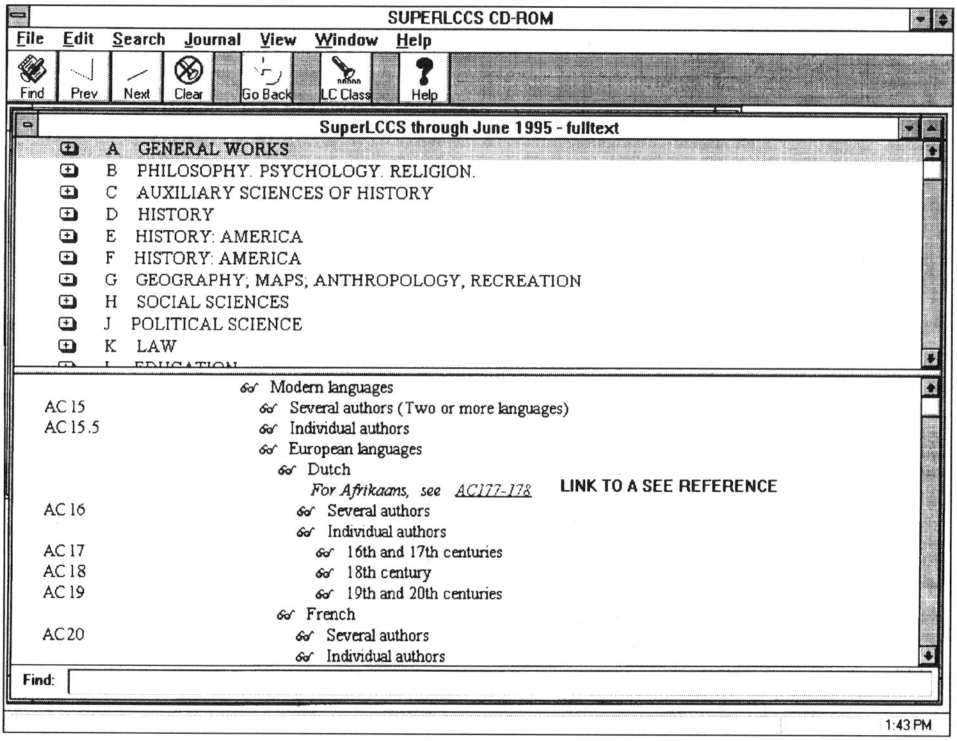

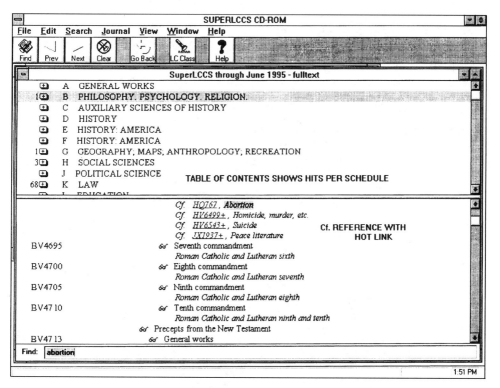

Figure 6.2 SuperLCCS Link to a See Reference

Figure 6.3 SuperLCCS "Hits"/Detailed View/Hot Links

```
┌──────────────────────────────────────────────────────────────────────┐
│ ▭                        SUPERLCCS CD-ROM                        ▼ │ ≑ │
├──────────────────────────────────────────────────────────────────────┤
│ File   Edit   Search   Journal   View   Window   Help                  │
│  🗇      ⌐      ╱      ⊗       ⌐╮     🖉        ？                        │
│ Find   Prev   Next   Clear   Go Back  LC Class   Help                   │
├──────────────────────────────────────────────────────────────────────┤
│ ▭             SuperLCCS through June 1995 - fulltext            ▼ │ ▲ │
├──────────────────────────────────────────────────────────────────────┤
```

KE226	6ʳ Particular offenses, A-Z
KE226.A2	6ʳ **Abortion**
KE226.M8	6ʳ Murder. Assassination
KE226.P6	6ʳ Political offenses
	Including treason, sedition, etc.
	6ʳ Particular trials
	Including records, briefs, commentaries and stories on a particular trial
KE228	6ʳ Early through 19th century. By defendant or by best known name, A-Z
KE229	6ʳ 20th century. By defendant or by best known name, A-Z
	6ʳ Civil trials **VALUE ADDED GALE NOTE EXPANDS ON STANDARD**
KE234	6ʳ Collections **LC NOTE. TOP LINE SHOWS A HIGHLIGHTED HIT**
	6ʳ Particular trials **FROM A WORD SEARCH AND A Cf. REFERENCE**
	KE228
	GALE NOTE The development takes the place of the Library of Congress note " see note above KE228 "
	Including records, briefs, commentaries and stories on a particular trial
	Class individual trials with "Particular cases" or "Particular companies" only if specifically provided for in the schedule, e.g. KE3234, Railway labor disputes; KE4655, Contested elections; KE2649.C3, Litigation involving the Canadian Broadcasting Corporation
KE236	6ʳ Early through 19th century. By plaintiff, A-Z
KE237	6ʳ 20th century. By plaintiff, A-Z
	6ʳ Legal research. Legal bibliography
	Methods of bibliographic research and how to find the law
KE250	6ʳ General Table
	GALE NOTE To develop this number integrate the subtopics into the table structure

```
├──────────────────────────────────────────────────────────────────────┤
│ Find:  │abortion│                                                       │
├──────────────────────────────────────────────────────────────────────┤
│                                                              1:59 PM    │
└──────────────────────────────────────────────────────────────────────┘
```

Figure 6.4   SuperLCCS with Added Gale Note

```
┌──────────────────────────────────────────────────────────────────────┐
│ ▭                        SUPERLCCS CD-ROM                        ▼ │ ≑ │
├──────────────────────────────────────────────────────────────────────┤
│ File   Edit   Search   Journal   View   Window   Help                  │
│  🗇      ⌐      ╱      ⊗       ⌐╮     🖉        ？                        │
│ Find   Prev   Next   Clear   Go Back  LC Class   Help                   │
├──────────────────────────────────────────────────────────────────────┤
│ ▭             SuperLCCS through June 1995 - fulltext            ▼ │ ▲ │
├──────────────────────────────────────────────────────────────────────┤
```

	6ʳ Austronesian languages Table
AC166-167	6ʳ Malay Table
AC168-169	6ʳ Indonesian Table
AC176	6ʳ Other, A-Z Table **LINKS TO TABLES**
AC176.J39-.J392	6ʳ Javanese Table
	6ʳ African languages Table
AC177-178	6ʳ Afrikaans Table
AC179-180	6ʳ Bantu Table
AC189	6ʳ Other, A-Z Table
AC189.A45	6ʳ Amharic Table
AC189.M34	6ʳ Malagasy Table
AC189.S9	6ʳ Swahili Table
AC190	6ʳ Hyperborean languages, A-Z
AC195	6ʳ American Indian languages, A-Z
AC200	6ʳ Collections for Jewish readers
	6ʳ Inaugural and program dissertations
	Prefer classification by subject in Classes B-Z
AC801	6ʳ American (United States)
AC811	6ʳ English
AC817	6ʳ Dutch
AC819	6ʳ Finnish
AC821	6ʳ French
AC825	6ʳ Belgian
AC831	6ʳ German and Austrian
AC835	6ʳ Hungarian

```
├──────────────────────────────────────────────────────────────────────┤
│ Find:  │                                                       │        │
├──────────────────────────────────────────────────────────────────────┤
│                                                              2:06 PM    │
└──────────────────────────────────────────────────────────────────────┘
```

Figure 6.5   SuperLCCS Links to Tables

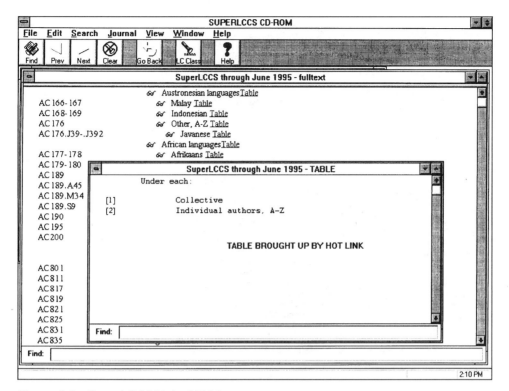

Figure 6.6 SuperLCCS Linked Table

(+) sign that when clicked produces an expanded view of the outline. That view collapses when the button marked with a minus (–) sign is clicked. When the user selects a particular schedule and subportion of the table of contents, the corresponding detailed view is displayed in the lower pane. When users are satisfied that they are in the correct area, they can request a detailed view and the full schedule appears (figure 6.7). Navigation in this area is not as smooth as it might be. During testing volunteers regularly followed trails that led to blank screens.

Once users start scrolling into the actual schedules, the table of contents disappears from the screen, and the detailed view appears. By clicking on the button marked Go Back, users can return to where they were. In addition, there are two other common ways in which to do a search. The first is to click on the Find button. This displays a dialog box into which the user types a search argument. (See figure 6.8.) The search results are the equivalent of a keyword search for the term as it appears across all Library of Congress Classification schedules. This can be most useful to a person who is not fully familiar with the various places a term might appear. For example, a standard search on the word *diabetes* takes a user initially into the H, Social Sciences, schedule. (See figure 6.9.) A more specific search on the words *diabetes mellitus* is needed for this type of keyword search to go directly to Class R, Medicine (figure 6.10), where most of the material on diabetes will be found.

```
┌──────────────────────────────────────────────────────────────────────────┐
│ ▬                         SUPERLCCS CD-ROM                          ▼│▲│ │
│ ▬  File   Edit   Search   Journal   View   Window   Help                 ▲│ │
├──────────────────────────────────────────────────────────────────────────┤
│  🗲      ⌐      /      ⊗       ⌐⌐      🖌      ?                             │
│ Find   Prev   Next   Clear   Go Back  LC Class  Help                      │
├──────────────────────────────────────────────────────────────────────────┤
```

                        ⊞ U - Uz
                        ⊞ V - Vz
                        ⊟ W - Wz
                            Wabash College, Crawfordsville, Ind. Table
                            Wagner College, Grymes Hill, Staten Island, N.Y. Table
                            Wake Forest University, Winston-Salem, N.C. Table

LD5721.W57-.W66   ∞ Walla Walla College, College Place, Wash. Table
LD5721.W67-.W76   ∞ Wartburg College, Clinton, Ia. Table
LD5731.W17-.W26   ∞ Washburn Municipal University, Topeka, Kans. Table
                        Also known as Washburn University
LD5731.W2637-.W2646 ∞ Washington Christian College, Washington, D.C. Table
LD5731.W37-.W46   ∞ Washington College, Chestertown, Md. Table
LD5731.W47-.W56   ∞ Washington College, Washington College, Tenn. Table
LD5731.W567   ∞ Washington Missionary College, Washington, D.C. Table
LD5731.W57-.W66   ∞ Washington State College. Pullman, Wash. Table
LD5740-5759   ∞ Washington (State) University. Seattle, Wash. Table
LD5780-5799   ∞ Washington University, St. Louis, Mo. Table
LD5820-5839   ∞ Washington and Jefferson College, Washington, Pa. Table
LD5860-5879   ∞ Washington and Lee University, Lexington, Va. Table
                   ∞ Watertown, Wis. Sacred Heart College, *see* LD4785.S47+
LD5887   ∞ Wayland College, Plainview, Tex. Table
LD5889.W37-.W46   ∞ Wayne University, Detroit, Mich. Table
LD5891.W37-.W46   ∞ Waynesburg College, Waynesburg, Pa. Table
LD5891.W57-.W66   ∞ Weaverville College, Weaverville, N.C. Table
LD5901.W27-.W36   ∞ Wesleyan University, Middletown, Conn. Table
LD5901.W4   ∞ West Chester State College, West Chester, Pa. Table
                        Formerly West Chester Academy; West Chester, Normal School; State Teachers College

Find: [   ]
                                                                    2:18 PM

Figure 6.7 SuperLCCS Detailed View of LC Classification

Figure 6.8 SuperLCCS Search Box

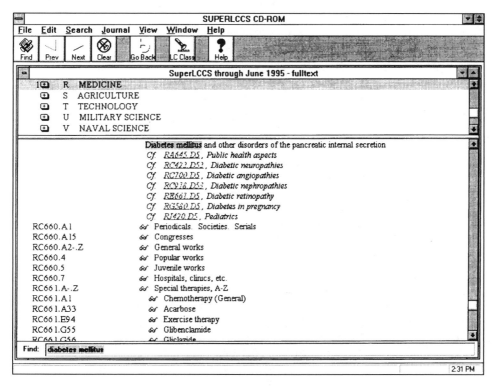

```
┌──────────────────────────────────────────────────────────────────────────┐
│ ─                          SUPERLCCS CD-ROM                         ▼│≑│   │
├──────────────────────────────────────────────────────────────────────────┤
│ File   Edit   Search   Journal   View   Window   Help                       │
│ ✒       ⌐̣     ╱      ⊗        ┌̣┐       ╲̖̖       ❓                          │
│ Find   Prev  Next   Clear    Go Back  LC Class   Help                       │
│ ┌────────────────────────────────────────────────────────────────────┐    │
│ │ ─               SuperLCCS through June 1995 - fulltext        ▼│▲│   │    │
│ ├────────────────────────────────────────────────────────────────────┤    │
│ │     ⊞   E   HISTORY: AMERICA                                    ‡│    │
│ │     ⊞   F   HISTORY: AMERICA                                     │    │
│ │     ⊞   G   GEOGRAPHY; MAPS; ANTHROPOLOGY; RECREATION            │    │
│ │   3⊞   H   SOCIAL SCIENCES                                       │    │
│ │     ⊞   J   POLITICAL SCIENCE                                   ‡│    │
```

HD9675.H67-.H674   𝄞 Hormones (General) Table
HD9675.H86-.H864   𝄞 Hypoglycemic agents Table
                             Cf. *HD9995.D53-.D534* **Diabetes** *treatment equipment*
HD9675.I45-.I47   𝄞 Insulin Table
                             Cf. *HD9995.D53-.D534* **Diabetes** *treatment equipment*
HD9675.I48-.I484   𝄞 Interferon Table
HD9675.I52-.I54   𝄞 Iodine Table
HD9675.O65-.O654   𝄞 Opium Table
HD9675.O75-.O754   𝄞 Osteoporosis drugs Table
HD9675.Q5-.Q7   𝄞 Quinine Table
HD9675.R47-.R474   𝄞 Respiratory agents Table
                             Cf. *HD9995.R48-.R484* *Respiratory therapy equipment industry*
HD9675.S83-.S834   𝄞 Steroids Table
HD9675.S96-.S964   𝄞 Sunscreens Table
HD9675.V33-.V334   𝄞 Vaccines Table
HD9675.V5-.V53   𝄞 Vitamins Table
HD9675.W44-.W444   𝄞 Weight loss preparations Table
                    𝄞 Precious stones
HD9676   𝄞 General Table
HD9677   𝄞 Diamonds Table

Find: ▐ diabetes

                                                        2:29 PM

Figure 6.9   SuperLCCS Search Results for "Diabetes" in "H"

```
┌──────────────────────────────────────────────────────────────────────────┐
│ ─                          SUPERLCCS CD-ROM                         ▼│≑│   │
├──────────────────────────────────────────────────────────────────────────┤
│ File   Edit   Search   Journal   View   Window   Help                       │
│ ✒       ⌐̣     ╱      ⊗        ┌̣┐       ╲̖̖       ❓                          │
│ Find   Prev  Next   Clear    Go Back  LC Class   Help                       │
│ ┌────────────────────────────────────────────────────────────────────┐    │
│ │ ─               SuperLCCS through June 1995 - fulltext        ▼│▲│   │    │
│ ├────────────────────────────────────────────────────────────────────┤    │
│ │   1⊞   R   MEDICINE                                             ‡│    │
│ │     ⊞   S   AGRICULTURE                                         │    │
│ │     ⊞   T   TECHNOLOGY                                          │    │
│ │     ⊞   U   MILITARY SCIENCE                                    │    │
│ │     ⊞   V   NAVAL SCIENCE                                       ‡│    │
```

                     Diabetes mellitus and other disorders of the pancreatic internal secretion
                         Cf. *RA645.D5*, *Public health aspects*
                         Cf. *RC422.D52*, *Diabetic neuropathies*
                         Cf. *RC700.D5*, *Diabetic angiopathies*
                         Cf. *RC918.D53*, *Diabetic nephropathies*
                         Cf. *RE661.D5*, *Diabetic retinopathy*
                         Cf. *RG560.D5*, *Diabetes in pregnancy*
                         Cf. *RJ420.D5*, *Pediatrics*
RC660.A1   𝄞 Periodicals. Societies. Serials
RC660.A15   𝄞 Congresses
RC660.A2-.Z   𝄞 General works
RC660.4   𝄞 Popular works
RC660.5   𝄞 Juvenile works
RC660.7   𝄞 Hospitals, clinics, etc.
RC661.A-.Z   𝄞 Special therapies, A-Z
RC661.A1   𝄞 Chemotherapy (General)
RC661.A33   𝄞 Acarbose
RC661.E94   𝄞 Exercise therapy
RC661.G55   𝄞 Glibenclamide
RC661.G56   𝄞 Gliclazide

Find: ▐ diabetes mellitus

                                                        2:31 PM

Figure 6.10   SuperLCCS Search Results for "Diabetes Mellitus" in "R"

Clicking again on the search button returns the initial search, which may be further refined if need be. All of the hypertext links continue to be available. Various search options include the following:

- ► single caption
- ► single note
- ► exclude notes
- ► limit by one class
- ► limit by two classes
- ► limit by three classes
- ► exclude one class
- ► limit by one subclass
- ► limit by two subclasses
- ► limit by three subclasses
- ► standard

A standard search, however, puts no limitations on the search.

Searches can make use of the Boolean operators and, or, and not. The operators function in the expected way. That is, *and* means that the specified words must all appear in the search statement—useful to narrow a search. The operator *or* means that any of the specified words must appear in the result—useful when the user has a group of synonymous terms and does not know which term is used in the Library of Congress Classification. *Not* allows the user to eliminate words that occur after the word *not* in the search statement. The proximity operator *within* (*X* number) *words of* (the user supplies the word or words) can also be useful when looking for a phrase.

Two wildcard characters are available. The asterisk (*) allows multiple character variations on a word to be used in the search argument, and the question mark (?) enables the search argument to accommodate single-character variations. Stop words and keywords that are listed in the manual can be used only in limited ways. A very few words are so commonly used in the schedules that they may never be used as search words. In the process of constructing a search, the user has the option of either typing words into the search box or copying them onto the clipboard using Windows cut-and-paste techniques.

It is also possible to search by LC Classification number. To do this the user clicks on the button at the top of the screen marked LC Class, and a dialog box will prompt for the desired class number. (It is also possible to do a call-number search from the search dialog box.) This type of search is resource intensive, and in the course of testing, *out of memory* errors were encountered when performing these types of searches.

One useful feature of the searching dialog box is that it contains the history of a user's previous searches. If a user wishes to repeat a particular search, it is only necessary to highlight that search in the dialog box and click on the Find button. This can be handy if a user dismissed a search but later determined that it had led to the best result.

When a search is executed, SuperLCCS CD annotates the table of contents portion of the screen. To the left of each class or subclass in the table of contents the number of occurrences of the requested search will appear, as was seen in figure 6.3. By using the Next and Previous buttons, users can move forward or backward from one occurrence of the term or search to the next. When finished with a particular search, it is wise to clear the search from any internal buffers before going on to the next search.

Bookmarks and Frequent-User Annotations

Frequent users of portions of the classification schedules may wish to set bookmarks to enable a speedy return to the same area of the text. Bookmarks can be set either from the keyboard or by clicking on the bookmark button. In addition to placing the mark, a user has the option of keeping the bookmark private or giving open access to it. Such decisions can be made individually for each bookmark by clicking on the appropriate button.

Notes on local decisions about use of individual portions of the classification can be inserted into the text by clicking the button marked Note (not shown). This invokes a work screen into which a user can type the text of any note desired in addition to assigning a name for the note. These notes can be created either by typing the data into the note box or by cutting and pasting text onto the clipboard and then into the dialog box. These, too, can be marked either private or public. During a search, the system will display all public as well as a user's private notes. The notes can also be edited. As new versions of the software are received, the notes are copied from the existing version of the software to the new version as part of the installation process.

It is also possible to create personal hyperlinks between class numbers. These can be either one-way or bidirectional links. By using a series of annotations consisting of personal hyperlinks and bookmarks, it is possible to personalize SuperLCCS CD for a particular institution or individual user. By accessing the Annotation Manager, users can get a listing of all their annotations.

Journal Functions

SuperLCCS CD allows the user to open a journal window and record and play back the activity during a session. These journals may be saved for a later time. Users must first create their journals by pulling down the menu from the menu bar at the top of the screen. From the menu, they click on New to create a new journal and then on Record to enter transactions into their journals. A button marked Stop ends a recording session, and a Pause button temporarily interrupts a session. These buttons work just like their counterparts on a tape recorder. Journals may be saved as either public or private files and can be renamed.

Although experienced classifiers will probably see no need to use the journal function, the truly significant value of journals lies in their potential to create training tools for teaching the classification system to new catalogers as well as for learning SuperLCCS CD itself. This is precisely the sort of tool that should be used—namely, an online tool—to create tutorials for the newly emerging technical environments.

Copying Text to a Bibliographic Record

Buried in an appendix to the SuperLCCS CD manual are instructions for copying and pasting schedule entries from the schedules to the clipboard and then from the clipboard to a bibliographic record. While useful for longer numbers, it is almost as efficient to copy shorter numbers directly into the bibliographic record by rekeying them.

Comments

This is a useful and very usable product. Until LC finishes inputting and proofing its classification data, this will be the only complete version of the LC Classification schedules available in machine-readable form. It installs easily and does what it claims to do. Improvements in the operation of the product are being made with each release, along with updates to the schedules themselves.

The downside of the software is the price. The cost of SuperLCCS CD is comparable to a complete run of the same product in paper. For a moderate additional sum, a site license for up to eight simultaneous users may be obtained. If additional simultaneous sites are needed, contact Gale Research for specific pricing. For most libraries, eight simultaneous users will actually suffice since it is unlikely more than eight would be using SuperLCCS CD at the same time. It is worth stressing that the strength of this version of the LC schedules is its completeness and the manner in which the software searches across all of the schedules.

Classification Plus

Classification Plus is the CD-ROM version of the LC Classification schedules issued by the Library of Congress Cataloging Distribution Service. Catalogers who are used to using the Library of Congress Cataloger's Desktop will be familiar with the look and operation of Classification Plus because the same search engine is used for both. The system requirements are similar to those for SuperLCCS CD and the Cataloger's Desktop.

One of the great strengths of Classification Plus is that it and Cataloger's Desktop share the same search engine and user interface (FolioViews). Furthermore, ALA is releasing the electronic version of the *Anglo-American Cataloging Rules*, 2nd edition (Revised), as AACR2-e under FolioViews. This has tremendous implications for the library profession as a whole, and for technical services in particular, because it will enable the development of uniform training approaches to what is likely to become a standard for development of documentation and tools within the profession. This may well lead to a flattening of the learning curve associated with integrating these tools (as opposed to their content) into departmental workflows: learn one and, in effect, learn them all.

Installation

Installation instructions are clear and easy to follow. (System and network requirements are listed in the appendix at the end of this chapter.) For the most part, the software is self-installing, with the user required to specify only the drive and desired directory name. Once the programs have been installed, the user need only place the desired CD-ROM in the disk drive and double-click on the icon to open the software. Network installations are equally straightforward. If the user also has the Cataloger's Desktop installed on the workstation, the two applications will share the search engine and other common files. Up to seven different infobases from both products may be open at any one time. The user need only answer the questions relating to an installed version of the Cataloger's Desktop to take advantage of this option.

Manual

The documentation is in two parts: a reference card and a software user's manual. Included in the software manual is a short tutorial that helps users become familiar with the techniques to move about the various databases. Telephone help is also available during normal business hours.

Online help files are available and are generally fairly useful. Help is always available from the tool bar at the top of the screen. The help files are more closely related to the content of Classification Plus than to the use of the disk.

It is worth commenting on the philosophy held by the developers of Cataloger's Desktop and Classification Plus from the Cataloging Distribution Service at the Library of Congress. It is their firm belief that the ease of use of the product should be inversely proportional to the size of the required printed documentation. That is, the smaller the required printed documentation, the easier the product should be to use. To be successful, the product development specialists in the Cataloging Distribution Service have provided multiple, often redundant learning- and help-file approaches. They have succeeded very admirably in this attempt. One result of this philosophy is that the Cataloging Distribution Service has no plans to prepare a formal instruction manual.

Contents

The Classification Plus CD-ROM contains separate files for each of the Library of Congress Classification schedules. Each schedule is a separate infobase, and the only way to move between the schedules is where a hot link occurs due to a reference within the text. Also on this CD-ROM are the *Library of Congress Subject Headings (LCSH). LCSH* is in a separate file with hypertext links to Library of Congress Classification. Users must consult the Cataloger's Desktop to reach the Subject Cataloging Manual: Subject Headings, the Subject Cataloging Manual: Classification, or the Subject Cataloging Manual: Shelflisting. Catalogers whose workstations have only a single CD-ROM drive will be swapping CD-ROM disks often to make use of the two complementary tools. It is much better, if local institutional logistics permit, to plan for providing networked access to all of the CD-ROM cataloging tools.[1] Barring that, in a locale where a cataloger is using a stand-alone workstation, it is worth considering attaching multiple CD-ROM drives to that workstation.

Searching

Users can search Classification Plus in a variety of different ways. When users open the program, a welcome screen appears. At the welcome screen users click for a list of searchable files and then click on a particular infobase to begin searching. (See figure 6.11.) The screens will be very familiar to users of the Cataloger's Desktop because they follow the same design and layout. This is very beneficial for users who are wary of using workstations in place of their familiar paper tools as they have only one software system to learn even though they are using several programs. A full range of Boolean operators is available in the query

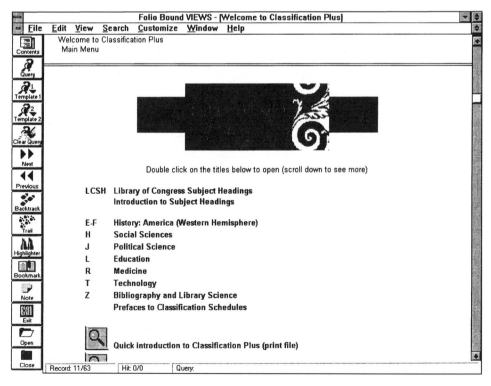

Figure 6.11 Classification Plus List of Infobases

mode. While complex searches are available, they will likely be used only by expert searchers.

Users must first choose an infobase, then click on the Query button. The flexibility of the query dialog box allows users of Classification Plus to enter either a class number search or a word search in the same box. The query box consists of a large dialog box into which the user keys the query. Above the box are two windows, one that supplies a list of words and the other that reports the number of hits. When the user executes the search, the number of hits resulting from the search appears at the bottom of the screen (figure 6.12). By using the navigation buttons for Next or Prev(ious), users can move about in the results file. At any time, it is possible to jump about by taking advantage of hypertext links between files.

When using LC's special tables to build numbers within an outlined scheme, the user must first get to the proper base-class number (figure 6.13) and then invoke the hot link to the table. In figures 6.13 and 6.14, the user has started with a search on diabetes and then jumped by means of a hypertext link to the tables associated with this classification number. The level of detail available in the tables (figure 6.14) is identical to that found in the printed versions of the file. One feature missing from Classification Plus is a small workspace where the user can build the number online for later transfer to a bibliographic record.

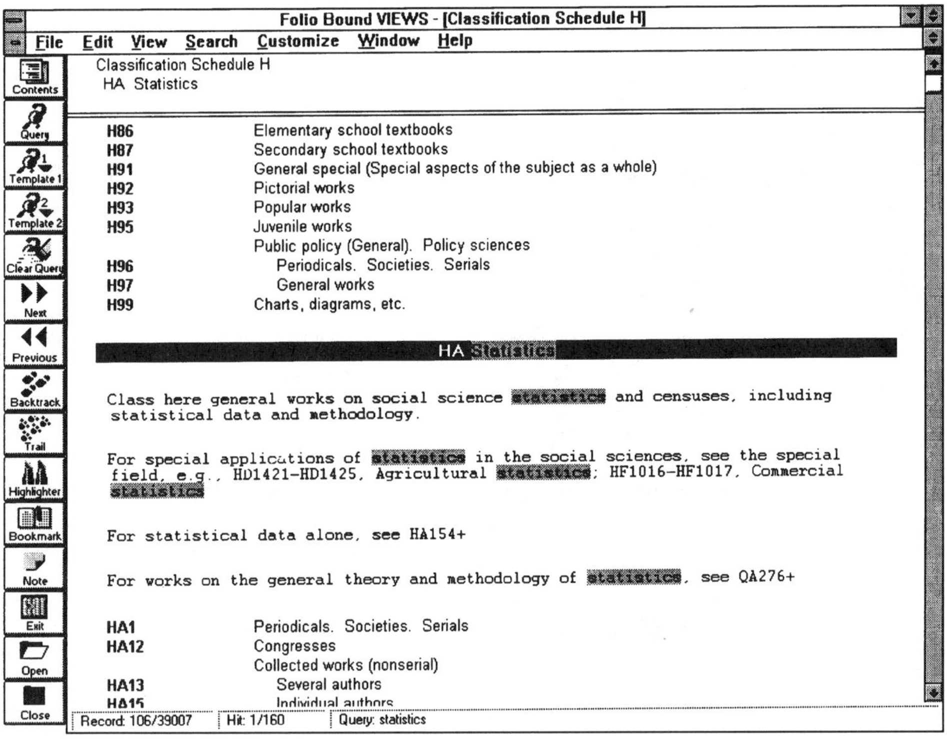

Figure 6.12 Classification Plus Search Results for "Statistics" in "HA"

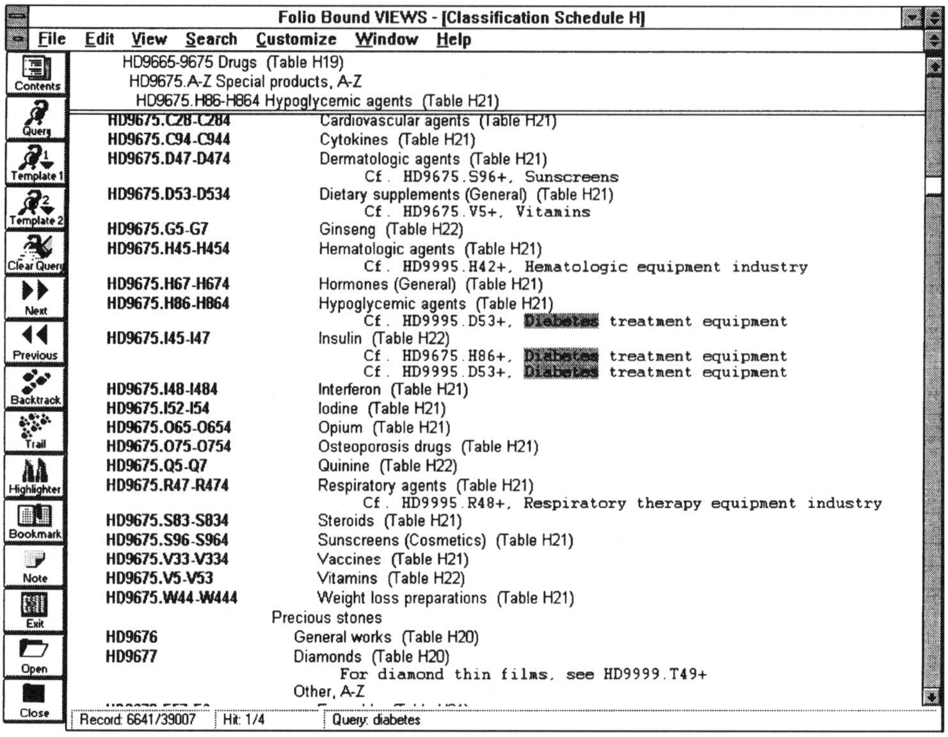

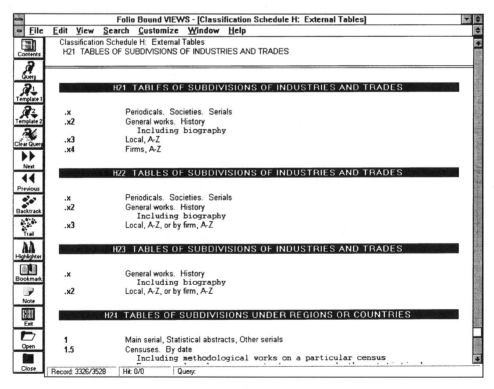

Figure 6.13 Classification Plus Link to a Table

Figure 6.14 Classification Plus Linked Table

One of the useful features of Classification Plus is the availability of the Library of Congress Subject Headings (figure 6.15) on the same CD-ROM. Because many MARC subject authority records for the Library of Congress Subject Headings contain suggested class numbers, many catalogers move back and forth between the two tools using the subject headings to suggest class numbers and the classification schedules to suggest words for subject headings. The hypertext links connect suggested class numbers found in subject headings with that part of the classification schedule (figure 6.16). In addition, many catalogers also consult their own shelflist, manual or online, to see how their library has used specific numbers in the past. The ability for many users of Classification Plus to be able to check call numbers in one window, their shelflist in another window, and perhaps their subject index in a third window will make the task of assigning and verifying class numbers much easier, quicker, and more accurate.

An interesting feature of Classification Plus is the ability to add one's own links between parts of the classification. This is the "Jump" function. These have the potential to be particularly useful in conjunction with local classification decisions.

Journals

The record-and-play method of tracing one's activity is not available in Classification Plus. The Backtrack button enables the user to retrace the

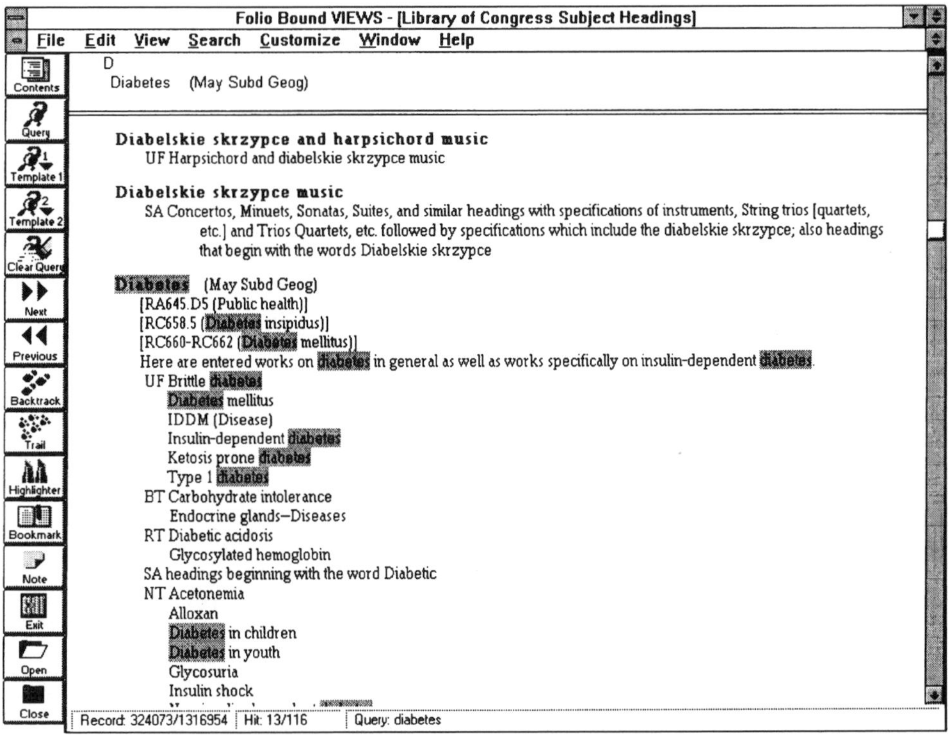

Figure 6.15 Classification Plus View of LCSH with Links

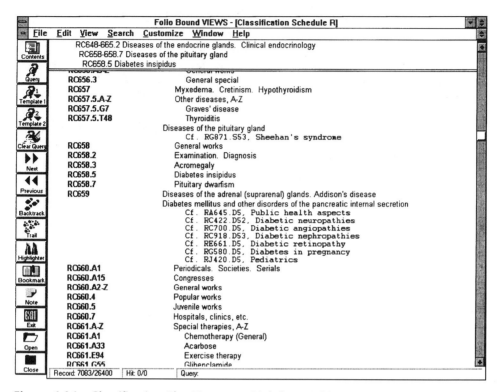

Figure 6.16 Classification Plus Hypertext Link from LCSH to RC658.5

logic of a search within a single session. It is a regular function of the FolioViews software and appears as a large button on the left hand side of the screen. While it does not allow a user in the role of potential trainer to record and play back a session later, it is possible to retrace one's steps from the current session. Backtrack is also useful as a navigation tool. The Trail function allows a user to review a session from the beginning. These two functions oppose each other in that one goes from the end to the beginning while the other goes from the beginning to the end.

Bookmarks and Notes

Users can add bookmarks as well as make notes in "shadow files," which are similar to little "yellow sticky" notes. The bookmark function is easy to use and allows users to place markers to frequently consulted portions of the schedules. Unfortunately, these personal annotations do not carry forward to the next version of the software, so they are of limited value in recording variations in local practices with regard to the application of Library of Congress Classification. It would be far more worthwhile if these notes could be retained. If users could carry the notes forward, they could be an online replacement for the instruction cards that many libraries insert in their shelflist to document exceptions to the norm. Developers at the Library of Congress Cataloging Distribution Service have heard about the lack of a reconcilable "shadow file" that can be carried forward, but they have been reluctant to implement such a feature in Classification Plus for technical reasons having to do with the nature of the schedules and the reconciliation process itself.

Copying Text to a Bibliographic Record

No specific instructions were included to copy text to a bibliographic record, most likely because this is a Windows capability that is assumed. Because many neophyte Windows users will be using Classification Plus, it would have been helpful to include this type of instruction. The significance in hammering home this type of Windows practice in users new to Windows is that simple copying techniques that avoid the need to rekey data will improve accuracy.

Comments

Classification Plus is a well-designed product that resembles other CD-ROM cataloging tools issued by the Library of Congress. The look and feel of the other products is clearly visible and a positive feature. The uncluttered screens of Classification Plus result in remarkable readability. The movement between screens and the query techniques will be familiar to users of the Cataloger's Desktop. The ability to use Cataloger's Desktop and the online, electronic classification as implemented in Classification Plus simultaneously brings users closer to the complete and all-encompassing technical services workstation. However, it may require equipment such as a CD-ROM tower or multiple CD-ROM drives that many technical services departments can only dream of having.

One drawback to Classification Plus is the lack of many parts of the Library of Congress Classification schedules, a situation that will prevail until all schedules have been reviewed for quality by LC and have been released. Product development staff at the Library of Congress have stated that new schedules will appear in each new release as the data are converted and pass quality assurance.

A major selling point for Classification Plus will be the substantially lower price since the Library of Congress is engaged in creating this product for its own internal technical services staff and can make the product available as an adjunct to that process. Moreover, purchasers who buy both Cataloger's Desktop and Classification Plus can obtain a package price that is about one-third the cost of Gale Research's SuperLCCS CD. However, Gale Research has an advantage until Classification Plus is complete because its product, SuperLCCS CD, is already complete and offers the purchaser the opportunity to cease subscribing to paper products now.

Summary

Classification Plus and SuperLCCS CD are two competitive products. The data in each product are the same. However, the data are structured differently, and the search engines for retrieval are different. Although starting from similar points, future product developments could result in the two products going in different directions. Both are useful, and each will have its own proponents.

Note

1. Putting all of the files on a networked hard drive, or even a local hard drive, is not as daunting as it once was. Cataloger's Desktop has matured at about 120 megabytes. While the Library of Congress does have a number of further infobases to add to Cataloger's Desktop, the product now contains most of the infobases it is ever likely to contain. Classification Plus, by comparison, comprises more than 225 megabytes, although approximately 75 percent of that is the Library of Congress Subject Headings. The remaining 25 percent consists of classification schedules. When completed, Classification Plus will probably comprise 350 megabytes overall. A 1-gigabyte network drive will be more than ample to hold both products.

APPENDIX
▼
System and Network Requirements for SuperLCCS CD and Classification Plus

SuperLCCS CD

System requirements for installation of SuperLCCS CD on a single, stand-alone workstation are as follows, as specified in the manual for the first release version of the product:

▶ IBM or compatible personal computer with an 80386 or higher CPU

▶ 4 to 8 megabytes or more RAM

▶ 8.5 megabytes hard disk space for full installation

▶ MS-DOS or PC-DOS 3.1 or higher

▶ Microsoft Windows 3.1 or higher, or Microsoft Windows version 3.0 with Multimedia Extensions

▶ ISO 9600 compatible CD-ROM with cables and interface card (double-speed or faster)

▶ MS-DOS CD-ROM extensions (MSCDEX) version 2.0 or higher or MSCDEX version 2.2 or higher with MS-DOS 4.0 or higher

▶ mouse

▶ VGA color monitor recommended, but CGA or EGA monitors will work

▶ printer (optional)

Network requirements include

▶ Novell, 3Comm, IBM Token Ring, or other Net BIOS-compatible network

▶ MS-DOS CD-ROM extensions

▶ ISO 9600 compatible CD-ROM drive with cables and interface card

▶ 8.5 megabytes hard disk drive space for full installation

▶ parallel or serial port for printer attachment (optional)

Each workstation attached to the network must meet these requirements:

▶ IBM or compatible PC/XT/AT or PS/2 with at least an 80386 or higher microprocessor

▶ MS-DOS or PC-DOS 3.1 or higher

▶ Microsoft Windows (as for stand-alone installation)

▶ 4 to 8 megabytes of RAM

▶ mouse

▶ VGA color monitor (recommended) with display on CGA or EGA monitor

Classification Plus

The system requirements for use of Classification Plus are almost identical to those needed for SuperLCCS CD. For the stand-alone workstation environment they include

- ▶ IBM PC/AT compatible computer with an Intel compatible 80386 (or greater) processor
- ▶ Microsoft Windows 3.1 or OS/2 version 2.1 or greater installed on local system
- ▶ for Microsoft Windows users, MS-DOS version 5.0 (or higher)
- ▶ for Windows users, at least 4 megabytes of RAM (8 for OS/2 users)
- ▶ one CD-ROM drive with Microsoft extensions
- ▶ at least one hard drive with at least 2 megabytes of free space
- ▶ monitor capable of displaying graphics and a compatible video card (EGA/VGA recommended)
- ▶ Microsoft-compatible mouse (recommended but not required)

In a networked environment, Classification Plus can support up to 125 users. For best response time, it is recommended that the program files be copied to the LAN server and then installed from the LAN to the workstation. Additional precautions are suggested to protect the security of the data. On the network the requirements are

- ▶ 80386 or greater Intel-compatible processor
- ▶ 8 megabytes of RAM (more RAM means better speed across the network)
- ▶ network software
- ▶ MS-DOS 5.0 (or higher)
- ▶ one CD-ROM drive with Microsoft extensions
- ▶ on peer-to-peer networks, SHARE.EXE must be loaded for all of the options to be available
- ▶ at least 2 megabytes of free disk space (depending upon the installation options selected)

The networked workstation requires

- ▶ 80386 or greater Intel-compatible processor
- ▶ 4 megabytes of RAM
- ▶ 500 kilobytes or more of free disk space
- ▶ monitor capable of displaying graphics (EGA or better)
- ▶ Microsoft-compatible mouse (recommended but not required)

CHAPTER

7

Dewey for Windows

Diane Vizine-Goetz
and
Mark Bendig
OCLC Online Computer Library Center, Inc.

▼ When researchers in the OCLC Office of Research obtained access to the machine-readable version of the Dewey Decimal Classification (DDC), they undertook a project to transform the DDC into a workstation-based classifier's tool. This was only one part of a series of ongoing research initiatives at OCLC to investigate the broad range of catalogers' tools and cataloging productivity enhancers.

Previously, use of the machine-readable DDC has been limited to online editorial support, production of the printed DDC, and select research projects. The release of the compact disc-based Electronic Dewey system by OCLC Forest Press in 1993 marked the start of classifier access to the Dewey Decimal Classification from a personal computer (PC) workstation. A new Windows version of the software, Dewey for Windows (DFW), which extends the functionality of the original DOS product, was released in mid-1996. The Electronic Dewey product represented a major milestone in providing access to machine-readable classification data: It was the first system to provide interactive user access to a general classification scheme. As such, it was one of the first successful building blocks of what is now recognized as the technical services workstation.

The computerization of the DDC began with the production of DDC 19 in 1979 from computer-based photocomposition tapes. This development and the end-user oriented DDC Online Project conducted by Karen Markey in the early 1980s prompted Forest Press to commission Inforonics to develop an online editorial support system (ESS) for

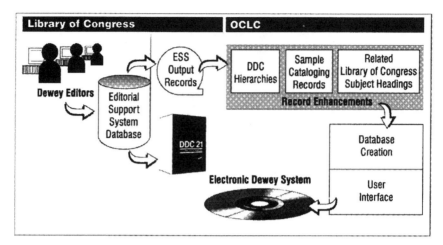

Figure 7.1 Creating the Electronic Dewey System

the Dewey Classification.[1] John Finni and Peter Paulson have provided an important historical description of the development of the Dewey ESS.[2] The resulting system and database were used by the Dewey editors to create DDC 20 in 1989. This was, in fact, the first classification ever produced using an online editorial support system. Access to the machine-readable version of DDC enabled staff members in the OCLC Office of Research to prototype the Electronic Dewey software. (See figure 7.1.)

In an article describing the development and implementation of the *USMARC Format for Classification Data,* Rebecca Guenther identified six potential uses for online classification data:

1. authority control for classification data
2. maintenance and printing of classification schedules
3. improving subject access
4. providing classifier assistance
5. maintenance of classification numbers in bibliographic files
6. providing the basis for an online shelflist[3]

The electronic version of DDC can be used in each of these ways.

Editorial Support System

The machine-readable version of the twenty-first edition of the DDC (DDC 21) consists of seventeen files, one for each of the ten main Dewey classes and seven auxiliary tables. These files are used to produce both printed DDC and the CD-ROM database components of the electronic Dewey products. The terms *electronic Dewey database* and *DDC database* used in the remainder of this chapter describe the CD-ROM version of the DDC.

In the editorial support system format, all of the information associated with a given schedule or table number is stored in a single record for that number, including relative index entries and manual information. A portion of the ESS record for DDC number 025.04, "Information storage and retrieval systems," is shown in figure 7.2. Although this record structure facilitates control and maintenance of classification data, it also produces some large records that pose browsing and display difficulties in a PC-based classifying system. In the printed DDC, the tables, schedules, index, and manual are presented separately for user convenience. This approach was partially adopted in the DDC database. Manual information is extracted from ESS records to produce separate manual records that can be individually searched and displayed. The interface provides additional methods for displaying and comparing detailed classification records. (See the discussion "Dewey for Windows User Interface" later in this chapter.)

ESS records contain coding specifically developed to support editing and printing DDC data. Since the release of Electronic Dewey, additional coding has been introduced to support the development of classifier assistance features in Dewey for Windows and its successors. For example, the alphabetic tags "ieh" and "iph" shown in figure 7.2 are used to identify relative index entries that appear in the printed Relative Index (for example, "Automated information systems" and Computer network resources," respectively). The tag "inh" is used for index terms that will appear only in the electronic Dewey database (for example, "Campus-wide information systems—information science"). This distinction allows for the addition of a wide range of indexing vocabulary that can be used in future versions to provide customized views of the classification.

ESS records also contain coding from the *USMARC Format for Classification Data*. In figure 7.2, the 685 field is used to indicate that the meaning of class number 025.04 has been changed through the addition of topics that were previously classed in another Dewey number, 001.59. USMARC tag 685 contains information about the history and use of a classification number. The date the change was implemented is also given (subfield $d). Such information may be used in the future to assist in the maintenance of classification numbers in bibliographic records.

Classification Record Enhancements

Figure 7.1 shows three of the five major ways ESS records are enhanced as they are processed to form the DDC database. The five enhancements are

1. creation of DDC hierarchies
2. mapping of *Library of Congress Subject Headings (LCSH)*
3. inclusion of sample bibliographic records
4. addition of segmentation information
5. expansion of built number information

ESS Tag	Text of field
en	025.04
eh	Information storage and retrieval systems
nin	Including recall, precision, relevance
nch	Class here search and retrieval in information storage and retrieval systems; front-end systems; comprehensive works on online catalogs integrated with information storage and retrieval systems, on automated storage, search, retrieval of information; interdisciplinary works on databases
nce	Class information storage in 025.3
nse	For computer science aspects of information storage and retrieval systems, of databases, see 005.74
nse	for information storage and retrieval systems devoted to specific disciplines and subjects, see 025.06
nsw	For a specific kind of information storage and retrieval system, see the kind, for example, online catalogs 025.3132
nsa	See also 658.4038011 for management use of information storage and retrieval systems
nsm	See Manual at 004.678 vs. 025.04, 384.33; also at 005.74
ieh	Automated information systems
inh	Campus-wide information systems—information science
iph	Computer network resources
ieh	Data banks
ieh	Data bases
ieh	Databanks
ieh	Databases
ieh	Databases—information science
iph	Front-end systems
iph	Front-end systems—information science
iph	Full-text databases
iph	Full-text databases—information science
ieh	Information storage and retrieval systems
iph	Internet resources
ieh	Online information systems
iph	Precision (Information science)
ieh	Recall (Information science)
iph	Relevance (Information science)
isa	Automated information systems
isa	Online information systems
685	21$t Recall, precision, relevance, irrelevance $i all formerly located in $b 001.59 $d 19890306 $2 20

Figure 7.2 ESS Record for 025.04, "Information Storage and Retrieval Systems"

These enhancements provide information not available in the print edition. This is, in fact, one of the strengths of the electronic version of the DDC, namely that it is possible to include much more information on a CD-ROM product than in its print equivalent. The editors of the printed DDC must constantly bear in mind that it is used worldwide and that its size and corresponding cost is an issue of significant consequence in many areas of the world where it is used. The CD-ROM, on the other hand, has ample room to include all sorts of information that cannot be easily accommodated within the restrictions imposed on the print edition. The enlarged body of information in the electronic version is in addition to the ease of use associated with a product that is built around electronic searching and hypertext links, which is one of the bonuses that come with using a properly designed electronic document.

DDC Hierarchies

Each record in the DDC database is supplemented with information relating to broader and narrower Dewey classes. This enhancement allows users to view any class number in the context of the Dewey hierarchy. In this regard, the DDC hierarchies are similar in function to the summaries in the printed DDC; both provide an overview of the structure and progression of hierarchy in the DDC scheme. In the Dewey for Windows system, hierarchy information also provides more efficient navigation among classes than is possible with print. The hierarchy information associated with DDC number 005.71, "Data communications," is shown in figure 7.3.

The interface takes advantage of the hierarchical information as the user moves to broader and deeper levels of the classification by clicking on the Hierarchy button or pressing shortcut keys. From the new location the user can execute the Hierarchy command again to move to more general or specific classes that make up the current hierarchy. A detailed description of the user interface is discussed later in this chapter.

0 00	Generalities
00 0	Generalities
005	Computer programming, programs, data
005.7	Data in computer systems
005.71	Data communications
005.711	Programming
005.712	Programming for specific types of computers
005.713	Programs

Figure 7.3   Hierarchy Information for DDC 005.71

Library of Congress Subject Headings

For schedule numbers, the electronic Dewey database includes up to five Library of Congress subject headings that have been frequently used with a given class number. The associations are based on a statistical analysis of LC-contributed records in OCLC's WorldCat with DDC 20-based class numbers. The LC subject headings included in the DDC database are a source of additional lead-in terminology for topics in the Dewey Classification and may provide assistance in assigning LC subject headings. They are not intended as a substitute for the print or electronic versions of the *Library of Congress Subject Headings (LCSH)*. However, this approach—where a user can see statistical correlations between classification numbers and subject headings—is a first step in what could be a very significant additional use of online classification products in general. This approach would take the hypertext links being embedded in the Library of Congress Classification Plus beyond one-to-one links and beyond the additional links being added to Classification Plus by LC's cataloging policy and support office in conjunction with the Cataloging and Distribution Service. The approach could comprise the beginnings of an expert systems add-on to the classification process.

For example, the following top five headings are used with DDC number 005.133, "Specific programming languages":

> C (Computer program language)
>
> PASCAL (Computer program language)
>
> C++ (Computer program language)
>
> Ada (Computer program language)
>
> BASIC (Computer program language)

They provide useful index terms not found in terminology used in Dewey captions, notes, or relative index terms.

The DDC 21 database also includes many DDC/*LCSH* links that have been reviewed editorially. In addition to providing supplemental vocabulary for topics already represented in class schedules, linking DDC with *LCSH* provides a mechanism for allowing new topics to be represented in the classification even if each is not supplied with its own number. The inclusion of statistically mapped and editorially reviewed *LCSH* links in the indexes improves users' ability to locate appropriate topic areas.

Sample Bibliographic Records
Showing DDC/*LCSH*

A sample bibliographic record is provided for most schedule numbers in the database. These records contain selected fields from the set of LC-contributed MARC records used to generate the DDC/*LCSH* mappings just described. These records are intended as an example of how a given

DDC number is used with the top-listed subject heading. As such, they provide specific guidance to catalogers in use of the classification numbers and targeted subject headings.

The sample bibliographic record for DDC number 005.133, "Specific programming languages," and the LC subject heading used most frequently with this number, "C (Computer program language)," is shown below:

OCLC: 28926380

010 93-083472

050 QA76.73.C15 $b P458 1993

082 005.13/3 $2 20

100 Perry, Gregory J.

245 Absolute beginner's guide to C / $c Greg Perry.

260 Carmel, Ind. : $b Sams Pub., $c c1993.

650 C (Computer program language)

Segmentation Marks

One aid to help librarians determine the logical place to shorten or reduce a DDC number is the segmentation provided in Dewey class numbers assigned to bibliographic records by the Decimal Classification Division at the Library of Congress. The segmentation is indicated by a prime mark (') or slash (/). DDC numbers can consist of one to three segments. These segments identify abridged numbers and help classifiers choose broad or close classification.

Segmentation marks are not available in the printed DDC, and so they represent still another value-added component of the electronic DDC. They were added to the database for both schedule numbers and built numbers using software that derives the segmentation information from LC-contributed bibliographic records in the OCLC WorldCat. The results were manually reviewed before they were included in the DDC database.

Built Numbers

Built numbers are DDC numbers that have been synthesized by the application of Add instructions provided in the notes for a schedule or table number. The DDC database includes separate records for built numbers that are included in the Dewey Relative Index. Records for built numbers include index terms and the nearest matching DDC schedule number with its caption. The following record is an example of a built number record in the DDC database. It is the built number record information for the Relative Index entry "Microcomputers—communications—programs" (DDC number 005.7136).

Built Number: 005.7/136

Best Match Class #: 005.713

Best Match Caption: Programs

DDC Index Terms: Microcomputers—communications—programs

                    Microcomputers—interfacing—programs

LC Subject Terms: CompuServe (Videotex system)

                    Communications software

                    Electronic mail systems

The fields labeled "Best match class #" and "Best match caption" indicate the source of the Add instruction applied to create the built number or the base number to which a standard subdivision has been added. For example,

Class Number: 005.7/13

Caption: Programs

Notes: Add to base number 005.713 the numbers follow-
             ing 005.3 in 005.31-005.39, for example, commu-
             nications programs for digital microcomputers
             005.7136

The DDC Database

The DDC database is composed of records that correspond to entries in the printed schedules, tables, or manual. Each record contains several fields that describe different types of information that may be included in records. A typical record contains the following fields:

Class number

Caption

Note(s)

DDC (Relative) Index term(s)

Indexes

For each field, words, phrases, or numbers are assembled into one or more keyword or phrase indexes. Keyword indexes contain an entry for each significant word in an indexed field, for example, 005.74 (class number). A phrase index entry contains all the words in an indexed field, treated as a unit, for example, "database design" (DDC Relative Index terms). The DFW system provides a range of searching capabilities, including Boolean, proximity, and truncation.

Figure 7.4 includes a definition and sample query for each of the nine indexes provided for searching and scanning.

Index	Searches for	Sample Query
Basic index	Keywords from captions, notes, relative index entries, Dewey class numbers	Sorting 005.748
Captions (words)	Keywords from captions	Data files
Captions (phrases)	Captions as phrases	"Data files and databases"
Dewey number	Dewey class numbers	005.74 T1—068
Relative index (words)	Keywords from DDC relative index entries	Query languages
Relative index (phrases)	DDC relative index entries as phrases	"Database query languages"
LCSH (words)	Keywords from *LCSH*	PASCAL
LCSH (phrases)	*LCSH* as phrases	"PASCAL computer program language"
Notes (words)	Keywords from notes	Validation

Figure 7.4   DDC Database Indexes

Dewey for Windows System Design

The DFW system consists of three main parts:

1. DDC database
2. OCLC's Newton search engine
3. user interface

A diagram of the overall system is shown in figure 7.5.

The user interface was implemented using Microsoft Visual BASIC (VB) version 3.0, which offers a complete programming and debugging environment during product development. VB allows the developer to create an executable file that contains the application code. The end user does not need to own VB. Using VB, windows that will appear on the screen can be designed quickly and easily. Buttons, list boxes, and other objects in the application windows can be moved, resized, relabeled, and colored through simple menu choices. Once windows are designed, snippets of BASIC code are attached to the objects, such as code to handle the button that was just pressed or code to run when resizing windows. Taken together, the windows and the code snippets constitute the DFW user interface.

Although VB offers a built-in database capability, DFW requires a more sophisticated database-access program (often referred to as a search engine). DFW uses a special version of OCLC's Newton search engine. To make the Newton software accessible to the VB user interface code, a dynamic link library (DLL) that contains the Newton code along with a

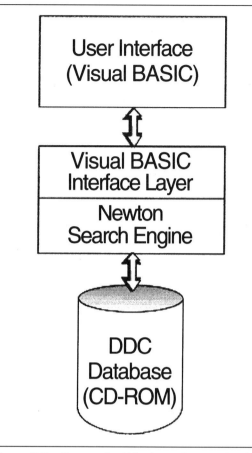

Figure 7.5 Dewey for Windows System Design

small amount of VB-to-Newton interface code was created. A DLL permits multiple applications to use its subroutines and functions, sometimes simultaneously. The DLL created for DFW also allows other Windows-based programs developed at OCLC to have full Newton search-engine functions from the beginning of development. DFW uses the same database structure as the earlier DOS-based Electronic Dewey product. Users should be able to use the Windows-based version with relative ease since the database structure is similar.

Dewey for Windows User Interface

During the course of product development, it was determined that to effectively search, navigate, and browse the DDC electronically requires a user interface tailored for content and structure. For a variety of reasons that will become clear in the following discussion, it was decided that the best method to achieve that goal was to design "single-function windows."

Each function performed by DFW is associated with a type of window specifically designed for that function. For example, one function is to display the DDC hierarchy centered on a specified DDC number. This information is displayed in a DDC hierarchy window, which is designed for one purpose only—to display hierarchies for specified DDC numbers. Among the eleven window types are windows to display search results, indexes, and DDC numbers.

Figure 7.6 (where the query is "database" using the truncation feature) shows a typical DFW screen with several window types: index window, a DDC hierarchy window, a search results window, and a DDC number window.

Fixed Display Views

DFW permits the user to have many windows open at once. Because of the potential proliferation of open windows, the screen display could become disorganized and confusing, not just to novice users but even to experienced Windows users who would nonetheless still have to juggle, rearrange, and resize a variety of open windows. To alleviate problems associated with multiple windows, DFW offers fixed views. A *view* is an arrangement of windows, which can be reestablished at any time. Each view supports a particular operation or represents a particular approach to classifying. For example, the browse view (figure 7.7) features

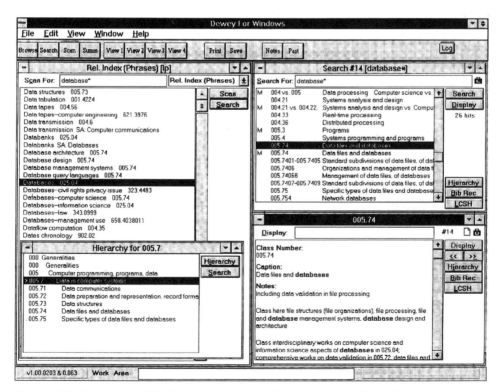

Figure 7.6 Dewey for Windows with Index, Hierarchy, Search, and DDC Number Windows

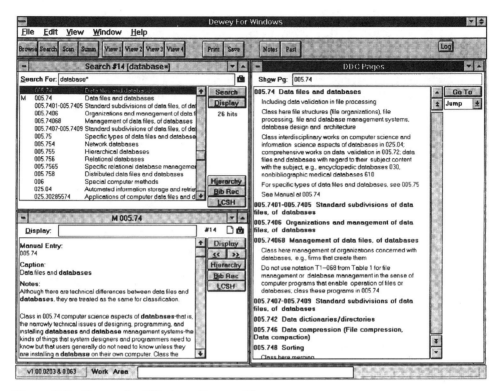

Figure 7.7 Dewey for Windows Browse View

a large DDC pages window and smaller search results and DDC number windows. Using this view, the user searches the DDC for specific keywords, views the text of the entries retrieved, and displays the DDC pages for those numbers. In the DDC pages window, schedule and table entries are displayed one after another, much as they appear in the printed version of the DDC. This display is particularly useful for viewing adjacent numbers, tables of precedence, and local notes.

After selecting and using a fixed view, the user can open additional windows in the usual way. For example, figure 7.8 shows the search view, which consists of one search results window and one DDC number window with an open *LCSH* window. This window displays the *LCSH*/DDC number mapping. The original view can be restored with one click of the mouse.

DFW offers four views—browse, search, scan, and summary. The first three correspond with principal approaches to using the database for document classification. The summary view provides orientation to DDC structure by enabling the user to coordinate or to move to broader or to deeper levels of the Dewey hierarchy. In addition, the user can set up to four custom views. These views, which may contain any combination of window types, are retained in a local file and are available each time the user runs DFW. Figure 7.9 shows a customized view that includes a search results window, two DDC number windows, and a hierarchy window.

Figure 7.8 window (Dewey For Windows):

File Edit View Window Help

Browse Search Scan Summ View 1 View 2 View 3 View 4 Print Save Notes Past Log

Search #14 [database*]

Search For: database*

M	004 vs. 005	Data processing Computer science vs. Co...	Search
	004.21	Systems analysis and design	Display
M	004.21 vs. 004.22.	Systems analysis and design vs. Computer	26 hits
	004.33	Real-time processing	
	004.36	Distributed processing	
M	005.3	Programs	
	005.4	Systems programming and programs	
	005.74	Data files and databases	
M	005.74	Data files and databases	
	005.7401-005.7405	Standard subdivisions of data files, of databa	
	005.7406	Organizations and management of data files,	
	005.74068	Management of data files, of databases	
	005.7407-005.7409	Standard subdivisions of data files, of databa	
	005.75	Specific types of data files and databases	
	005.754	Network databases	
	005.755	Hierarchical databases	
	005.756	Relational databases	
	005.7565	Specific relational database management sy	
	005.758	Distributed data files and databases	
	006	Special computer methods	
	025.04	Automated information storage and retrieval	

005.74

Display: #14

Class Number:
005.74

Caption:
Data files and **databases**

Notes:
Including data validation in file processing

Class here file structures (file organizations), file processing, file and **database** management systems, **database** design and architecture

Class interdisciplinary works on computer science and information science aspects of **databases** in 025.04; comprehensive works on data validation in 005.72; data files and **databases** with regard to their subject content with the subject, e.g., encyclopedic **databases** 030, nonbibliographic medical **databases** 610

For specific types of data files and **databases**, see 005.75

See Manual at 005.74

DDC Index Terms:
Architecture (Computer science)–**databases**
Data files
Database architecture
Database design
Database management systems
Database query languages
Databases–computer science
File management systems–computer science
File organization–computer science
File processing–computer science

Display << >> Hierarchy Bib Rec LCSH

LC Headings for 005.74

CLASS # FREQUENCY: 148

HEADINGS COUNT: 17

COUNT	PCT	HEADING
102	68.92%	Data base management
21	14.19%	Data base design
8	5.41%	File organization (Computer science)
4	2.70%	Hard disk management
1	0.68%	Virtual computer systems

v1.00.0203 & 0.063   Work Area

Figure 7.8   Dewey for Windows Search View with Open *LCSH* Window

Figure 7.9 window (Dewey For Windows):

File Edit View Window Help

Browse Search Scan Summ View 1 View 2 View 3 View 4 Print Save Notes Past Log

Search #14 [database*]

Search For: database*

M	004 vs. 005	Data processing Computer science vs.
	004.21	Systems analysis and design
M	004.21 vs. 004.22.	Systems analysis and design vs. Compu
	004.33	Real-time processing
	004.36	Distributed processing
M	005.3	Programs
	005.4	Systems programming and programs
	005.74	Data files and databases
M	005.74	Data files and databases
	005.7401-005.7405	Standard subdivisions of data files, of dat
	005.7406	Organizations and management of data f
	005.74068	Management of data files, of databases
	005.7407-005.7409	Standard subdivisions of data files, of dat
	005.75	Specific types of data files and database
	005.754	Network databases

Search Display 26 hits Hierarchy Bib Rec LCSH

M 005.74

Display: #14

Manual Entry:
005.74

Caption:
Data files and **databases**

Notes:
Although there are technical differences between data files and **databases**, they are treated as the same for classification.

Class in 005.74 computer science aspects of **databases**–that is, the narrowly technical issues of designing, programming, and installing **databases** and **database** management systems–the kinds of things that system designers and programmers need to know but that users generally do not need to know unless they are installing a **database** on their own computer. Class the

Display << >> Hierarchy Bib Rec LCSH

005.74

Display: #14

Class Number:
005.74

Caption:
Data files and **databases**

Notes:
Including data validation in file processing

Class here file structures (file organizations), file processing, file and **database** management systems, **database** design and architecture

Class interdisciplinary works on computer science and information science aspects of **databases** in 025.04; comprehensive works on data validation in 005.72; data files and

Display << >> Hierarchy Bib Rec LCSH

Hierarchy for 005.7

000	Generalities
000	Generalities
005	Computer programming, programs, data
005.7	Data in computer systems
005.71	Data communications
005.72	Data preparation and representation, record formats
005.73	Data structures
005.74	Data files and databases
005.75	Specific types of data files and databases

Hierarchy Search

v1.00.0203 & 0.063   Work Area

Figure 7.9   Dewey for Windows Custom Display View Example

Drag-and-Drop Interaction

DFW is designed so that nearly all operations can be performed from the keyboard. Each operation also has an on-screen button to actuate it, and most have a menu command as well. These three modes of interaction have become conventional with graphical user interfaces (GUIs), such as Windows. Moving beyond these standard modes, DFW uses a further level of interaction called "drag-and-drop." This type of capability is very familiar to users of the Macintosh interface and is familiar also to those who use it in the Windows file manager.

In a drag-and-drop user interface, every element of data appearing on the screen is envisioned as a physical object that can be "picked up" (using the mouse), "dragged" across the screen, and "dropped" onto a window. This "dropping," in turn, causes an action to take place. For example:

> An entry in a search results list, representing a DDC number retrieved by a previous search, can be dragged to a DDC hierarchy window and dropped into its data area, causing a display of the hierarchy centered on that DDC number.

> An entry appearing in an index window can be dragged to a search results window and dropped into its data area, initiating a search for that term.

By defining a single function for each window type, drag-and-drop actions in any given window are unambiguous. Dropping something onto a DDC hierarchy window can only mean "display the DDC hierarchy for this" since that is the only function of that window type. In addition, the views are set up as tiled (nonoverlapping) window arrangements to facilitate drag-and-drop among the various windows.

Once the user is accustomed to drag-and-drop, this technique will most likely become the preferred mode of interaction. Even selecting an item and clicking a button to display a retrieved DDC record seems cumbersome when drag-and-drop is available as an alternative.

Other Features

One of the most useful features of the DFW system is the ability to annotate the DDC. Users can add their own electronic notes to the schedules, providing an ability analogous to annotating the print edition to reflect classification decisions. Local notes along with the published notes are displayed in the DDC pages window. The annotation feature may also be used to store user-supplied built numbers. Figure 7.10, where the search is for two adjacent terms, "computer" and "communications," shows a user-supplied note for the microcomputer communications program, ProComm Plus. The record for Dewey number 005.713, "Data communications programs," has been annotated to include the built number 005.71369 for ProComm Plus (shown in the DDC pages window). User-supplied notes are displayed before published notes and in a contrasting color (blue) to distinguish them from Dewey notes. The next time a book about ProComm Plus is classified, the number need

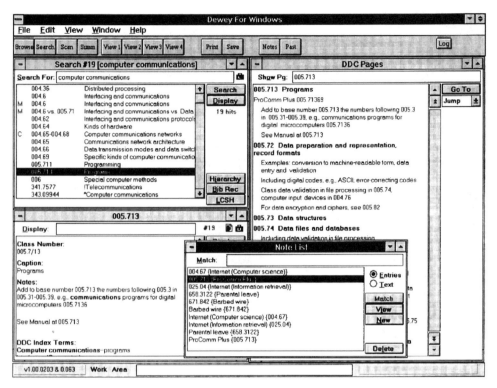

Figure 7.10   Dewey for Windows Browse View with Open Note List Window

not be built again. Annotations can be carried over from one CD-ROM update to the next and thus preserve local numbers without the need to manually transfer annotations.

The past searches window provides a history of all actions performed during the current session including search requests, DDC number displays, index window displays, and DDC pages displays. These actions can be reissued or restored by using the Restore button in the past searches window (figure 7.11) or by using drag-and-drop. The past searches window can also be used to construct new queries by restoring the text of one or more previously entered queries. For example, the query "file management systems or database*" displayed in the past searches window in figure 7.11 was constructed by combining the text of search #1 and search #14 from the past searches window. After the text of a previous query is restored to the "Search For: [input line]:" of the search window, the query can be modified. The search "file management systems or database*," for example, can be edited to "file management system* and database*."

Hardware/Software Compatibility and LAN Operations

Dewey for Windows requires a microcomputer capable of running Windows version 3.1 or higher. A minimum of an 80486-based machine is recommended for satisfactory performance. A color monitor, CD-ROM

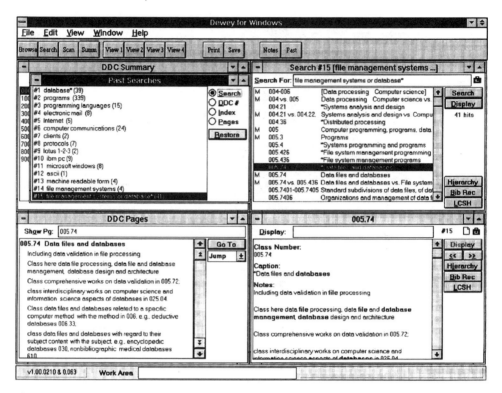

Figure 7.11   Dewey for Windows Summary View with Open Past Searches Window

drive, and a minimum of 8 megabytes of memory are also required. DFW will run on all versions of Windows 3.1 and higher, including Windows, Windows for Workgroups, Windows NT, and Windows '95.

Users of the earlier DOS-based product expressed great interest in sharing access to the DDC CD-ROM among workstations. The DOS program could not be used in this way, and it is now clear that this limitation was one of its major drawbacks. Its design was strictly a standalone application that ran on a single workstation, with no networking capabilities. DFW gains a degree of network functionality simply by virtue of its being a Windows application. Windows itself provides low-level mechanisms for sharing databases and executable files in ways that are largely transparent to the controlling application.

Now, however, the Windows-based product Dewey for Windows is LAN-compatible in that the database may be loaded in a single CD-ROM drive. When the CD-ROM is placed in a networked CD drive—that is, one that can be simultaneously "attached" to a number of workstations—and when a separate copy of the software is running on each workstation, each copy of DFW sees the database files as if they were connected directly to that workstation. The attaching and sharing of the networked CD drive is handled by Windows and/or by the network operating system (for example, Netware or Lantastic). This database sharing is provided without significant coding changes from the stand-alone version of the program as a consequence of the low-level, transparent sharing of the database files. This is one of the major new benefits to be derived from DFW and one that will enable wider acceptance because PCs and networking technology are now rapidly reaching the stage where they are common even in smaller, less affluent libraries.

The degree to which DFW constitutes a successful component of a technical services workstation may be measured by its ability to coexist and interact with other tools and applications running on the same workstation at the same time. As is the case with LAN operation, DFW benefits in this regard simply by virtue of being a "well-behaved" Windows application. The coexistence of multiple applications on screen and in memory at the same time is handled by Windows itself. No special coding is required within applications to realize this level of multitasking.

Beyond mere coexistence is the desirability of interaction between and among concurrent applications. This interaction can take two principal forms: data transfer between applications and control of one application by another. With only a small amount of special-purpose coding, DFW can transfer data to and from other applications, such as OCLC's Passport for Windows (the access program for OCLC). The mechanism is formally known as dynamic data exchange (DDE) but is actually the familiar Windows copy-and-paste function. Data of various kinds, such as DDC numbers retrieved using DFW, are copied into a data object known as the Windows clipboard, from which it may be pasted into any other application. The process serves as a substitute for switching to the target program and then rekeying the data.

Writing applications that control others requires mastery of the complex and difficult Object Linking and Embedding (OLE) standard from Microsoft, now referred to as "ActiveX." ActiveX-compliant applications are written to go beyond the limited DDE functions. The ActiveX standard allows programs to actually issue commands to each other, among other things. In effect, the target program becomes, momentarily, the "slave" of the controlling program. This scheme has the potential to more tightly integrate the component applications of a technical services workstation.

Summary

Dewey for Windows represents one of a growing number of software tools being developed for use by catalogers and classifiers. Although the product has value in its own right as a stand-alone application, its true strength emerges when it is combined with other tools to form a technical services workstation worthy of the name. In general, the more tightly integrated the components are, the more efficient the resulting TSW will be. Since individual applications cannot "know" what else is running on the workstation, this integration presently takes the form of user-initiated data interchange between applications by way of the Windows-provided copy-and-paste functions, for example.

Future generations of DFW and other TSW component applications may be expected to make increasing use of standards such as OLE and its successors. These standards permit the creation of "smarter," more tightly integrated sets of tools to comprise extremely focused, efficient technical services workstations.

In addition, a number of improvements to DFW itself may be envisioned. Such evolutionary steps as an enhanced annotation feature, hypertext links to follow "See" and "See also" type references, and more built numbers may be followed by revolutionary changes in hardware and in operating systems that permit new levels of functionality, particularly with respect to interapplication communications and control.

Notes

1. Karen Markey and Anh Demeyer, *Dewey Decimal Classification Online Project: Evaluation of a Library Schedule and Index Integrated into the Subject Searching Capabilities of an Online Catalog: Final Report to the Council on Library Resources,* OCLC Research Report Series, OCLC/OPR/RR-86/1 (Dublin, Ohio: OCLC, 1986).

2. John J. Finni and Peter J. Paulson, "The Dewey Decimal Classification Enters the Computer Age: Developing the DDC Database and Editorial Support System," *International Cataloging* 16, no. 4 (Oct./Dec. 1987): 46–8.

3. Rebecca S. Guenther, "The Development and Implementation of the USMARC Format for Classification Data," *Information Technology and Libraries* 11, no. 2 (June 1992): 120–31.

PART

III

Productivity Enhancers
Macros and
Programmatic Approaches

Northwestern University's Toolkit

Gary L. Strawn
Northwestern University Libraries

▼ For many years, computing resources at Northwestern University Libraries resided in the central mainframe computer, which housed NOTIS, the library's integrated library management system.[1] Users (both public and staff) interacted with the mainframe via 3270-type dumb terminals. The situation was not materially altered when a very few staff members received AT-class (80286) personal computers in the mid-1980s. Although NOTIS is powerful, fast, and ably performs many routine tasks, it was not possible to add to it every feature that might promote the efficiency of technical services operations. Yet, the very nature of the hardware configuration rendered impossible any approach that did not rely exclusively on the central computer.

The acquisition in about 1990 of a few personal computers (PCs) with 80386 processors (chiefly in the guise of OCLC workstations) inspired Northwestern University Libraries staff to write several productivity programs for the DOS operating system. One of these programs loads batches of records in the USMARC communication format into the NOTIS system. Another works with OCLC's Cataloging MicroEnhancer Plus to search the OCLC database for materials newly cataloged at Northwestern, automatically add Northwestern's holding symbol to existing OCLC records, and contribute original bibliographic records created on NOTIS—all without much assistance from an operator. (A cataloger makes a final search of the OCLC WorldCat before this program contributes a new record.) Many programs transform data. For example, one program reformats a file of MARC records into a library's quarterly accession list, while another converts sections H 1095 through H 1200 of the Library of Congress *Subject Cataloging Manual: Subject Headings* into MARC authority records for "free-floating" *LCSH* subdivisions. These programs were not made widely available because they had rather crude interfaces, their functionality was specialized, and access to computers that could run them was limited. However, their success encouraged us to believe that useful bibliographic processing could nevertheless take place on PCs despite their being removed from the NOTIS mainframe computer.

The computing situation changed dramatically with the wholesale replacement of 3270-type terminals with PCs running 3270-emulation software and with the decision to move to the Microsoft Windows operating environment. Originally, workstations were connected through the existing terminal network, but all were eventually reconnected to a local area network dedicated to staff functions. There are more than 200 staff workstations. The workstation model has changed over the years: Most of the installed machines now employ the 80486 processor, but Northwestern's current standard for new workstations specifies the Pentium processor. In addition to the programs described in this chapter, these workstations now have access to the Cataloger's Desktop files on CD-ROM from the Library of Congress, to the OCLC WorldCat through Passport, to the World Wide Web through Netscape Navigator, and to a full complement of PC applications.

With a computer on nearly every desk, nonmainframe computing was no longer restricted to just a few or to many but only one at a time on a shared computer basis. It would be extended to every staff member on an individual basis. One of the virtues of Windows is that it can run several programs at the same time (multitasking), and those programs can easily communicate with each other. As a result we suddenly had the ability to implement new system features and make them available to all by writing programs that ran on the new workstations. We could bring under the direct control of staff exactly the detailed functionality that had long been desired but was difficult to achieve on the mainframe system. The development of such programs required Windows-based terminal emulation software, a programming language, the support and participation of library staff at all levels, and lots of time.

The evaluation of the available Windows-based 3270 terminal emulation programs was based not only on the power they provided to end users but also on the tools they made available to program developers. The TCP3270 program from McGill University attracted our attention because it adds several different programming interfaces to a highly configurable set of terminal-emulation features. We eventually decided to use this program and selected the "EHLLAPI" interface to it. (EHLLAPI is the "Emulator High-Level Language Application Programming Interface"—an IBM-standard way for a program to interact with a mainframe terminal session.) With EHLLAPI, a local program running on a workstation may be viewed as a client that makes requests of a server, the TCP3270 program (which happens to be running on the same workstation). TCP3270 may, in its turn, be viewed as a client that makes requests of its own server, the mainframe NOTIS system. In this three-level client-server setup, the mainframe system is isolated from the local program and is unaware of its capabilities; as far as the mainframe system is concerned, it is dealing with a typist at a terminal. Similarly, the local program is heedless of the complexities of communication with the mainframe system. This arrangement has its disadvantages: The local program would be able to interpret the results of a database search more easily and efficiently if it communicated directly with the mainframe and exchanged information in an agreed-upon format. Instead, the local program must infer the results of a search by reading a set of terminal screen images prepared by the mainframe for user review. Because the local program is tied to NOTIS terminal screen displays, it would have to be completely rewritten before it could work with other integrated library systems. However, it has one major advantage: No changes of any kind need be made to the mainframe system before the local program will work.

TCP3270 offers easy access to EHLLAPI services from the Visual BASIC and C languages. Because it appeared we could get started more quickly with Visual BASIC than with C, we chose the former language. (Visual BASIC Professional version 3.0 is used at Northwestern.) The decision was a fortuitous one. Visual BASIC allowed us quickly to assemble the interface components for a new feature and then to supply the code behind the interface to make the feature work. In many cases, we could move from a suggestion to a working demonstration in an hour or two.

Development and Distribution

The workstation project started with a task simple enough to be the focus of an initial programming effort in a new language running under a new operating system, but one that would exercise all the essential functions needed to automate more-elaborate tasks in the future. A survey of frequently performed operations provided a candidate: claiming authority records.

Claiming Authority Records

Northwestern's authority file contains locally created records (including records for *Transportation Library Subject Headings—TLSH*—maintained by Northwestern's Transportation Library), as well as the complete files of Library of Congress Name Authority File, *Library of Congress Subject Headings (LCSH),* and the National Library of Medicine's *Medical Subject Headings (MeSH).* In NOTIS, reference tracings in an authority record do not appear as references in the public catalog until the record has been "claimed," that is, identified as containing a heading present in a bibliographic record. Claiming an authority record is a simple process. If the authority record comes from the Library of Congress or the National Library of Medicine and has never been claimed before, the cataloger issues the "claim authority record" command. For every record, regardless of source, the cataloger changes the name, subject, or series heading use codes (field 008, bytes 14–16) as appropriate.[2]

This authority claiming operation seemed well matched to our criteria for a first development project. It called for reading the NOTIS screen and typing text into it—operations to be performed by nearly every function envisionable—yet required only a small amount of program logic. The authority claiming program was working in a few days.[3] Because the abbreviation of the NOTIS claim authority record command is "clar," we named this first program "CLAR." Although vast amounts of code to do quite different things were added to it over the next eighteen months, the name of the original program has remained the name for our workstation program.

Automating Authority Records

With the claiming function working smoothly, the more challenging task of automating the generation of authority records followed. Most of the content of the typical authority record can be derived by rearranging information found in a bibliographic record, and so this transformation is a process ripe for automation.[4] A few library systems already include a low-level implementation of this capability, but the existing approaches had not completely solved the problem. We wanted our program to do as much of the work as possible so that the cataloger in most cases could simply approve the result of the program's efforts. CLAR spit out its first primitive authority records in March 1994. We posted the news almost immediately to the Autocat discussion list and received many useful criticisms and words of encouragement. These comments, together with feedback from catalogers who used the program in the following months, have caused CLAR's authority record creation module to be the subject of repeated expansion and revision. In fact, the code that automatically generates references has been completely rewritten twice.

It is important to stress that the authority creation module developed was "machine-assisted, operator-approved." This is quite different from purely machine-created authority modules, and the emphasis accordingly is on using the machine to do what it can do best but relying on the cataloger to pass the final judgment on the authority record. (See the appendix at the end of this chapter for specifications for machine-generated authority records.)

Added Features for CLAR

Dozens of new features were added to CLAR during the spring and summer of 1994. The buttons that invoke the various functions were arranged in several different patterns before finalizing the current single-panel array. The principle behind the program's design was that functions should be "generic": the program should support not just Northwestern University Libraries' local needs but should, where applicable, conform to national standards or national customary practice. Indeed, the development of CLAR has led to the discontinuation by Northwestern University Libraries of many local conventions at variance with national practice. In addition, CLAR was expected to work not only with

Northwestern's version of NOTIS but also with the current version of the unmodified system distributed by Ameritech Library Services. With care in developing the approach and in designing the code, the Northwestern program could be used at other NOTIS libraries.

Most original catalogers at Northwestern University Libraries started using CLAR in August 1994, just after they received their workstations. Copy catalogers were introduced to the program over the next several months as additional workstations were installed. As a result of the use of the program by this expanded and very exacting audience, requests for enhancements, changes, and fixes were received over the next year in a constant and heavy stream. Currently, more than thirty catalogers in Northwestern University's main library building (including the Music and Transportation Libraries) and catalogers at Northwestern's downtown Chicago campus use the program.

Two Versions: CLAR and CLARR

Following the announcement of machine-generated authority records, a number of other institutions expressed interest in acquiring the program for their own use. This interest increased substantially when the program was described at the fall 1994 NOTIS Users' Group Meeting and at the American Library Association's 1995 midwinter meeting. Northwestern University Libraries, however, decided that it did not wish to undertake distribution and support of the program. Instead, the library (through an office of the university) sought a vendor who might be interested in making the program available to others and be willing to handle user support. While waiting for a vendor to come forward, the university allowed Northwestern University Libraries to designate a number of other libraries as beta test sites, and a few libraries did install the program and use it successfully.[5] The first of these was Indiana University, which received the program after a pair of live on-site demonstrations in February 1995.

CLAR exists in two versions: the version used at Northwestern, with 54 buttons (figure 8.1), and the version used everywhere else, with 42 buttons (figure 8.2). (The non-Northwestern version of CLAR is officially known as "CLARR," but most catalogers simply call the program "the Toolkit.") The function buttons in the Toolkit have different amounts of coding behind them, which is one measure of the complexity of the operations they perform. For example, there are only a few lines of code behind the button that copies a whole variable field from a bibliographic record to the Windows clipboard, but there is well over a half megabyte of source code behind the call number button. With a few minor differences (chiefly tied to efficiencies to be gained by exploiting the peculiar capabilities of Northwestern's online system), the Northwestern and non-Northwestern versions share the same body of code and work in the same manner.

The first user documentation for the Toolkit was a brief, text-only description of each of the program's buttons, called up from within the program itself. The complexity of the program eventually led to the preparation of a user's manual. Making copies for everyone was a logis-

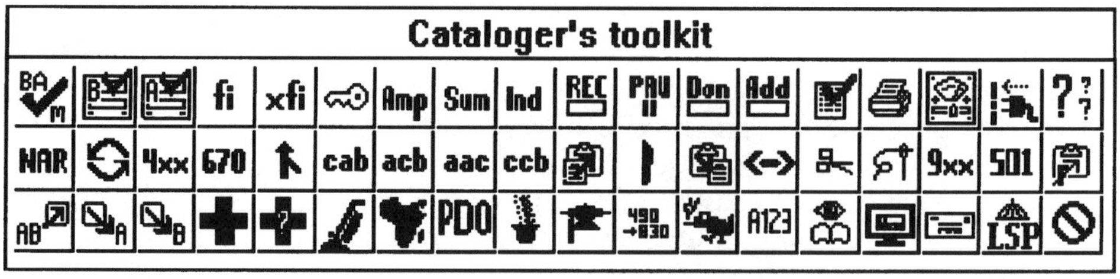

Figure 8.1 CLAR Toolkit Buttons Used at Northwestern

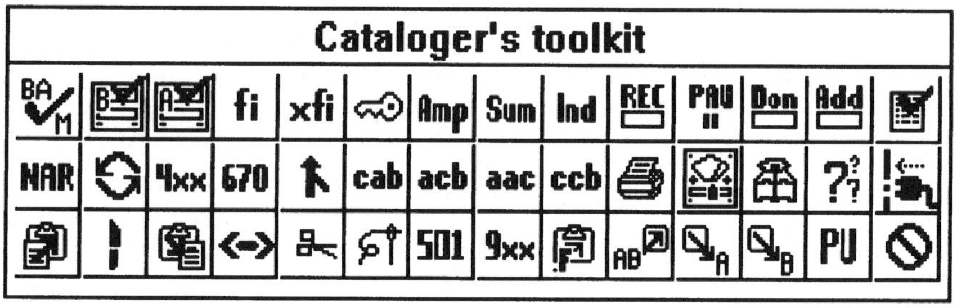

Figure 8.2 CLARR Toolkit Buttons Used at Other Institutions

tical problem compounded by the constant revision to which the text was subject as the program changed. The printed documentation was eventually converted into a set of documents with HyperText Markup Language (HTML) coding and mounted on the library's World Wide Web server. Staff within Northwestern University Libraries, at beta test sites, and other interested parties around the world now have ready access to the current version of the program's documentation at http://www.library.nwu.edu/clarr.

Outline of Features

The buttons on the toolbar are organized into functionally related groups, and their actions are summarized in the following sections. (The membership of a button in a particular group is signaled by the background color used for the button's icon, which is not apparent from the black-and-white illustrations in this chapter.) The buttons can be arranged to suit each cataloger's preferences. Detailed descriptions of a few especially notable buttons follow the summaries.

Bibliographic and Authority Record Validation and Verification

The BAM button (the first button on the top row of the toolbar in figures 8.1 and 8.2) validates the MARC content designation of a bibliographic or authority record and inspects the access points in the record for consistency with other records in the local system. (This operation is described in detail later in the chapter.) The validation and verification routines prepare summaries of their findings, which the cataloger can review and act on as appropriate. Among the possible actions is the creation of an authority record from a heading listed in the verification report. The two buttons to the right of the BAM button recall the most recent bibliographic and authority verification reports.

Authority Record Creation and Manipulation

The first nine buttons on the middle row of the toolbar in figures 8.1 and 8.2 allow the cataloger to create a new authority record from a heading in a bibliographic record without first verifying the entire bibliographic record, add various kinds of references or a 670 field to an existing authority record, manipulate an authority record's heading use codes (field 008, bytes 14–16) for proper display of references in the online catalog, and merge two authority records for the same entity into a composite.

Macro Recording and Playback

With the macro buttons (the REC button and the next four buttons on the top row of the toolbar in figures 8.1 and 8.2) the cataloger can capture a sequence of keystrokes and button presses and assign the sequence to a keyboard shortcut. Using macros allows the cataloger to automate repetitive operations. A simple macro might perform a straightforward heading change. On the other hand, a complex macro might assist in the creation of a brief bibliographic record by calling up a workform, filling in default fixed field values (pausing for unpredictable ones, such as country of publication and language codes, and the last two digits of the date of publication), and prompting the cataloger for standard variable fields.

Variable Field Manipulation

The cataloger can use the last nine buttons on the middle row of the toolbar in figure 8.1 (beginning with the Copy to Clipboard button) or the first nine buttons in the third row in figure 8.2 to perform a number of editing functions, among them:

- copy, cut and paste text, including text that wraps to more than one line[6]
- save any number of whole fields from authority and bibliographic records and paste them into other authority or bibliographic records (changing the tag and sometimes the contents of the field at the time of the transfer, as needed)
- manipulate long fields
- convert provisional NOTIS fields (temporary fields input by acquisitions staff when there is no record for an item in the local copy of the LC MARC bibliographic file or in the OCLC WorldCat) into their nonprovisional, standard, USMARC equivalents
- generate a set of "With" notes for individually cataloged items in a single container by identifying each bibliographic record in its turn

Using these buttons allows the cataloger to build a record with the minimum of new typing—reducing the likelihood of error and the need for proofreading. (The button labeled *PU* in the third row of figure 8.2 is a NOTIS-specific button to change the transaction code of a record. It appears on the current version of each toolbar.)

Functions Available Only at Northwestern

Additional buttons (the Cross in the bottom row of the toolbar in figure 8.1, and the next nine buttons) provide assistance for tasks such as Northwestern's Africana conference paper indexing and retrospective conversion projects, for the conversion of not-traced series into traced series, and for work with call numbers. A Dissertation button supports the generation of brief bibliographic records for Northwestern's doctoral dissertations: A student assistant fills in an online form with information from the dissertation's title page, and the Toolkit generates the bibliographic and holdings records. Some of these functions, such as the Africana conference papers button, are probably of use only to catalogers at Northwestern. Others, such as the dissertation and call number buttons, may be of more general interest but are here tailored exclusively to Northwestern's processing needs. In any case, these buttons do not meet our criterion that functions be "generic," so they are not available to non-Northwestern users.

Miscellaneous Functions

Catalogers have the following capabilities not yet mentioned but also grouped among the functions available from the buttons in figure 8.1. They can

> send an annotated copy of the current NOTIS screen image as an E-mail message
>
> print an annotated copy of the NOTIS screen image
>
> save and recall bibliographic and authority records
>
> search the local database and manipulate search results
>
> move records into and out of the local system in the USMARC communication format

The Eye over a Book button (third row in figure 8.1) allows a cataloger to convert ASCII text into variable fields in a bibliographic record. It is possible for a cataloger to use a scanner to capture the image of a title page or table of contents, use optical character recognition (OCR) software to convert the image into a text file, and load the text file into the Toolkit. Then, by selecting portions of the text and clicking buttons, the cataloger can manipulate the text into a basic bibliographic description or a fully formatted contents note.

Verification and Validation of Bibliographic and Authority Records

The Toolkit can compare the headings in a bibliographic record against headings and references in locally held authority records and headings in other locally held bibliographic records. (Similar functionality is available in some online library systems.) The verification feature allows the cataloger quickly to determine how the headings in a bibliographic record fit into the local catalog.

To do so, the Toolkit extracts from the bibliographic record the access points that are, or could be, under authority control and breaks them into separately verifiable units. For example, it breaks a name-title heading into two separate headings for the purposes of verification: the name by itself and the name plus the title.

Bibliographic Field

    600 10 $a Shakespeare, William, $d 1564-1616. $t Hamlet.

Verified as

    600 10 $a Shakespeare, William, $d 1564-1616.
    600 10 $a Shakespeare, William, $d 1564-1616. $t Hamlet.

The Toolkit treats a topical subject heading with subdivisions as several headings: the main heading by itself, then the main heading plus the first subdivision, then the main heading plus the first two subdivisions, and so on.

Bibliographic Field

    650 2 $a Aspirin $x adverse effects $x videocassettes.

Verified as

    650 2 $a Aspirin
    650 2 $a Aspirin $x adverse effects
    650 2 $a Aspirin $x adverse effects $x videocassettes.

The Toolkit extracts geographic subdivisions from topical headings, reconstitutes the original geographic name headings, and attempts to verify them against geographic name authority records. This is because there will almost never be an authority record for the heading with a geographic subdivision actually included in it. The cataloger will want to know whether the geographic subdivisions are in an acceptable form and whether the geographic subdivisions are inserted at the proper point in the headings. Of course, when reconstructing a geographic name from two subdivisions, the Toolkit must recognize exceptions to the general *LCSH* pattern, such as extinct cities and places in Australia.

Bibliographic Field

    650 0 $a Aspirin $z Michigan $z Detroit $x Congresses.

Verified as

    650 0 $a Aspirin
    650 0 $a Aspirin $x Congresses.
    651 0 $a Detroit (Mich.)

The Toolkit searches each extracted heading against locally held authority records. If there is an authority record for the heading or if the heading matches a cross reference, it stops work on the heading. Otherwise, the Toolkit does a second search to see if there are any additional bibliographic records that contain the heading. If there is no authority record and the heading is a topical heading, the Toolkit also checks the last subdivision against a database of free-floating subdivisions for the appropriate subject heading system *(LCSH, MeSH or TLSH)*. In its current incarnation, the Toolkit is able only to determine that a subdivision is valid in a particular subject heading system and that any geographic subdivision has been applied correctly. The ability to determine that a topical heading string has been assembled according to rule is the focus of ongoing development.

Figure 8.3 shows a typical example of the Toolkit's bibliographic heading verification report. Information about the headings is in the large window, arranged in three columns. The first column holds up to three codes to represent the results of its searches for information about each heading. (The top line of the report contains the codes "+n" in this column.) These verification codes are followed by the tag, sequence number, and indicators of the source field ("650/1: 0:" in the top line). The third column contains a normalized version of the heading itself, preceded by a NOTIS search code ("fsl=science" in the top line). The following paragraphs explain some of the dozens of codes used in the first column of this report.

Lines with a plus sign (+) as the first code in the first column (such as the very first line in the report in figure 8.3) show headings extracted from the bibliographic record that match headings in authority records.

Verification results for: NU/AGU5980

```
+n    650/1: 0:   fsl=science
+n    650/1: 0:   fsl=science—study and teaching elementary
+n    650/2: 0:   fsl=mathematics
+n    650/2: 0:   fsl=mathematics—study and teaching elementary
+n    650/3: 0:   fsl=natural history
0+f   650/3: 0:   fsl=natural history—study and teaching elementary
+n    650/4: 0:   fsl=bats
00f   650/4: 0:   fsl=bats—study and teaching elementary
+n    650/5: 0:   fsl=activity programs in education
+n    650/6: 0:   fsl=interdisciplinary approach in education
00    700/1:10:   fx =BAUCHER CAROLYN
0+a   700/2:10:   fx =CORDEL BETTY
+C    700/3:10:   fx =hillen judith
?c    700/4:10:   fx =WINKLEMAN GRETCHEN
00    700/5:10:   fx =ANDERSON MARGIE
00    700/6:10:   fx =DAHL BRENDA
+C    710/7:20:   fx =aims education foundation
```

| JX | Modify search term | Recall bib. record | Create authority | Print report |
| XT | Explain status | Recall hldg. record | Validation errors | Hide list |

Figure 8.3   Toolkit Bibliographic Verification Report

Lines with a zero (0) as the first code (such as the line in the report in figure 8.3 for "natural history—study and teaching elementary") show headings with no authority record. If the second code in such a line is a plus sign (as is the case in figure 8.3 for "CORDEL BETTY"), there is at least one other bibliographic record in the local system that contains the heading. Lines with zeroes as the first two codes ("bats—study and teaching elementary" and "BAUCHER CAROLYN") contain headings that appear nowhere in the local system except in the bibliographic record being verified.

A question mark (?) as the first code labels a heading that requires special attention. In the case of the problem heading "WINKLE-MAN GRETCHEN," there is an authority record in Northwestern's file for the heading "Winkleman, Gretchen, 1930– ".

The third code in the first column contains additional information. The code "f" (for example, in the report line for "natural history—study and teaching elementary") means that the last subdivision in the heading is an authorized *LCSH* subdivision. The code "a" ("CORDEL BETTY") means that at least one of the bibliographic records that contains this heading—not counting the record being verified—was prepared according to *AACR2R* conventions.

A computation based on the codes in the first column of the verification report allows the Toolkit to make a provisional judgment about the fitness of each of the headings in the bibliographic record. The Toolkit shows headings that appear to warrant cataloger review in uppercase letters; it shows headings that are probably acceptable in lowercase letters. This typographical convention makes the unsupported or otherwise doubtful headings more obvious. The cataloger is expected to review the verification report and treat as appropriate each potential problem identified by the Toolkit (by changing the heading in the bibliographic record, creating a new authority record, and so on) before completing work on the bibliographic record.

The process behind the button that does this work does not simply check headings, it inspects the entire bibliographic record. The NOTIS system performs a coarse inspection of MARC content designation, but it does not evaluate such matters as the repeatability of subfields. Moreover, NOTIS does not verify coded data elements from extensive or open-ended lists (for example, the place of publication code). The NOTIS system also does not evaluate the consistency of data present in different parts of the record. For instance, NOTIS does not compare any 043 field with geographic information in subject headings and does not compare 034 and 255 fields. These gaps in the NOTIS system can cause problems when attempting to upload records to OCLC's WorldCat because the tests to which OCLC subjects incoming bibliographic records are much more detailed than the checks NOTIS makes. As a result, a second set of routines added to the verification button validates as much of the MARC content designation and coding in the record—including cross-field checks—as possible.

To make this feature work, we needed program-readable versions of the USMARC documentation. We downloaded the USMARC format and code lists from the Library of Congress's USMARC gopher site, copied other code lists from the Cataloger's Desktop, and wrote a program to digest them all into a set of indexed database files. The Toolkit queries these databases to gather information about the coding of a record, and appends a report of validation problems to the heading verification report (figure 8.4). As is the case with the heading verification report, the cataloger is expected to resolve each problem. At the cataloger's instruction, the Toolkit is able to fix a few of these problems by itself. Among the corrections it can make are to create or to manipulate the 043 field based on information in the subject headings.

Several months after the general introduction of the Toolkit, we added to it the ability to verify and validate an authority record in a manner similar to that used for bibliographic records. There are, of course, substantial differences of detail between the verification of authority and bibliographic records, and these had to be built into the program.

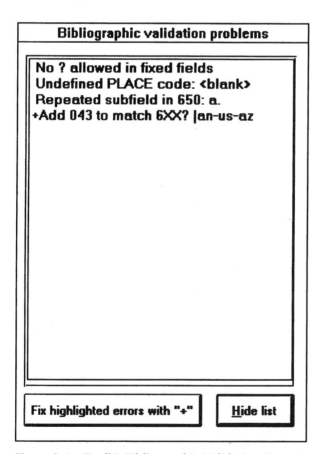

Figure 8.4 Toolkit Bibliographic Validation Report

Automated Creation of Authority Records

The cataloger can ask the Toolkit for a machine-generated authority record in two different ways:

1. The cataloger can verify a bibliographic record that contains the heading of interest, highlight the heading in the verification report, and click a button on the verification report itself.
2. The cataloger can click the cursor on a heading in the bibliographic record and click a button on the toolbar.

In either case, the Toolkit pours the necessary information into a common routine that checks for a duplicate authority record, requests a workform, and eventually writes a proposed new authority record into the NOTIS window. The process by which the cataloger generates an authority record from a nonheading field—for example, creating an authority record for a series-like phrase from a note—is only slightly more complicated than the basic authority generation routine, involving three or four additional clicks of various buttons.

The Toolkit's authority record is as complete as it can be within the design constraints imposed on ourselves: namely, *the program should do everything that it reliably can do, and no more.* The cataloger should not have to review the record for things that need to be deleted. (An outline of the specifications the Toolkit uses to create authority records is given in the appendix to this chapter.) Instead, the cataloger should be confident that everything present in the record is acceptable and should be concerned chiefly with the *addition* of information that could not be supplied automatically. Figure 8.5 shows a personal name authority record created by the Toolkit. The cataloger has not yet made any change to the record and will probably not need to make any change.

It is important to note that the Toolkit does not add an authority record to the local database. It simply draws a *proposed* authority record on the screen. Once it has finished drawing the proposed authority record, it is the cataloger's responsibility to review the record for completeness and make any necessary changes to it. If the record is acceptable, the cataloger can add the record to the local system by pressing <Enter>. If the cataloger does not feel that the proposed authority record should be added to our local system, he or she can easily clear the screen and destroy all trace of the record.

The Toolkit offers several features for modifying authority records in the local system, including records it has just created. Among these features are buttons that allow the cataloger to

> rotate text in the authority record (from any access field or from a 670 field) into references

> create a reference based on a heading in another authority record (for example, the cataloger can add a name/title reference to an authority record for a title heading simply by showing the Toolkit the authority record for the name heading)

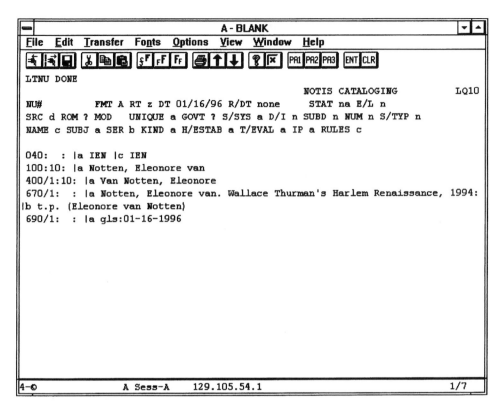

```
┌──────────────────────────────────────────────────────────────────────┐
│ ▬                        A - BLANK                            ▼ ▲ │
├──────────────────────────────────────────────────────────────────────┤
│ File   Edit   Transfer   Fonts   Options   View   Window   Help       │
├──────────────────────────────────────────────────────────────────────┤
│ [toolbar icons]                                                        │
│ LTNU DONE                                                              │
│                                            NOTIS CATALOGING      LQ10  │
│ NU#        FMT A RT z DT 01/16/96 R/DT none     STAT na E/L n          │
│ SRC d ROM ? MOD   UNIQUE a GOVT ? S/SYS a D/I n SUBD n NUM n S/TYP n    │
│ NAME c SUBJ a SER b KIND a H/ESTAB a T/EVAL a IP a RULES c             │
│                                                                        │
│ 040:    : |a IEN |c IEN                                                │
│ 100:10: |a Notten, Eleonore van                                        │
│ 400/1:10: |a Van Notten, Eleonore                                      │
│ 670/1:  : |a Notten, Eleonore van. Wallace Thurman's Harlem Renaissance, 1994: │
│ |b t.p. (Eleonore van Notten)                                          │
│ 690/1:  : |a gls:01-16-1996                                            │
│                                                                        │
│                                                                        │
│                                                                        │
│                                                                        │
│                                                                        │
│                                                                        │
│                                                                        │
│                                                                        │
│                                                                        │
├──────────────────────────────────────────────────────────────────────┤
│ 4-◉        A Sess-A    129.105.54.1                            1/7    │
└──────────────────────────────────────────────────────────────────────┘
```

Figure 8.5   Toolkit Simple Personal Name Authority Record

convert a variant heading in a bibliographic record into an "earlier established heading" reference

add 670 fields based on bibliographic records

The authority record in figure 8.6 is an outstanding example of the Toolkit's capabilities: It contains exactly twelve characters that the cataloger had to enter from the keyboard (the word "cover" and the initialism "MDPWP" together with its preceding semicolon-space, all in the 670 field). The remainder of the record was created by the Toolkit, prompted by the cataloger's clicking on buttons.

Assistance with Call Numbers

Northwestern University's main library uses the Dewey Decimal Classification for most materials.[7] The use of Dewey means that, for bibliographic records with a suggested number in an 082 field, catalogers normally complete the number with a Cutter block and workmarks—a process often called "shelflisting" the number. For exceptions and for records without a suggested Dewey classification number, catalogers assign the complete call number themselves.

```
═══════════════════════════════════════════════════════════
─│                    A - BLANK                       ▼│▲
File  Edit  Transfer  Fonts  Options  View  Window  Help
[icons toolbar]
LTNU DONE                                         CSA2239
                                  NOTIS CATALOGING        LQ10
NU# CSA2239 FMT A RT z DT 01/16/96 R/DT none      STAT na E/L n
SRC d ROM ? MOD   UNIQUE n GOVT ? S/SYS a D/I n SUBD n NUM a S/TYP a
NAME a SUBJ a SER c KIND a H/ESTAB a T/EVAL a IP a RULES c

040:  : |a IEN |c IEN
130: 0: |a Maseru development plan working paper
410/1:10: |a Lesotho. |b Dept. of Lands, Surveys, and Physical Planning. |b
Physical Planning Division. |t Maseru development plan working paper
430/2: 0: |a MDPWP
642/1:  : |a nr 3A |5 IEN
643/1:  : |a Maseru, Lesotho |b Physical Planning Division, Dept. of Lands,
Surveys and Physical Planning |b Swedeplan
644/1:  : |a f |5 IEN
645/1:  : |a t |5 IEN
646/1:  : |a s |5 IEN
670/1:  : |a Prochazkova-Costa, Dana. Preservation of historical buildings and
sites in Maseru, 1986/87 i.e. 1987: |b cover (Maseru development plan working
paper; MDPWP)
690/1:  : |a gls:01-16-1996



4-©          A Sess-A    129.105.54.1                  1/7
═══════════════════════════════════════════════════════════
```

Figure 8.6   Toolkit Series Authority Record

Soon after the Toolkit was made available, catalogers began to ask for some kind of online Cutter table to help simplify the shelflisting of a Dewey number. We were confident, however, that we could offer something more elaborate than a simple table lookup. One of the catalogers found a version of the three-figure Cutter table on the Internet. This file, although it contained errors and did not appear to us to be free from questions of copyright, nevertheless allowed us to perform some rudimentary but encouraging experiments with call numbers. Eventually, we located an "official" source for the machine-readable Cutter table. It is part of the Professional Collection CD-ROM available from Libraries Unlimited, of Englewood, Colorado. The Cutter table on the CD-ROM is in an encoded format (which cannot be processed directly) and is available through its supplied viewer in read-only mode; it is not possible to copy-and-paste from the screen display into a bibliographic record. Libraries Unlimited agreed to supply us a tab-delimited ASCII text file of the Cutter table. While we waited for delivery of the table, we held meetings with catalogers to describe in some detail the kinds of things that might be possible and to solicit ideas from them.

First, we converted the local call number documentation into an algorithm and translated that algorithm into a set of routines. Two experienced catalogers (one copy cataloger, one original cataloger) were given access to the new call number button while it was in the early stages of development. They double-checked the Toolkit's work and reported every case in which the call number produced by the program was not exactly the same as the call number they would have constructed on their own. Dozens of undocumented exceptions and unusual cases came to light in the extended period of testing and development, with each requiring small or large changes to the growing body of code.

After several months' worth of design and programming, the code behind the call number button was comprehensive and stable enough for wider use. All catalogers were introduced to the new button at a series of training sessions, during which the steps the Toolkit uses to determine the proper call number were described in detail. Again, catalogers were encouraged to report all call numbers that did not conform to their expectations. Perhaps because catalogers view this button as so important to their work, they have taken this responsibility very seriously. After continuing refinement, we now have a feature of far more than passable accuracy: Fewer than a dozen of the thousands of uses of the button each month now generate call numbers that require some adjustment to the program.

The call number button does four different things, depending on the location of the cursor when the cataloger clicks the button:

1. If the cursor is on a name heading or a title in the bibliographic record, the Toolkit determines the Cutter number for that piece of text and pastes it into the appropriate slot in the NOTIS holdings record.

2. If the cursor is on a topical subject heading, the Toolkit performs a series of searches on the heading and permutations of it. To do this, it uses the locally defined NOTIS search that retrieves subjects only when they are the *first* subject heading in the bibliographic record. This search is based on the assumption that the first subject heading—at least in the case of *LCSH* headings—is the subject heading most closely related to the classification number. The Toolkit produces a list of the classification numbers associated with the subject heading and its permutations, ranked by frequency of occurrence (figure 8.7), and prompts the cataloger to make a choice. If the cataloger selects one of the numbers in the list (or supplies a different number), it completes the call number.

3. If the cursor is on a copy statement in a NOTIS holdings record, the Toolkit inserts the call number it has assigned most recently.

4. Finally, and most importantly, if the cursor is at the top of the screen (the cursor's "home" position), the Toolkit attempts to determine the complete call number. The following paragraphs describe the major points it considers in its attempt to identify the proper call number for an item. Much detail—the handling of videorecordings of feature films, to cite only one exception among dozens—is omitted.

```
┌──────────────────────────────────────────────────────────────┐
│                    Classification summary                      │
├──────────────────────────────────────────────────────────────┤
│  Here are the classification numbers most closely associated with your │
│  subject heading                                               │
│  OCCULTISM--CONGRESSES                                         │
│                                                                │
│  Please examine these numbers, and select an appropriate action.│
│  ┌Number from 082 field─────────────────────────────┐         │
│  │  (none)                                           │         │
│  │                                                   │         │
│  │                              ┌──────────┐         │         │
│  │                              │ Use 082  │         │         │
│  │                              └──────────┘         │         │
│  └───────────────────────────────────────────────────┘         │
│  ┌Number(s) from index──────────────────────────────┐         │
│  │ OCCULTISM--CONGRESSES                        ▲    │         │
│  │     1 133                                         │         │
│  │ OCCULTISM                                         │         │
│  │    56 133                                         │         │
│  │     8 133.4                                       │         │
│  │     4 001.9                                       │         │
│  │     3 189.5          ┌──────────────┐             │         │
│  │     2 133.03         │ Use this one │        ▼    │         │
│  └──────────────────────└──────────────┘───────────┘          │
│  ☐ Class in 016  ┌─────────────┐ ┌─────────────┐ ┌────────┐   │
│                  │Use different #│ │ Bib. record │ │ Cancel │  │
│                  └─────────────┘ └─────────────┘ └────────┘   │
└──────────────────────────────────────────────────────────────┘
```

Figure 8.7   Toolkit Classification Number Summary for a Topical Heading

Classed series. The Toolkit inspects the authority record for each series heading in the bibliographic record. If Northwestern classes any of the series together, it uses the call number in the series authority record, completing it with information from subfield $v of the series heading.

Other editions. The Toolkit attempts to determine if Northwestern has already cataloged other editions of the same work. (It occasionally asks the cataloger if an item with a similar title is truly a variant edition.) If Northwestern's catalog contains a record for another edition of the same work, it uses the call number for the existing edition as the basis for the call number of the new edition.

Goethe, Schiller, and "classical" authors. If the main entry or first subject heading is for Johann Wolfgang von Goethe, Friedrich Schiller, or an ancient or medieval Greek or Latin author, the Toolkit stops all work on the item.[8] Northwestern uses elaborate, locally devised arrangement schemes for these authors— a different scheme for each. Given the small number of items by or about any one of these authors currently received at

Northwestern, we decided that there was insufficient justification for the substantial programming effort required to automate the assignment of these call numbers. (Such work might be undertaken in the future, if deemed worthwhile.) The cataloger must supply the complete call number.

Shakespeare. If the main entry or first subject heading is for William Shakespeare, the Toolkit uses Northwestern's locally devised Cuttering scheme. In contrast to the schemes for Goethe, Schiller, and "classical" authors, the arrangement of Shakespeare materials is simple and straightforward, and Northwestern is constantly adding new items by and about Shakespeare. These different conditions seemed to justify the programming time required to bring the Shakespeare scheme online.

Africana materials. Materials destined for Northwestern's Africana collection that meet certain criteria are arranged according to a locally developed classification and Cuttering scheme. The Toolkit is able in most cases, with occasional cataloger assistance, to build the complete call number.

Computer programming languages. If the first subject heading in the bibliographic record is for a computer programming language, the Toolkit uses a special Dewey classification number and assigns a Cutter for the name of the programming language.

Belles-lettres. If the item being cataloged is belletristic in nature— the Toolkit identifies potential items by picking up clues from the bibliographic record, but the cataloger makes the final determination—the Toolkit gathers classification number information from other belletristic works by the same author. (The report is similar to the list shown in figure 8.7.) If the cataloger decides that one of these numbers is appropriate, it completes the call number.

Biography or corporate history. If the first subject heading in the bibliographic record is for a person or corporate body (including a name/title heading), the Toolkit looks for other items about the same entity. If it finds such an item, it uses its call number as the basis for the call number for the current item.

With the cursor at the top of the screen the Toolkit will also attempt to assign a call number in the following miscellaneous cases:

If there is an 082 field in the record, the Toolkit bases the proposed call number for the item on the classification number in the 082 field. (Northwestern's NOTIS system does not directly support the 09X fields. An incoming 092 field—an OCLC-defined field for a locally assigned Dewey Decimal Classification number—is retagged 082, with a second indicator of "4.") When a bibliographic record contains an 082 field, the Toolkit normally uses the proposed number but it cannot decide that this is appropriate until it has ruled out all exceptions.

If there is no 082 field in the bibliographic record and if the first subject heading in the bibliographic record is a topical heading, the Toolkit produces a summary of the classification number usage for the heading (similar to that shown in figure 8.7). The cataloger may choose one of these classification numbers for use in the item being cataloged.

If there is no 082 field and if the local bibliographic file contains no items on the same subject, the Toolkit prompts the cataloger for a classification number. If the cataloger supplies a number, the Toolkit shelflists it as if it had come from an 082 field. If the cataloger does not supply a number, the cataloger must later formulate the entire call number.

In this work, the Toolkit calls on a common set of routines to determine how the item should be Cuttered; assign the Cutter block; and add workletters, translation marks, dates, and oversize designators to call numbers. When assigning Cutters, the Toolkit examines the bibliographic records for previously cataloged materials with the same classification number. Wherever necessary, it "slides" the Cutter for the new work to fit it into proper alphabetical order.[9]

At the end of this process—which, depending on conditions, may take only a second or two—the Toolkit in most cases has derived a unique, shelflisted call number for the item being cataloged and has written the call number into the proper slot of the NOTIS copy holdings record. As with the authority records it creates, this finished call number is merely a proposal: No permanent change has yet been made to any record. The cataloger is expected to evaluate the proposed call number for suitability and to accept it, correct it, or reject it altogether.

Conflict Resolution

The NOTIS mainframe system can produce a report that points out certain types of inconsistencies between headings in bibliographic records, on the one hand, and headings and references in authority records, on the other. At a typical NOTIS library, a member of the catalog management team, using the printed conflict report, searches each problem heading, evaluates the situation, and takes appropriate action to resolve the problem. When Northwestern University Libraries loaded the entire Library of Congress Name Authority File into our local system in 1995, we suddenly acquired many hundreds of thousands of new errors, and we certainly had no hope of resolving them in the traditional manner in any reasonable time. The new "conflict resolver" program, which borrows some code from the Toolkit, was our solution to this predicament.

Rather than print the report on paper, we now download the NOTIS conflict report to a workstation as an ASCII file. (Because there are so many errors to correct, we work with one letter of the alphabet at a time.) The conflict resolver program reads the report and decides, on its own, what action to take. (In terms of the program familiar to most NOTIS users, this program handles errors 1 through 4: duplicate authority records for the same heading and miscoding of bytes 14 through 16 of field 008.)[10] When the conflict resolver cannot decide how to handle a situation, it writes a message to a log file. For example, the program can merge information from two authority records for the same heading into a composite and delete the duplicate. If both of the records are from the Library of Congress, however, the program reports the problem for cataloger review. The program can handle up to about 1,800 problems per hour, reducing hundreds of pages of error reports into a few pages of difficult situations that require expert attention.[11] With this new program, we can perform in a few hours work that once required many weeks.

All batch heading changes were once processed on the mainframe, which sometimes caused scheduling problems, so we turned heading corrections over to another PC-based program. An authorized cataloger can now simply click a button when a heading conflict is in a NOTIS window, and a program on another computer performs the correction. We use a different workstation program to perform more-complex changes. The program was originally designed to move an oversize designator from one point to another within a group of call numbers, but we have added many other types of unusual changes to its repertoire. Northwestern also now loads *MeSH* authority records with a workstation program. (It is not yet certain whether we will also load LC name and *LCSH* records with the same program.) In the future, the authority loader could work directly with the heading correction program to process incoming authority records and handle many changed headings without operator involvement. Similarly, the next version of the conflict resolver program will pass some categories of conflicts between headings and references to the correction program for immediate resolution. Beyond the catalog department, workers in preservation, acquisitions, and serials have all asked for Toolkits tailored to their own specific processing needs. Enthusiasm for all these projects is tempered somewhat by the library's decision to identify a replacement for the NOTIS system in fiscal year 1997, and consequently, we will write these new workstation programs only if they can be completed quickly enough to allow us to recoup the investment in programming time.

Next Steps

The Toolkit has by now reached a certain level of maturity. We expect that most future work on it will probably be in the area of maintenance and expansion of existing features rather than in the exploration of new territory. Potential areas for investigation might include linking its import and export functions to OCLC through Passport for Windows, or the call number generation button could be supplemented by a connection to Forest Press's release of the Dewey Decimal Classification as

Dewey for Windows. These enlargements would require that future versions of Passport for Windows and Dewey for Windows be written to respond to requests from other programs such as the Toolkit—a capability not present in the initial versions. Another obvious avenue to explore would be the extension of the call number button to the Library of Congress Classification. Although buttons are no longer being added weekly to the Toolkit, the programming staff at Northwestern does not suddenly find themselves idle. We have begun to develop new programs that employ techniques similar to those used in the Toolkit.

Conclusions

The Toolkit's functions may be considered in light of their relation to the current local integrated library management system, the local system of the near future, and the concept of the technical services workstation. The program overcomes some deficiencies in our current system, such as the lack of keyword searching in staff mode, that will probably not be problems in the next system or even in future versions of the current system. It provides editing capabilities that users expect to be part of any MARC record editor running in a graphical environment. The Toolkit provides elaborate text-manipulation routines, such as the creation of authority records from bibliographic headings, that should be an integral part of the standard technical services workstation of the future. Last, but not least, the Toolkit provides some functions tailored to Northwestern's own needs, such as the generation of call numbers, that catalogers at Northwestern must be able to continue to enjoy as a local add-on to any future technical services workstation and local system.

While working on the Toolkit and related programs, the belief that PCs can greatly enhance technical services operations has been confirmed. With these programs the productivity of individual catalogers and the throughput of materials have increased, all the while maintaining, or even increasing, the quality of the finished bibliographic and authority records. At a time when technical services staff levels are constantly being scrutinized and, unfortunately, often reduced, Northwestern University Libraries has with these programs been able to expand and enhance its program of catalog management and authority control.

Through first-hand experience, catalogers at Northwestern University now have a clear idea of just how much it is possible to expect and demand from a workstation-based online system. They are going to expect from the next local system at least the same level of functionality they now enjoy at their NOTIS workstations, and they are not going to accept excuses from developers and vendors for local systems that clearly fail to measure up to these expectations. I hope that pressure from technical services staff who have used or seen these and similar programs developed elsewhere will finally persuade the developers of the coming generation of library automation systems to add productivity features that will make a real difference to the work of technical services. Northwestern has demonstrated that much more is possible than is represented by available products in the library automation marketplace and that savings of effort and time can be realized from judicious allocation of programmer resources. It is up to each of us to make sure that the features we need to do our work well in this time of retrenchment are available to all.

Notes

1. Northwestern University Library began the development of a mainframe-based library management system, eventually dubbed "NOTIS," in 1967. After twenty years of hard work, marketing and most development staff for NOTIS were spun off by Northwestern University as an independent corporation that eventually became part of Ameritech Library Services. Northwestern's heavily modified version of release 5.0.2 contains many features not available at other NOTIS installations.

2. The NOTIS system distinguishes in bytes 14–16 of field 008 between headings that are appropriate for use in a particular manner (code "a" as defined in *USMARC Format for Authority Data*) and headings that have actually been used in locally held bibliographic records (non-MARC code "c"). Code "c" causes reference tracings in an authority record to appear in corresponding public-catalog displays.

3. It is an amusing historical footnote to this development process that most of this time was spent building a subroutine that could press the <Enter> key and reliably wait until NOTIS had formulated a response.

4. There is only an extremely small body of literature related to the machine generation of authority records. Although some of the references described therein are now made only in rare cases, I believe that the most valuable is still Douglas Anderson, "Automatically Generated References in Minimal-Level Authority Records," *Information Technology and Libraries* 10 (Dec. 1991): 251–62.

5. The Academic Division of Ameritech Library Services later announced that it would undertake the distribution of CLAR to existing NOTIS customers.

6. TCP3270 provides copy and cut functions only for text that can be contained within a rectangle; its paste function overwrites text, while the Toolkit inserts text.

7. The Music, Law, Health Sciences, and Transportation Libraries use the Library of Congress Classification; most government documents in the main library are arranged according to the Superintendent of Documents scheme. Materials in Special Collections are arranged according to a bewildering number of ad hoc schemes.

8. The Toolkit identifies "classical" authors by the presence of a specially formatted classification number in the 082 field of the authority record for each author.

9. A long-standing practice at Northwestern (now discontinued) was not to attempt to "slide" Cutters to keep materials in strict alphabetical order but simply to assign arbitrary expanded Cutters in the general neighborhood of the "best" Cutter number. As a result, the Toolkit must be able to deal with ostensibly contradictory situations such as 574.875 B615 Biomembranes, 574.875 B6152 Biogenesis and turnover of membrane macromolecules, 574.875 B6154 Biochemistry of lipids and membranes, and 574.875 B6155 Biomembrane structure and function.

10. Those familiar with the printout generated by the NOTIS conflict and error detection report should note that the conflict resolver program described here considers the NOTIS report to be only a list of *potential* problems. The conflict resolver re-searches each reported heading and uses its own set of rules to determine what action, if any, it should take.

11. This speed is achieved by a computer with an 80486 processor running at 66 MHz on a Saturday. (The program's speed varies somewhat, depending on the mix of problems in the report and the time of day.) The same program running on a computer with a 90 MHz Pentium processor can handle up to about 2,700 problems per hour. At the time of this writing, the conflict resolver program had corrected more than 500,000 database errors.

APPENDIX
▼
Specifications for Machine-Generated Authority Records

This appendix describes the authority record the Toolkit creates from a controlled-access field in a bibliographic record during a workstation session under direct cataloger control. (A *controlled-access field* is a bibliographic field, or group of bibliographic fields, under authority control: 1XX, 1XX+240, 400–440, 600–651, 700–730, 800–830. Northwestern University Libraries' NOTIS system does not index the 655–658 and 755 fields, which can also be under authority control. The Toolkit could easily be modified to create authority records from these fields.) It uses a similar model to create an authority record from a noncontrolled field in a bibliographic record (such as an authority record for a series-like phrase created from a note field).

"Fixed Fields" (Leader and 008 Field)

The Toolkit supplies correct values for each leader and 008 field position, here described in terms of the *USMARC Format for Authority Data*. Fixed-field elements not listed here (such as record status, type of record, and date of record creation) are supplied by the NOTIS system itself.

Encoding level (leader/17): blank

Direct/indirect geographic subdivision (008/06): blank for topical headings; "n" for other headings

Romanization scheme (008/07): the "fill" character

Kind of record (008/09): "a"

Descriptive cataloging rules (008/10): "n" for topical headings; for other headings, derived from the descriptive cataloging code (leader/18) in the source bibliographic record ("c" if bibliographic leader/18 is "a"; "a" in other cases)

Subject heading system/thesaurus (008/11): for headings derived from bibliographic 6XX fields, a translation of the bibliographic second indicator; for headings derived from other bibliographic fields, the local institution's default subject system code

Type of series (008/12): for series headings: "b" if entered under personal name, "a" in other cases; "n" for nonseries headings

Numbered/unnumbered series (008/13): for series: "a" if subfield $v is present in the original heading, "b" in other cases; "n" for nonseries headings

Heading use—main or added entry (008/14): "b" for topical heading; "a" for other headings (For 008/14-16, the Toolkit uses the non-MARC code "c" [a NOTIS convention] in the appropriate position(s) instead of code "a" to reflect the manner in which the heading is used in the bibliographic record from which the heading was extracted.)

Heading use—subject added entry (008/15): "a"

Heading use—series added entry (008/16): "a" for series headings; "b" for other headings

Type of subject subdivision (008/17): "n"

Type of government agency (008/28): the "fill" character

Reference evaluation (008/29): "a" if the Toolkit generates references at the same time it generates the original authority record; "n" in other cases (If the cataloger later uses the Toolkit to add references to an authority record, it changes the reference evaluation code "n" to "a.")

Record update in process (008/31): "a"

Undifferentiated personal name (008/32): "a" for personal name headings; "n" for all other headings

Level of establishment (008/33): "a"

Modified record (008/38): blank

Cataloging source (008/39): "d"

040 Field

The Toolkit supplies a default 040 field consisting of an NUC code in subfields $a and $c. The Toolkit uses the local institution's NUC code, supplied on an options screen during program installation.

Extraction of Authority Heading (1XX Field)

The Toolkit extracts from the bibliographic record the portion of the variable field or fields from which it is to create an authority heading. It removes those subfields that do not form part of the uniform heading (for example, it removes subfields $e, $u, and $4). The program adjusts the tag, indicators, and terminal punctuation of the source field so that they conform to the specifications for authority 1XX fields.

The Toolkit allows the cataloger to create an authority record for less than the full heading, if desired.

Bibliographic Field

    650 0 $a Pottery, Fulah $x Exhibitions

Desired Authority Heading

    150 0 $a Pottery, Fulah

Citation of Source (670 Field)

The Toolkit generates subfield $a of the 670 field by manipulating information from the bibliographic record.

> 1XX field (the "name" portion only; for example, the Toolkit omits subfield $d from personal names)
>
> 240 field
>
> 245 field subfields $a, $n, $p
>
> 250 field subfield $a
>
> 260 field subfield $c

The Library of Congress has reduced the number of elements that *must* be included in subfield $a of an authority record's 670 field—provided that the reduced set of elements still unambiguously identifies the item from which the information is extracted. (This reduction was made in an attempt to lessen the effort required to create an authority record.) Since the Toolkit can generate a full 670 field with no work on the part of the cataloger, and because it is not possible in any case for it easily to determine whether or not a particular less-than-full identification is adequate, it provides all available information for every item.

If the Toolkit finds the heading, or a variation of it, in the 245 or 260 field, it pastes it into subfield $b of the 670 field. The program allows for differences in capitalization and diacritical marks and can find versions of names that differ in fullness; it can also find names whether they are given in forename–surname or the less common surname–forename order. If it cannot find some form of the heading being established in the 245 and 260 fields, it asks the cataloger for assistance. The Toolkit usually assumes that the information in the 245 or 250 field came from the title page and uses the location designation "t.p." in the 670 field. It makes other assumptions in special circumstances. For example, it uses "series t.p." for series headings and "title frames" for video recordings. (This location designation within the 670 field is the one piece of information that cannot be predicted reliably. Catalogers must assume this information is incorrect until they have verified it.)

Series-Related Fields

If the heading being established is a series heading, the Toolkit supplies additional variable fields:

> 022 (ISSN): subfield $x from the series heading (if any)
>
> 642 (series numbering example): subfield $v from the series heading (if any) in subfield $a, and an NUC code in subfield $5
>
> 643 (series place and publisher/issuing body): subfields $a and $b from the 260 field of the bibliographic record, with internal punctuation removed

644 (series analysis practice): the code for the default series analysis practice ("f") in subfield $a, and an NUC code in subfield $5

645 (series tracing practice): the code for the default series tracing practice ("t") in subfield $a, and an NUC code in subfield $5

646 (series classification practice): the code for the default series classification practice ("s") in subfield $a, and an NUC code in subfield $5

Automatic Generation of References

The Toolkit makes every effort to generate references that are predictably required for personal-name headings based on information in the heading or present elsewhere in the record. (It generates references only when the personal name appears without extensions such as topical subdivisions.) The program also makes one name/title reference for a name/title heading generated from the complete 1XX+240 fields. (This reference is from the 1XX+245 subfields $a, $n, and $p.) The idea is to provide references clearly required for a particular heading, while avoiding references the cataloger will only have to delete.

The following samples (the headings do not represent known individuals!) show the kinds of references the Toolkit generates automatically when it creates the initial proposed authority record. It carefully adjusts indicators and the contents of subfield $q to match each reference. At the American Library Association's 1996 midwinter meeting, MARBI (the interdivisional ALCTS/LITA/RASD USMARC advisory committee) voted to make the first indicator code "2" in personal name headings obsolete and redefined the first indicator code "1" to mean simply "Surname" to align the British and American MARC formats. After these changes have been approved at all levels and published, the Toolkit will be modified to conform to them. (It contains a suite of tools that make the generation of references beyond this automatic minimum a simple matter.) The examples include a 670 field when it contains information the Toolkit uses to generate an automatic reference. A few examples are included to show cases where it deliberately does *not* generate a reference that is usually not wanted. Occasional reference is made in the examples to *Library of Congress Rule Interpretations (LCRIs)*.

Reference for Multiple-Element Surname

100 20 $a Schleswig-Holstein-Augustenburg, Friedrich Christian von, $d 1952-

400 20 $a Holstein-Augustenburg, Friedrich Christian von Schleswig-, $d 1952-

400 10 $a Augustenburg, Friedrich Christian von Schleswig-Holstein-, $d 1952-

400 20 $a Von Schleswig-Holstein-Augustenburg, Friedrich Christian, $d 1952-

100 10 $a Ley, Alexander von der, $d 1952-

400 10 $a Von der Ley, Alexander, $d 1952-

Following *LCRI* 26.2, the Toolkit does not generate a reference tracing for Der Ley, Alexander von, $d 1952- .

100 10 $a De La Boop, $d 1952-

400 10 $a La Boop, $c De, $d 1952-

400 10 $a Boop, $c De La, $d 1952-

Note the use of subfield $c in this case; cf. *LCRI* 22.5D.

Reference for Variation in Fullness of the First Forename

100 10 $a Boop, B. E. $q (Betty E.), $d 1952-

400 10 $a Boop, Betty E., $d 1952-

100 10 $a Smith, Hastings Alexander, $d 1952-

400 10 $a Smith, H. A. $q (Hastings Alexander), $d 1952-

670       $a Winchell, Paul. You can do it, kid, 1995: $b t.p. (H.A. Smith)

When the Toolkit moved the statement of responsibility from subfield $c of the 245 field to subfield $b of the 670 field, it noted that the statement of responsibility varied from the established heading in the fullness of the first forename. It automatically used this variant form as the basis for a reference.

100 20 $a Boop Rodriguez, B. $q (Betty), $d 1952-

400 20 $a Boop Rodriguez, Betty, $d 1952-

400 10 $a Rodriguez, B. Boop $q (Betty Boop), $d 1952-

The Toolkit does not generate a reference tracing for Rodriguez, Betty Boop, $d 1952- .

Reference for Variation in Fullness of Surname

100 10 $a B., Betty E. $q (Betty Elizabeth Boop), $d 1952-

400 10 $a Boop, Betty E. $q (Betty Elizabeth), $d 1952-

100 20 $a Smith B., Betty $q (Smith Boop), $d 1952-

400 20 $a Smith Boop, Betty, $d 1952-

400 10 $a B., Betty Smith $q (Boop), $d 1952-

400 10 $a Boop, Betty Smith, $d 1952-

Reference for Variation in Fullness of Both Surname and Forename

100 10 $a Boop R., B. $q (Betty Boop Rodriguez), $d 1952-

400 20 $a Boop Rodriguez, B. $q (Betty), $d 1952-

400 20 $a Boop R., Betty $q (Boop Rodriguez), $d 1952-

400 10 $a R., B. Boop $q (Betty Boop Rodriguez), $d 1952-

400 10 $a Rodriguez, Betty Boop, $d 1952-

Reference for Title of Nobility, etc.

100 10 $a Boop, Betty, $c Countess of, $d 1952-

400 00 $a Betty, $c Countess of Boop, $d 1952-

100 10 $a Boop, Bob, $c Count of Boop, $d 1952-

The Toolkit does not create a reference tracing for Boop, Bob Boop, $c Count of, $d 1952- .

Reference for Multiple-Element Forename Headings

100 00 $a Mobutu Sese Boop, $d 1952-

400 10 $a Boop, Mobutu Sese, $d 1952-

400 20 $a Sese Boop, Mobutu, $d 1952-

100 00 $a Betty E. $q (Betty Elizabeth), $d 1952-

400 00 $a Betty Elizabeth, $d 1952-

400 10 $a E., Betty $q (Elizabeth), $d 1952-

400 10 $a Elizabeth, Betty, $d 1952-

Reference for "Incomplete" Names

100 10 $a La Boop, $c Madame de $q (Marie-Madelaine Pioche de La Vergne), $d 1952-

400 10 $a La Boop, Marie-Madelaine Pioche de La Vergne, $d 1952-

400 10 $a De La Boop, $c Madame $q (Marie-Madelaine Pioche de La Vergne), $d 1952-

400 10 $a Boop, $c Madame de La $q (Marie-Madelaine Pioche de La Vergne), $d 1952-

Additional reference tracings (from "Pioche" and following words in subfield $q) are needed for this heading. However, it is impossible for the Toolkit to distinguish between this heading and others of similar construction for which such references are not desired (see the following example). It leaves the generation of these reference tracings to the cataloger—they can be added to the record with the click of a button.

100 10 $a Sigaud de la Fond, $c M. $q (Joseph Aignan), $d 1952-

400 20 $a Sigaud de la Fond, Joseph Aignan, $d 1952-

400 10 $a De la Fond, Sigaud, $c M. $q (Joseph Aignan), $d 1952-

400 10 $a La Fond, Sigaud de, $c M. $q (Joseph Aignan), $d 1952-

400 10 $a Fond, Sigaud de la, $c M. $q (Joseph Aignan), $d 1952-

100 10 $a Smith, $c Mr. $q (John Seymour), $d 1952-
400 10 $a Smith, John Seymour, $d 1952-

100 10 $a S., $c Mr. $q (John Seymour Smith), $d 1952-
400 10 $a S., John Seymour $q (Smith), $d 1952-
400 10 $a Smith, John Seymour, $d 1952-
400 10 $a Smith, $c Mr. $q (John Seymour), $d 1952-

100 20 $a Smith B., $c Mr. $q (John Seymour Smith Boop), $d 1952-
400 20 $a Smith B., John Seymour $q (Smith Boop), $d 1952-
400 20 $a Smith Boop, John Seymour, $d 1952-
400 20 $a Smith Boop, $c Mr. $q (John Seymour), $d 1952-
400 10 $a B., Smith, $c Mr. $q (John Seymour Smith Boop), $d 1952-
400 10 $a Boop, Smith, $c Mr. $q (John Seymour), $d 1952-

Reference for Name Consisting Solely of Initials

100 00 $a E. R. $q (Elizabeth Rodriguez), $d 1952-
400 10 $a ER $q (Elizabeth Rodriguez), $d 1952-
400 00 $a Elizabeth Rodriguez, $d 1952-
400 10 $a R., E. $q (Elizabeth Rodriguez), $d 1952-
400 10 $a Rodriguez, Elizabeth, $d 1952-

100 20 $a Q Q Q X Y Z
100 10 $a Z, Q Q Q X Y
400 10 $a QQQXYZ

Custom Applications
The Library of Congress Experience

David Williamson
Library of Congress

▼ Since the early 1990s the Library of Congress (LC) has been converting the aging, dumb-terminal population formerly used to connect to the LC online system, Multiple-Use MARC System (MUMS), to bibliographic work stations (BWS), which are being installed on individual catalogers' desktops. The BWS is an input/update terminal for the Library's computer catalog files as well as a personal computer (PC) capable of performing many work-related tasks (such as word processing and Internet access). Every BWS is configured with 16 megabytes of memory under OS/2 version 2.1 and TCP/IP (Transmission Control Protocol/Internet Protocol) for OS/2 version 2.0 with screen resolution of 1024 × 768 with 256 colors. The BWS is an off-the-shelf personal computer that is loaded with off-the-shelf software to carry out most of its functions.

To do the cataloging work, however, special software had to be written to enable use of the full ALA extended character set. LC contracted with Data Connections, a British company, to write the OS/2 program to enable input/update functions on the BWS as well as the extended character set. This is custom software written specifically for LC's BWS and mainframe interaction. Also, custom keycaps were created for the library. These keycaps replace the standard keycaps on an otherwise ordinary keyboard that contains the normal character set as well as the ALA extended set. Also written for the library was a program to enable the use of macros in cataloging. Catalogers can create approximately one hundred macros for use in their work. Currently this macro capability is limited to actual-keystroke types of commands.

At the heart of the BWS is the OS/2 operating system with its programming language interpreter, REXX, integrated into it. REXX is a powerful character manipulator. Any text source, such as an ASCII file or a screen image, can be parsed and the various elements manipulated in almost any way the programmer wants. This has proven to be very useful at LC. Staff in the Cataloging Directorate have been very successful in using a graphical version of REXX, VX-REXX by Watcom Software, to develop programs that automate many cataloging functions. This chapter will describe three of those programs and indicate the degree to which they have both compensated for shortcomings of the mainframe-based library automation system and proven to be major productivity enhancers for the Cataloging Directorate.

The programs being developed at LC fall under the Text Capture and Electronic Conversion (TCEC) project.[1] Initial programs were primarily concerned with using text from various sources (ASCII files, Internet screen captures, and scanned text), capturing that text by highlighting it with a mouse, and then using REXX routines to convert the text into MARC fields. Since those early experiments, TCEC has moved beyond just capturing and converting text to automating searches against the LC database and automatically generating name authority records.

On the MARC

The first TCEC experiment was developed in conjunction with the Electronic CIP Experiment.[2] In April 1993, the Cataloging-in-Publication Division at LC formed a study group to examine the feasibility of creating an electronic version of the cataloging-in-publication (CIP) process. Publishers were contacted to see if any were interested in participating in an experiment. In November 1993, the University of New Mexico Press submitted the first manuscript file for electronic processing. By February 1, 1997, a total of 1,502 manuscripts submitted by 58 publishers had been processed using these routines (compared with 651 manuscripts from 36 publishers the year before).

The program developed to assist in performing the cataloging of electronic manuscripts is called On the MARC. It can take text from any source (electronic file, Internet screen capture, or keyboard input) and convert that text into MARC fields. The cataloger supplies appropriate ISBD (International Standard Bibliographic Description) punctuation to the text, highlights the text to be converted, and then tells the program which field to create based on the highlighted text. Figure 9.1 shows the field and function keys on the left side of the program window, the upper text area, and the lower record-creation area.

Cataloging from Text

In figure 9.1, the text of the manuscript file is displayed in the upper window of the program. The publisher provided the general mock-up of the pages. The half title page, series page, and the title page are visible.

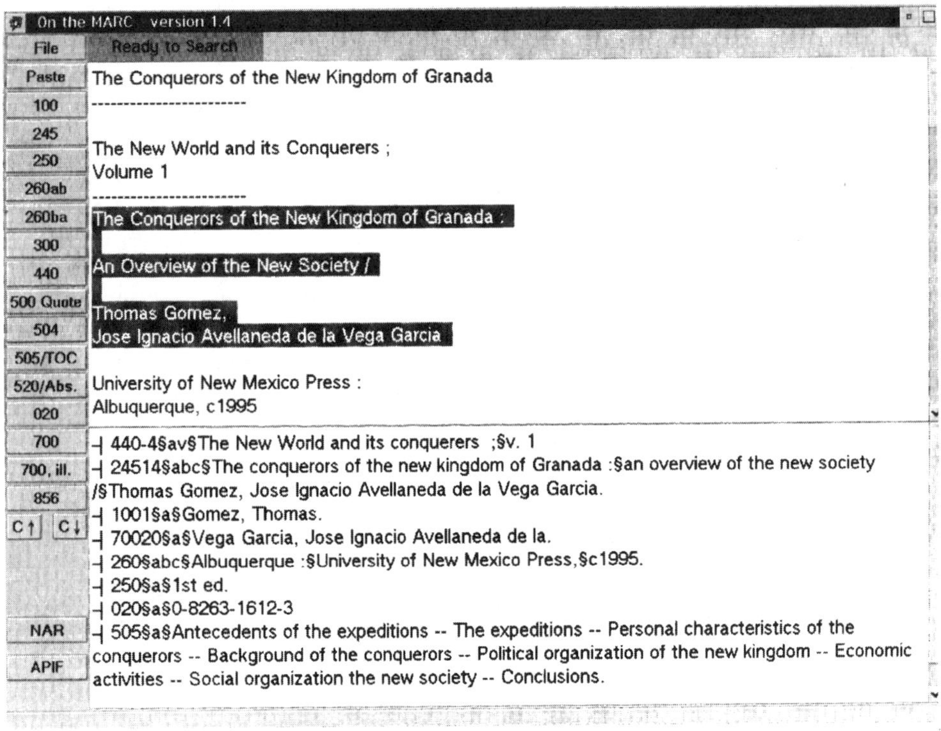

Figure 9.1 On the MARC Bibliographic Record Creation

The rest of the manuscript can be seen by scrolling down in the upper window. The cataloger inserts ISBD punctuation into the text of the manuscript. Since this is a copy of the manuscript that was read into memory, the original copy of the manuscript remains unchanged. Notice the punctuation added: semicolon after the series title, colon after the title, slash after the subtitle, comma after the first author's name, colon after the name of the publisher, and a comma after the place of publication. After inserting the ISBD punctuation, the data for a given field are highlighted. The cataloger then clicks on the button on the left side of the screen to tell the program which field to create. In figure 9.1, the 245 field information is highlighted, so the cataloger would click on the 245 button. The lower window for record creation shows the descriptive fields that were generated from this sample manuscript file.

A few features in figure 9.1 are particularly worth noting. The 100 and 700 fields were created from the text presented in direct order. The program, however, intelligently and automatically inverted the name in the 100 field. For the multiple surname in the 700 field, the cataloger inserts an asterisk at the entry element, and the program constructs the heading based on the location of the asterisk. In this example, the asterisk was placed just before the word *Vega*. (While this would not normally be the entry element, it is used for demonstration purposes.)

The 440 and 245 fields both have a second indicator value of "4." This is computer generated to ignore the initial article, *The,* in searching. Also in the 245 field, the first word of the title is uppercase while the rest of the words were automatically changed to lowercase. The cataloger can go back and uppercase any word ("Granada" in this example) by pointing the cursor at the word and double-clicking with the mouse.

The 250 field contains abbreviations for the edition statement. While not visible in the upper text window, the edition statement was given on the copyright page mock-up as *First Edition.* The program automatically substituted the correct abbreviations used in cataloging.

The elements for the 260 field are not presented in correct order, that is, place, publisher, date. Instead, the data are given as publisher, place, date. The program has two buttons related to the 260 field: 260ab and 260ba. The former is used when data are given in correct cataloging order (place : publisher, date) and the latter is used when the data elements are given in reverse order (publisher : place, date).

Finally, notice that the table of contents (TOC) is given. Since the TOC information is provided in electronic form, it can be easily captured and converted into a 505 field and included in the catalog record. TOC information is not normally included in catalog records manually produced due to the time it takes to key it and the possible introduction of transcription errors. When it can be done by capturing electronic text, it is easy to include the TOC.

Automated Searching and Name Authority Generation

On the MARC is a multithreaded program—one in which computer processes can be programmed to run as if they were separate programs. This has advantages over single-threaded programs. For instance, a cataloger can go through the manuscript file, highlight data, and tell the program to process it as appropriate. Whenever the cataloger creates a 100, 440, or 700 field, the program spawns a new thread that initiates a search against the LC database. The advantage in using a separate thread for searching is that the cataloging thread of the program would not be affected by a problem with the LC database search (for example, a system crash, if one occurs) and the cataloger would be able to continue cataloging without losing the record on the screen.

When the cataloger created the 100 field in figure 9.1, the name "Gomez, Thomas" was searched against the LC database. The results of the search were brought to the foreground of the display in an LC terminal session window. The cataloger could then see the results of this initial search and go on to perform other searching if needed to find a name authority for this author.

In the case of the 700 field, the name "Vega Garcia, Jose Avellaneda de la" was searched against the LC database. Since the name used in this example is fictitious, no name authority record was found. So, in this case it would be necessary to create one for the heading. On the MARC is capable of generating a skeletal name authority record (NAR) *after* the 100, 245, and 260 fields have been created by the program (data needed for the skeletal NAR are in these three fields). The cataloger clicks anywhere on the line containing the 700 field to tell the program what heading needs an NAR. The cataloger then clicks on the NAR button to tell the program to make the NAR. A window pops up on the screen as shown in screen 1 of figure 9.2.

From this point, the cataloger can perform several functions. Notice that in screen 1 of figure 9.2 both authors' names are given in the 670 field. This is intentional in case there is wording other than the name elements that the cataloger might want to include. The cataloger simply highlights the extraneous data and deletes it. If a reference structure is needed—as is the case in this name that has several surname elements—the cataloger clicks anywhere on the 100 field so that the cursor is blinking somewhere on that line. The cataloger then clicks on the Ref button at the top of the box and references are created automatically as shown in screen 2 of figure 9.2.

Notice for the heading itself as well as for all references that the first indicator is properly set for single or multiple surnames. The program counts the number of words before the comma and assigns a value as appropriate. The program cannot distinguish surname elements from particles, for example, prepositions, so it may miscode a reference beginning with a particle.

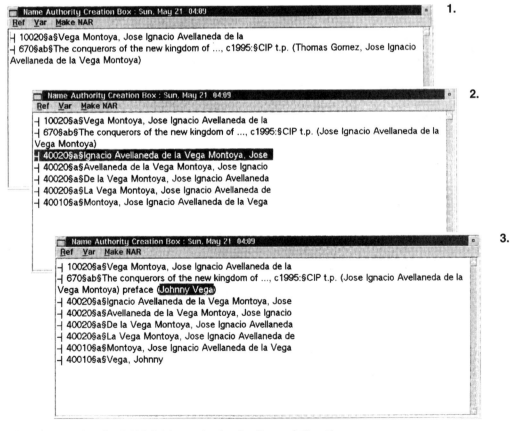

1.

Name Authority Creation Box : Sun, May 21 04:09
Ref Var Make NAR

⊣ 10020§a§Vega Montoya, Jose Ignacio Avellaneda de la
⊣ 670§ab§The conquerors of the new kingdom of ..., c1995:§CIP t.p. (Thomas Gomez, Jose Ignacio Avellaneda de la Vega Montoya)

2.

Name Authority Creation Box : Sun, May 21 04:09
Ref Var Make NAR

⊣ 10020§a§Vega Montoya, Jose Ignacio Avellaneda de la
⊣ 670§ab§The conquerors of the new kingdom of ..., c1995:§CIP t.p. (Jose Ignacio Avellaneda de la Vega Montoya)
⊣ 40020§a§Ignacio Avellaneda de la Vega Montoya, Jose
⊣ 40020§a§Avellaneda de la Vega Montoya, Jose Ignacio
⊣ 40020§a§De la Vega Montoya, Jose Ignacio Avellaneda
⊣ 40020§a§La Vega Montoya, Jose Ignacio Avellaneda de
⊣ 40010§a§Montoya, Jose Ignacio Avellaneda de la Vega

3.

Name Authority Creation Box : Sun, May 21 04:09
Ref Var Make NAR

⊣ 10020§a§Vega Montoya, Jose Ignacio Avellaneda de la
⊣ 670§ab§The conquerors of the new kingdom of ..., c1995:§CIP t.p. (Jose Ignacio Avellaneda de la Vega Montoya) preface (Johnny Vega)
⊣ 40020§a§Ignacio Avellaneda de la Vega Montoya, Jose
⊣ 40020§a§Avellaneda de la Vega Montoya, Jose Ignacio
⊣ 40020§a§De la Vega Montoya, Jose Ignacio Avellaneda
⊣ 40020§a§La Vega Montoya, Jose Ignacio Avellaneda de
⊣ 40010§a§Montoya, Jose Ignacio Avellaneda de la Vega
⊣ 40010§a§Vega, Johnny

Figure 9.2   On the MARC Name Authority Record Creation

The program is designed to create references from any element after the first element to the right of the comma. This resulted in an incorrect reference as highlighted in screen 2 of figure 9.2. The cataloger simply needs to highlight any unwanted reference and press the <Delete> key. The program is not capable of distinguishing forenames from surnames, so it may occasionally generate bad references. Both instances are examples of the fact that cataloger review and approval is an integral part of the program. The BWS and its associated programs cannot create records or references without cataloger approval.

The cataloger can edit the text displayed in the NAR box. If a variant form of a name is found in the electronic file, the cataloger can cite this form and create the reference structure needed. For example, if the name "Johnny Vega" is found in the preface, the cataloger can type this information into the 670 field, highlight the variant name, and then click on the Var button at the top of the screen. This operation will generate a new reference at the bottom of the box as seen in screen 3 of figure 9.2.

If, in turn, a reference is also needed from this variant form, the cataloger can click on this variant reference as was done formerly in the case of the 100 field, and then can click on the Ref button again to generate automatically all possible references from this entry as well.

On the MARC has at this point created most of the descriptive fields of the bibliographic record and has created an NAR as well—all based on the screen image of the electronic manuscript file. From here, the cataloger would send these two records into the LC database. The bibliographic record is sent to the database by clicking on the APIF (Automated Process Information File [LC's in-process file]) button. The NAR is sent by clicking on the Make NAR button near the top of the NAR window. Once the records are in the database, the cataloger then can review them and make any adjustments needed or add anything else not done by On the MARC.

Other Sources of Data

On the MARC can be used with more than just ASCII manuscript files supplied by publishers. Catalogers searching OPACs on the Internet can capture screen images of records and paste those into the upper text window of the program. Depending on the way the data are presented, the cataloger can highlight the fields presented and create a record for use in the LC system. This is useful when a library's OPAC does not offer another way for catalogers to capture records for processing purposes at LC.

Another possibility is to use scanned text. Retrospective conversion projects often involve significant rekeying of data from catalog cards. It is possible, however, for cards to be scanned and then for the data in the individual fields to be highlighted in the resulting electronic text. Since ISBD punctuation is frequently already present on the cards, little editing of the data is needed if the scanning software is able to recognize the letters being scanned with a high degree of accuracy. With both of these possibilities, OPACs and scanned text, automatic searching of headings as well as automatic NAR generation is available for catalogers' use.

National Library of Medicine CIP

The Library of Congress Cataloging-in-Publication Division administers the CIP program; however, LC does not catalog all CIPs submitted for cataloging. The National Library of Medicine (NLM) assists LC with the CIP cataloging for items on clinical medicine.[3] Prior to fall 1995, NLM received the CIP paperwork from LC, did the cataloging of CIPs that were in scope for NLM, and sent the CIP paperwork back to LC. At that point technicians at LC would rekey the data into the LC system. This was a laborious and repetitive process, and one ripe for improvement.

Much of the workflow still remains the same, with one extraordinary exception. Realizing the import of the advances made with the TCEC experiments and eager to capitalize on it, the Cataloging Directorate, with the cooperation of NLM, initiated a project to automate much of the processing of NLM CIP records. Every day, a routine is run at NLM where all CIP cataloging records from the previous day are gathered and written to a file in MARC communications format. This automatic function does not require human intervention.

When the CIP paperwork comes back to LC, the technician does not rekey the CIP data into the LC system. Instead, the technician uses file transfer protocol (FTP) to connect to NLM over the Internet and retrieves the needed file of CIP records from NLM. The paperwork for each NLM CIP is dated so that the technician knows which file available from NLM has the CIP data for that day's titles. All paperwork for a particular day is gathered and processed at the same time for efficiency. The technician starts a TCEC program that immediately opens a file dialog box. The file dialog box presents the files that the technician has retrieved. The technician simply clicks on the file name for a particular day's CIP data, and the file is read. The program converts the records from MARC communications format to the LC internal format. All records from the file are converted at once, and the technician is presented with a window containing the first record from the file as seen in figure 9.3.

In figure 9.3, the LC card number for the first CIP in this file is shown. The technician can choose from among the other records in the file by clicking on the arrow to the right of the LC card number. The record for that CIP would then be displayed in the window. There are two buttons on the right side of the information area so that the technician can move from record to record either forward or backward through the available records. The darker box on the right displays the current record number in this file and the total number of records in the file (not visible in the figure). On the left side is the button that the technician uses to send the NLM data into the LC database.

The CIP Division at LC creates a skeletal record in the LC system as shown in figure 9.4. This allows the CIP Division to monitor throughput for an item and also indicates the status of the item if there is a question.

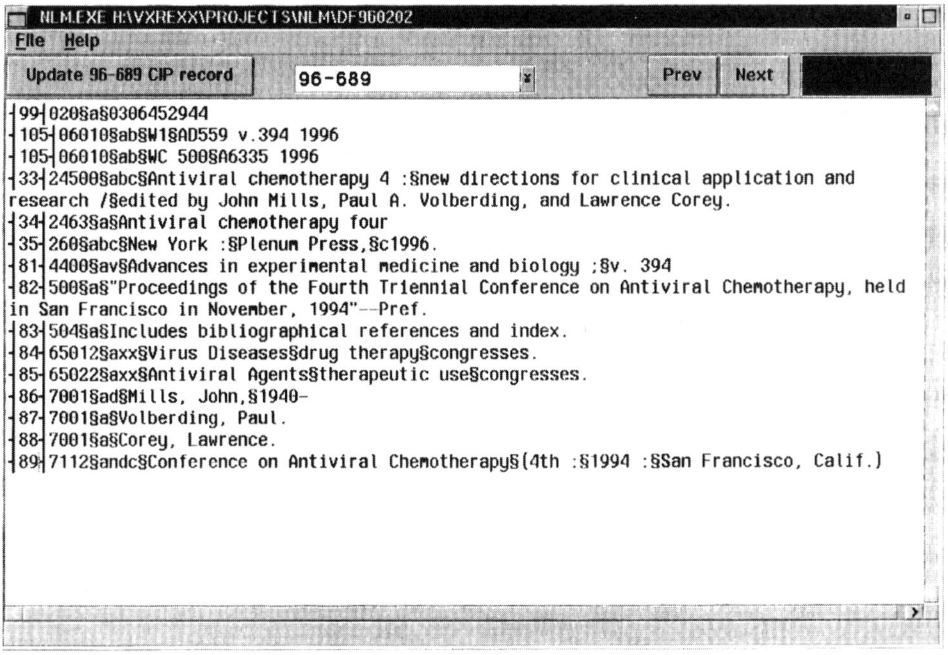

```
┌─ NLM.EXE H:\VXREXX\PROJECTS\NLM\DF960202                              ◦ □
 File  Help
┌──────────────────────┐ ┌──────────────────┐        ┌──────┬──────┐
│ Update 96-689 CIP record │ │ 96-689        ▼ │        │ Prev │ Next │
└──────────────────────┘ └──────────────────┘        └──────┴──────┘
─┤99┤020§a§0306452944
─┤105┤06010§ab§W1§AD559 v.394 1996
─┤105┤06010§ab§WC 500§A6335 1996
─┤33┤24500§abc§Antiviral chemotherapy 4 :§new directions for clinical application and
research /§edited by John Mills, Paul A. Volberding, and Lawrence Corey.
─┤34┤2463§a§Antiviral chemotherapy four
─┤35┤260§abc§New York :§Plenum Press,§c1996.
─┤81┤4400§av§Advances in experimental medicine and biology ;§v. 394
─┤82┤500§a§"Proceedings of the Fourth Triennial Conference on Antiviral Chemotherapy, held
in San Francisco in November, 1994"--Pref.
─┤83┤504§a§Includes bibliographical references and index.
─┤84┤65012§axx§Virus Diseases§drug therapy§congresses.
─┤85┤65022§axx§Antiviral Agents§therapeutic use§congresses.
─┤86┤7001§ad§Mills, John,§1940-
─┤87┤7001§a§Volberding, Paul.
─┤88┤7001§a§Corey, Lawrence.
─┤89┤7112§andc§Conference on Antiviral Chemotherapy§(4th :§1994 :§San Francisco, Calif.)
                                                                      ▸
```

Figure 9.3   TCEC Version of NLM CIP Record

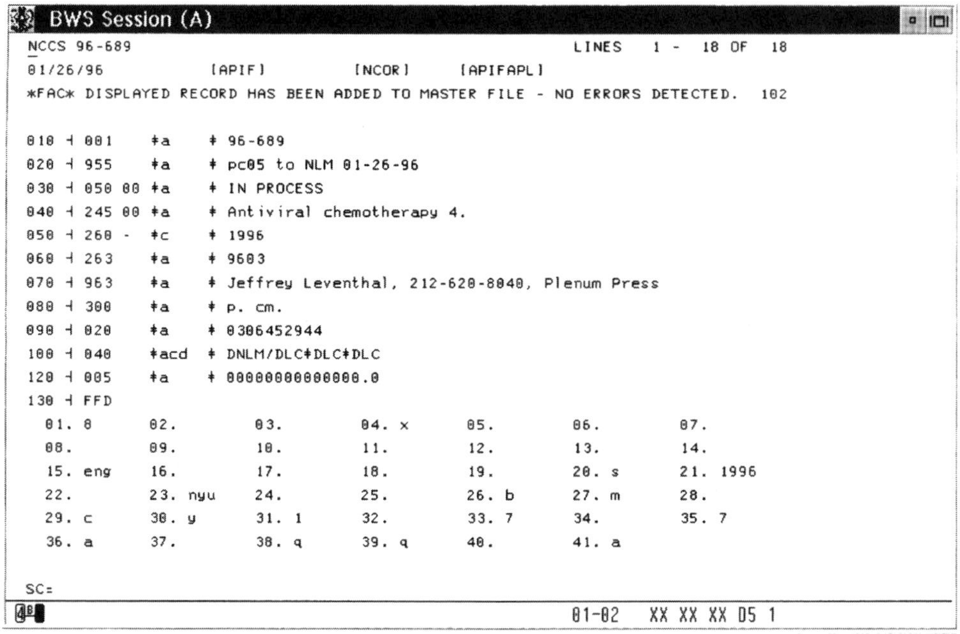

```
┌─ BWS Session (A)                                                    ◦ □
 NCCS 96-689                                            LINES   1 - 18 OF  18
 01/26/96         [APIF]         [NCOR]     [APIFAPL]
 *FAC* DISPLAYED RECORD HAS BEEN ADDED TO MASTER FILE - NO ERRORS DETECTED.   102

 010 ┤ 001    ‡a    ‡ 96-689
 020 ┤ 955    ‡a    ‡ pc05 to NLM 01-26-96
 030 ┤ 050 00 ‡a    ‡ IN PROCESS
 040 ┤ 245 00 ‡a    ‡ Antiviral chemotherapy 4.
 050 ┤ 260 -  ‡c    ‡ 1996
 060 ┤ 263    ‡a    ‡ 9603
 070 ┤ 963    ‡a    ‡ Jeffrey Leventhal, 212-620-8040, Plenum Press
 080 ┤ 300    ‡a    ‡ p. cm.
 090 ┤ 020    ‡a    ‡ 0306452944
 100 ┤ 040    ‡acd  ‡ DNLM/DLC‡DLC‡DLC
 120 ┤ 005    ‡a    ‡ 000000000000000.0
 130 ┤ FFD
   01. 8      02.        03.        04. x     05.       06.       07.
   08.        09.        10.        11.       12.       13.       14.
   15. eng    16.        17.        18.       19.       20. s     21. 1996
   22.        23. nyu    24.        25.       26. b     27. m     28.
   29. c      30. y      31. 1      32.       33. 7     34.       35. 7
   36. a      37.        38. q      39. q     40.       41. a

 SC=
 ┤9┤■                                          01-02    XX XX XX D5 1
```

Figure 9.4   Initial LC Version of NLM Record

The technician looks over the record in the program to make sure it corresponds to the NLM CIP printout that is supplied and to the skeletal record created by the CIP Division. If all is well, the technician clicks on the update button (in figure 9.3) that sends the NLM CIP data into the LC system. The program deletes the textual information in the 245 and 260 fields supplied by the CIP Division (see figure 9.4) and then inserts the NLM data into the record (figure 9.5). Notice in figure 9.3 that there are sequence numbers on the left side of each field in the NLM record. Those are supplied by the program, not by NLM. The skeletal record supplied by the CIP Division has fields in the same positions for all skeletal records. The program assigns sequence numbers based on the skeletal record field positions and where the NLM fields are to be inserted according to LC field input order. Thus, the fields go into the bibliographic record correctly.

```
 BWS Session (A)
 NCCS 96-000689                                    LINES   1 -  19 OF   34
 02/09/96        [APIF]        [NCOR]    [APIFAPL]
 *FAC* UPDATED MASTER FILE RECORD.                              186

 010 ⊣ 001   ┼a    ┼ 96-689
 020 ⊣ 955   ┼a    ┼ pc05 to NLM 01-26-96; sb26 to ASCD 02-09-96
 030 ⊣ 050 00 ┼a   ┼ IN PROCESS
 040 ⊣ 245 00 ┼abc ┼ Antiviral chemotherapy 4 :┼new directions for clinical app
 lication and research /┼edited by John Mills, Paul A. Volberding, and Lawrence C
 orey.
 050 ⊣ 246 30 ┼a   ┼ Antiviral chemotherapy four
 060 ⊣ 260 -  ┼abc ┼ New York :┼Plenum Press,┼c1996.
 070 ⊣ 263   ┼a    ┼ 9603
 080 ⊣ 963   ┼a    ┼ Jeffrey Leventhal, 212-620-8040, Plenum Press
 090 ⊣ 300   ┼a    ┼ p. cm.
 100 ⊣ 440 -0 ┼av  ┼ Advances in experimental medicine and biology ;┼v. 394
 110 ⊣ 500   ┼a    ┼ "Proceedings of the Fourth Triennial Conference on Antivir
 al Chemotherapy, held in San Francisco in November, 1994"--Pref.
 120 ⊣ 504   ┼a    ┼ Includes bibliographical references and index.
 130 ⊣ 650 12 ┼axx ┼ Virus Diseases┼drug therapy┼congresses.
 140 ⊣ 650 22 ┼axx ┼ Antiviral Agents┼therapeutic use┼congresses.
 150 ⊣ 700 1- ┼ad  ┼ Mills, John,┼1940-
 160 ⊣ 700 1- ┼a   ┼ Volberding, Paul.
 SC=
                                        01-02   XX XX XX D5 1
```

```
 170 ⊣ 700 1- ┼a   ┼ Corey, Lawrence.
 180 ⊣ 711 2- ┼andc ┼ Conference on Antiviral Chemotherapy┼(4th :┼1994 :┼San Fra
 ncisco, Calif.)
 190 ⊣ 020   ┼a    ┼ 0306452944
 200 ⊣ 020   ┼a    ┼ 0306452944
 210 ⊣ 040   ┼acd  ┼ DNLM/DLC┼DLC┼DLC
 220 ⊣ 060 10 ┼ab  ┼ W1┼AD559 v.394 1996
 230 ⊣ 005   ┼a    ┼ 00000000000000.0
 240 ⊣ FFD
   01. 8       02.        03.        04. x    05.      06.      07.
   08.         09.        10.        11.      12.      13.      14.
   15. eng     16.        17.        18.      19.      20. s    21. 1996
   22.         23. nyu    24.        25.      26. b    27. m    28.
   29. c       30. y      31. 1      32.      33. 7    34.      35. 7
   36. a       37.        38. q      39. q    40.      41. a


 SC=
                                        01-02   XX XX XX D5 1
```

Figure 9.5 Completed NLM/LC Record

Once the data are sent into the LC database, the program forces a record update transaction, and the NLM fields are actually added. Some MARC validation is performed, the fields are sorted by their sequence numbers, and the entire record is redisplayed. The technician can then review the record and make any adjustments needed. The completed record is shown in figure 9.5.

This new workflow has added a few steps to the NLM CIP process—FTP and use of a TCEC program—but the productivity increase has been dramatic. In the former, pre-TCEC workflow, the technician was able to rekey approximately twelve CIP titles per day (along with other work normally done by the technician). The new NLM CIP program is very easy to learn and use, and on the very first day using this new program the technician was able to process forty-two titles. That is a 350 percent increase in productivity!

Programs like the NLM CIP program use pieces of computer code written for other TCEC programs that can then be copied as needed. It is easy to write programs to convert data from one format to another, in this case from USMARC communications format to the LC MARC format. While microcomputer-based programs like this one can be completed in a week or two, major system changes involving the mainframe to enable it to import data directly into the LC automated system can take years to design and implement. Until the LC system is replaced or modified to take advantage of today's technological advances and requirements for cataloging, TCEC programs such as the NLM CIP program can provide quick, easy alternatives for automating cataloging operations while requiring fewer resources and less expense.

ClipSearch

While On the MARC and the NLM CIP program have been developed for specialized purposes, ClipSearch can be used by any cataloger at LC for daily work. ClipSearch was developed to take advantage of the LC BWS and the multitasking capabilities of the OS/2 operating system. The BWS software that allows catalogers to create and update LC records is a variation of the standard 3270 terminal-emulation software, adjusted for the ALA character set and OS/2. Catalogers can have up to three 3270 terminal sessions running concurrently, frequently called BWS session A, B, and C. A cataloger can perform input-update functions on book records in session A, name authority input-update functions on session B, and perhaps use the LC internal E-mail system in session C. All of these sessions are running concurrently, and the cataloger has only to change the focus on the screen to bring a session to the foreground.

ClipSearch was born almost by accident. The developers were working on another application for personal use in RLIN (Research Libraries Information Network) searching with the idea of using the OS/2 clipboard (equivalent to the Windows clipboard) as a trigger to start a process. Then the thought suggested itself: Could this be done in the BWS sessions? Could database searches be started? Is using the clip-

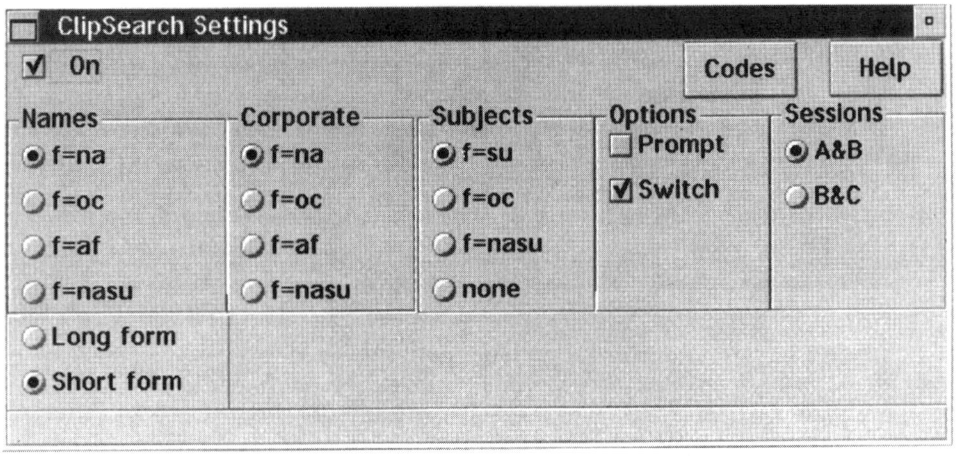

Figure 9.6   Initial View of ClipSearch

board a good trigger? After a few initial experiments, it became clear that a very useful program was in the making.

ClipSearch is a searching tool and name authority record generator. Catalogers can perform input-update functions in one BWS session, invoke ClipSearch with a hotkey combination, and have cataloging functions performed automatically in another session. When ClipSearch is started, users see the window shown in figure 9.6.

ClipSearch Options

The On check box lets the cataloger turn the searching capability on or off temporarily. There may be times when catalogers do not want to quit ClipSearch entirely but do not want ClipSearch to do searching completely automatically. Clicking on this check box will remove the checkmark and will disable searching. To start searching again, catalogers click on the box so the checkmark is visible again.

The Names, Corporate, and Subjects areas contain radio buttons that catalogers can choose for default file searching, depending on the type of heading being searched. In all cases, the "f=" directs the search to a particular LC database file. The files searched are

    na   name authority file

    oc   official catalog files (name authority files, all bibliographic files, in-process files, etc.)

    af   all files (includes files not included in the official catalog set of files)

    nasu name authority and subject authority files only

The Options area has two check boxes, Prompt and Switch. When checked, the Prompt check box causes ClipSearch to display the search it proposes to perform before actually running it so it can be adjusted if necessary. A window appears as shown in figure 9.7.

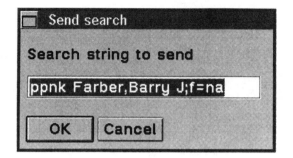

Figure 9.7 ClipSearch Search Box

Searching

The example in figure 9.7 shows that a search command "ppnk," for an LC-style personal name search, is being proposed. The name to be searched is given, and a file search qualifier for the name authority file is appended. Therefore, this name will be searched in the name authority file if the cataloger clicks on the OK button. The Cancel button can be clicked if the search is not to be run. To adjust the search, perhaps to change the file searched or to adjust the name, the cataloger simply edits the information in the space and then clicks on OK to run the search.

When checked, the Switch check box instructs ClipSearch to switch to the BWS session that has the search results when a search is run. This is an automatic switching, so catalogers do not have to change focus to another BWS session manually.

The Sessions area (figure 9.6) tells ClipSearch which BWS sessions to use. The first choice, A&B, tells ClipSearch that bibliographic record input-update will occur in BWS session A and that name authority work and automated searching will occur in BWS session B. The second choice tells ClipSearch that bibliographic work is in BWS session B and name authority work/searching is in BWS session C. This allows some flexibility when deciding which sessions to use for what functions.

Below the Names area are two choices, Long form and Short form. These indicate the type of personal name search to be run. Long form is seen in figure 9.7; that is, the entire name is searched as given in the bibliographic record. Short form indicates that an LC compression key search is to be run. The search command is still "ppnk," but the form of the name searched is the first five letters of the surname and the first letter of the forename.

While names are searched with the "ppnk" command, title searches use the "ptk" command. This search is similar to the OCLC 3,2,2,1 title search structure but uses the LC 3,1,1,1 search structure instead. This means the search uses the first three letters of the first word of the title followed by the first letter of the next three words of the title, if available. Corporate searches use the "find c" command and subject searches use the "find s" command. The "find" searches use the words in the field being searched in a keyword type of strategy. ClipSearch automatically discards one- or two-letter words from the search string as well as a list of common stop words such as *United* and *States*.

To use the basic features of ClipSearch, a bibliographic record must be displayed in the first BWS session. Figure 9.8 shows an example of a bibliographic record.

Notice in the 100 field for the author that the letter *a* in *Farber* is highlighted. This indicates that the BWS cut-and-paste operation has been initiated. Normally the cataloger would highlight a heading or some other text to be copied into the OS/2 clipboard for use elsewhere. In this case, however, only a single letter is highlighted. When the <Enter> key is pressed, the BWS software will copy that single letter into the OS/2 clipboard. ClipSearch scans the OS/2 clipboard every second to see if it has changed. If a single character is found, it is a signal to ClipSearch to perform some task. ClipSearch examines the character and, if it is a letter, scans the line that the cursor is on, looking to the left of the highlighted letter to find the tag of the field and then looking to the right to find the end of the field, wrapping to the next line if needed. ClipSearch then parses the field into its sequence number, tag and indicators, and subfield codes, and the individual subfields are examined, depending on the type of search to be performed. In this case, the 100 field tag tells ClipSearch to perform a personal name search against subfield "a" of this field. ClipSearch follows the rules programmed into it for performing personal name searches; constructs a search based on those rules, whether Long form or Short form is selected, and the file qualifier selected in the "Names" area; and either performs the search auto-

```
 BWS Session (A)
PAGE  95-95
06/20/95          [BOOKSM]          [NCRD]   [MUMS]          PAGE   1 OF  3
0*UPD* DISPLAYED RECORD HAS BEEN VERIFIED.                              112
¶

-- 010 ‡00 1‡a‡95-95¶
-- 020 ‡955‡a‡pb04 to sa00 01-19-95; sb02/desc 01-24-95; sb14 01-24-94 (subj.);
sb21 01-25-95; CIP ver. yk05 06-13-95¶
-- 030 ‡05000‡ab‡HF5438.4‡.F37 1995¶
-- 040 ‡100 1-‡a‡F rber, Barry J.¶
-- 050 ‡245 10‡ac‡Superstar sales manager's secrets /‡by Barry J. Farber.¶
-- 060 ‡260-‡abc‡Franklin Lakes, NJ :‡Career Press,‡c1995.¶
-- 090 ‡300‡abc‡127 p. :‡ill. ;‡22 cm.¶
-- 100 ‡500‡a‡Includes index.¶
-- 110 ‡020‡ac‡1564141683 (pbk.) :‡$8.99¶
-- 120 ‡650-0‡a‡Sales management.¶
-- 121 ‡08200‡a2‡658.8‡20¶
-- 123 ‡08200‡a2‡332.4/5‡20¶
-- 130 ‡040‡acd‡DLC‡DLC‡DLC¶
-- 140 ‡005‡a‡19950620165811.3¶
-- 160 ‡985‡a‡APIF/MIG¶
SC=--,--

                                        10-18  XX XX XX 81.1
```

Figure 9.8 LC Bibliographic Record Used for ClipSearch Searching

matically or else presents the prompt box shown in figure 9.7. If the Switch box is checked, the search results are seen immediately.

Once the initial search results are shown, other searches can be performed to find the desired information, if available. It is hoped that when searching the name authority file, an NAR will be found. If so, catalogers must determine if the heading on the NAR is to be used in the bibliographic record. If the NAR is the same as the heading already in the record, then nothing further needs to be done. If it is different, however, the NAR form of the name needs to be copied into the bibliographic record. ClipSearch can do this automatically. Looking at the third line of text in figure 9.8, the text "*UPD*" can be seen. What is important here are the asterisks. These also appear in name authority records in LC NAR screen displays. When a cataloger finds an NAR heading that needs to be copied into a bibliographic record, the cataloger puts the cursor on one of these asterisks and copies that asterisk into the OS/2 clipboard. ClipSearch is still scanning the OS/2 clipboard, and when it finds a single asterisk, that is an indication that a heading needs to be copied from the searching BWS session into the bibliographic input-update BWS session. ClipSearch calls up the MARC coded display of the NAR (if it is not already displayed), scans for the heading, and copies the heading (with diacritics) and MARC coding into program variables. Next the focus is changed so that the bibliographic record is brought to the foreground, and the subfield codes are pasted in followed by the heading.

Copying Headings and Generating NARs

The ability of ClipSearch to copy headings from the authority files is very useful. When adding new fields to a bibliographic record, the cataloger needs only to type the part of the heading that is to be searched. ClipSearch can search that part of the heading, find the authority record, and then copy back the entire correct heading. For example, searching a corporate name can frequently be difficult if the body is complex, as would be the case, for example, with a United Nations body. These bodies tend to use words common to many other corporate bodies, so performing a keyword search often retrieves many hits. If, however, the cataloger types in a unique initialism for the body in the bibliographic record and has ClipSearch search that initialism, the NAR for the body may well be found faster. Then ClipSearch can copy the spelled-out heading back into the bibliographic record automatically. A similar exercise could also be done for subject headings. For lengthy subject headings or for those that are difficult to search, the user can key an alternative form and let ClipSearch find the actual heading and copy it back into the bibliographic record.

Of course, this will work only when an authority record exists for the heading being searched. If no NAR exists, ClipSearch is capable of generating an NAR. The cataloger needs to input the heading into the bibliographic record as it will be established, including any qualifiers or dates the heading may need. To tell ClipSearch that an NAR is needed, the cataloger puts the cursor on the delimiter immediately to the left of the name to be used. ClipSearch is then invoked, and the skeletal NAR appears in the NAR creation window as described in On the MARC and shown in figure 9.2.

ClipSearch can also copy any field from any record into the record being updated. The cataloger searches the database as usual. If, after finding an appropriate record, the cataloger wants to copy a field back into the cataloging record, the cursor is put on one of the hyphens at the left side of the start of the field, as can be seen in figure 9.8. The same routine used to copy authority headings back into the cataloging record is used here to copy the field information back into the cataloging record.

The Codes Feature

Figure 9.6 shows two buttons in the upper right corner of the ClipSearch window, Codes and Help. Clicking on Codes causes a window to appear with a button for MARC codes and one for Lists. When the cataloger clicks on the MARC codes button, another window appears as shown in screen 1 of figure 9.9. Catalogers can then click on the type of MARC code list to be viewed: the language list, country list, or geo-

Screen 1

Screen 2

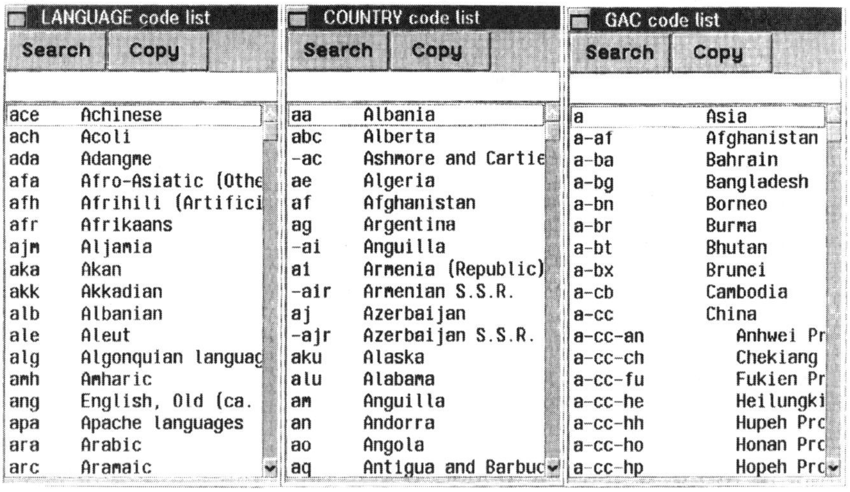

Figure 9.9 ClipSearch Types of MARC Codes

graphic area code (GAC) list. These lists can be left up and running and can be accessed in seconds by switching to them. This venture has proven to be faster and easier than other electronic means of providing these lists. Screen 2 of figure 9.9 shows sample displays from the three MARC lists.

Within each list, catalogers can perform free-text searches to speed up access to a particular code. The cataloger then highlights the information to be used and clicks on the Copy button, and the information is automatically copied into the OS/2 clipboard. The cataloger can then paste the information directly into the bibliographic record. Note that since the code being copied to the clipboard is longer than one character, it does not initiate a search in ClipSearch.

The Lists Feature

If the cataloger clicks on the button for Lists, another window appears as shown in figure 9.10. This window enables the cataloger to save commonly used fields and text. Rather than re-searching other records to find a set of fields that are usually used together, the cataloger can input the fields into the cataloging record once, copy them to the OS/2 clipboard, and save them in the lower box of this window. The next time the cataloger wants to use a group of fields in a bibliographic record, the fields are selected with the mouse, the Use button is clicked, and the fields are automatically copied to the OS/2 clipboard and can immediately be pasted back into another cataloging record. The fields

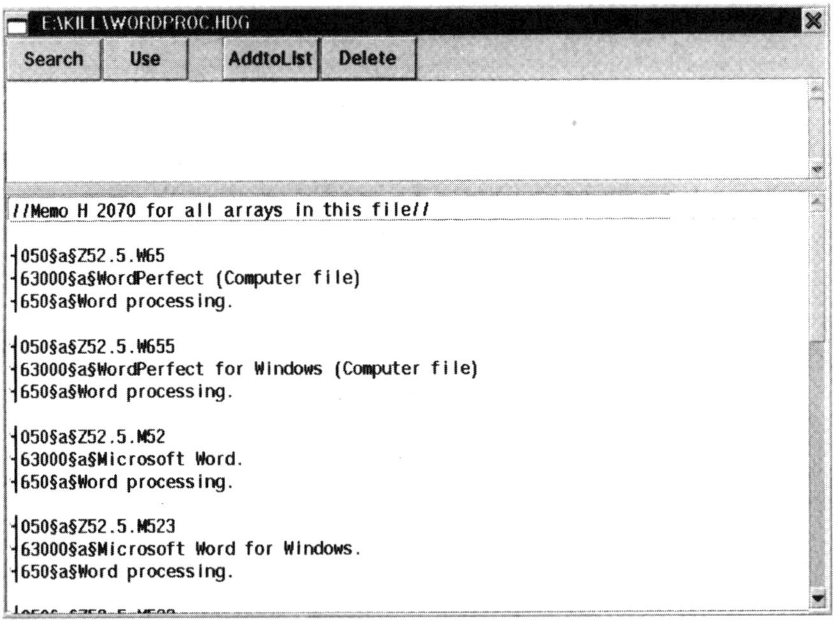

Figure 9.10   ClipSearch Lists Feature

can be input and arranged in any order. If the cataloger works in several different subject areas, multiple files can be created and stored and are available for use with a few mouse clicks. Any fields, text, or personal notes can be put into this feature for use at any time. Both this List feature and the MARC code lists can be left running on the BWS and easily brought to the foreground for use.

Online Help

The final feature is the online help facility. Detailed, hypertext help is available by clicking on the Help button in figure 9.6. The usual table of contents of the help file is provided, and the cataloger can use that to navigate through the help screens as well as by using the hypertext links. Also, an image map of the ClipSearch settings window is provided. A cataloger can click on the image map to get help on that area of the ClipSearch settings window; for example, clicking anywhere in the Names area of the image will bring up help about the file qualifiers and how ClipSearch formulates personal name searches.

ClipSearch Success

How successful has ClipSearch been as a tool for everyday cataloging? Experimental versions of ClipSearch were released to a small test group of about ten people in September 1995. These testers provided valuable feedback and good suggestions for enhancements to the program. In October 1995, the test group was expanded to about fifty people. Demonstrations were the only training provided along with a basic handout. Once other people outside the test group saw what ClipSearch could do, they began asking for the test version also. There were about fifty known testers and perhaps another twenty-five or thirty unauthorized users.

Version 1.0 was released on January 25, 1996. ClipSearch is being installed on all BWSs in the Cataloging Directorate as well as other areas that perform cataloging (for example, special collections cataloging). That represents 500 to 750 catalogers using BWSs that might use Clip-Search in 1996, with additional users as more machines are purchased. ClipSearch will be updated as new features are added. Cataloging staff using ClipSearch will be the source of new ideas and features.

How is ClipSearch being used? Certainly for "regular" cataloging, but also it has proven very useful for technicians performing copy cataloging. When examining a copy cataloging record, technicians are required to verify all access points. ClipSearch speeds up this process greatly, and since ClipSearch can automatically copy headings from authority records back into the copy cataloging record, there is less chance of transcription errors. Senior catalogers and supervisors are also finding ClipSearch useful in the review process. A trainee's bibliographic record can be checked quickly and easily.

Conclusion

The three programs explained here are just a few of the programs under development by cataloging staff. Other programs perform similar tasks such as record conversion from non-LC MARC formats to the LC MARC format, searching of records and saving results to a file for further study, and even converting information from World Wide Web forms into LC MARC records. As new tasks are needed, TCEC programs can be written in a relatively short time to accomplish a needed job. Adjustments to the programs are also quick and easy to implement. Mainframe applications can take several months or years to design, program, and implement. By using the BWS with OS/2, VX-REXX, and the library's special 3270 terminal-emulation software, the cataloging staff is able to go beyond the limits of the current mainframe system and create the automation functionality they need now to accomplish "more, better, faster, cheaper."

Notes

1. The TCEC team has four players. Richard Thaxter, automated operations coordinator, Special Materials Cataloging Division, and David Williamson, senior cataloger, Social Sciences Cataloging Division, are the primary VX-REXX programmers. Robert August, automated operations coordinator, Regional and Cooperative Cataloging Division, provides much of the online documentation support. Howard Sanner, senior cataloger, Social Sciences Cataloging Division, provides critical help with related C++ programming. This project was funded, in part, by a generous gift from the Edward Lowe Foundation.

2. Information about the Electronic CIP Experiment and the program On the MARC was condensed from the article by Beth Davis-Brown and David Williamson, "Cataloging in the Digital Age at the Library of Congress," *Cataloging and Classification Quarterly* 22, no. 3/4 (1996): 171–96.

3. Information about the NLM CIP project is expanded from my article "NLM CIP Productivity Enhancements," *LC Cataloging Newsline* 4, no. 4 (Mar. 1996).

PART

IV

Ergonomic and Training Issues for the Desktop Environment

Ergonomics and Design

Bruce Trumble
Harvard College Library

▼ The introduction of the technical services workstation promises significant gains in productivity. (In this chapter the term *workstation* will refer to the total environment, including furniture, lighting, etc. The computer proper will be referred to as the technical services workstation or TSW.) Many routine tasks can now be automated by the use of labor-saving techniques such as macros and cut-and-paste. In addition, the need to leave one's desk to consult various cataloging tools such as classification schedules and subject heading lists will be eliminated as these tools are brought online. Tasks such as filing new inserts to keep the *Library of Congress Rule Interpretations* up-to-date will also be eliminated. The Library of Congress Cataloger's Desktop has already accomplished much of this, and efforts in this direction will surely continue to the point where it will soon be unnecessary for the cataloger to consult any materials other than those accessible through the well-equipped TSW.

While acknowledging the importance of these innovations, it is important for technical services administrators to be aware that these improvements are not without potential pitfalls that can consume financial and other gains resulting from increased productivity. The most significant risk is the possibility of repetitive strain injuries (RSIs). Although there is a tendency to view tasks such as filing and manually consulting cataloging tools as completely expendable, they have value in that they provide the kind of variation that the human body requires to avoid excessive strain on individual body parts. It has become evident in the modern era that the human body has evolved as a working system and is not well suited to constant repetitive motions involving the same body parts. The advent of the industrial age and the introduction of assembly-line processes greatly limited the range of activities that workers were required to perform and correspondingly increased the risk of weakening the body in the most-involved areas with a concomitant threat of injury.

The arrival of the information age has exacerbated this hazard, and the resulting injuries have not been long in appearing. Librarians are information specialists, and so it is not surprising that the special hazards of the information age should strike them especially hard. The costs of ergonomic injuries can quickly erase the gains made from technological innovations, and the cost in human suffering to the injured staff members is considerable.

Although the dangers of repetitive motions are now well documented, methodologies of prevention and treatment are still being developed. The administrator faced with the task of planning for the introduction of the TSW is confronted with a variety of issues and is forced to make decisions sometimes based on less than complete information. When this is coupled with limited budgets and pressures for increased productivity—both factors commonly found in nonprofit institutions such as libraries, especially in times of economic constraint—the task becomes daunting indeed.

This chapter does not provide specific ergonomic advice. That is a task for trained ergonomists and competent medical professionals, and it clearly must be advice dispensed only after rigorous examination of local conditions. Moreover, there is a growing body of literature dealing with the specifics of prevention and treatment of ergonomic injuries. It does, however, provide an organized approach to managing all the various ergonomic issues that a library faces in the course of automating its technical services operations. A well-planned program of ergonomic policies and procedures can serve to minimize the number and seriousness of ergonomic complaints and allow technical services departments to exploit successfully the many advantages that increased automation can afford.

A Workplace Ergonomics Program

One of the key ways to address the problems posed by ergonomic hazards in the workplace is the development and implementation of a workplace ergonomics program, including the numerous policies necessary to coordinate the activities of the many offices that play a role in the prevention and treatment of injuries. The program must take into account education and training as well as workspace design and problem-resolution procedures. It must also do so in a manner that makes clear to all parties what their obligations are in the effort to minimize injury.

The Harvard College Library undertook this process by appointing the Standing Committee on Ergonomic Issues and Policy. Its charge was

to evaluate the current situation with respect to computer-related ergonomic safety in the workplace and to recommend steps to remedy iden-
tifiable deficiencies. The committee was composed of an equal number
of support-staff members and exempt staff, with ex-officio members
representing the Harvard College Library Human Resources and the
Harvard College Library Automation Office. After making site visits to
the libraries of the Harvard College Library system and conducting interviews with staff members and administrators, the committee reached
the conclusion that a new written policy was necessary to replace the
1991 report, *Ergonomic Issues in the Workplace,* which had been submitted by the Harvard College Library Joint Councils in a first effort to
enumerate the causes of the many ergonomic injury complaints that
the library was receiving. The standing committee's report was distributed to the Harvard College Library community in February 1996.

The report attempts to meet three main concerns:

1. Rights and responsibilities of the individual staff member, the
   supervisor, and the administration
2. Problem-resolution procedure
3. Policies of many of the offices involved in the problem-resolution
   procedure

After a brief overview of the nature of repetitive strain injuries and
other computer-related hazards, this chapter describes each of them and
highlights the elements necessary for preventing work-related injury.

Defining the Problem

Cumulative trauma disorders (CTDs), including repetitive stress injuries, are disorders of the musculoskeletal and nervous systems that
may be caused or aggravated by repetitive motions, forceful exertions,
vibration, mechanical compression, sustained or awkward posture, or
exposure to noise over an extended period of time. CTDs can affect
nearly all tissues—the nerves, tendons, tendon sheaths, and muscles—
with the upper extremities being the most frequently affected.

These injuries develop gradually over a period of weeks, months,
and years and result from repeated actions, such as twisting and bend-
ing the hands, arms, and wrists. *A common risk factor among these disorders is the use of force combined with repetitive motion over time.*[1] The most
common types of injuries associated with computer workers are the
repetitive stress injuries: carpal tunnel syndrome and tendinitis.

One reason these problems seem so common today is that the nature of the work performed in offices has changed drastically, especially
with the advent of automation. In the past, work often required use of
the entire body to perform a variety of tasks; today's jobs often entail
performing highly focused tasks restricted to a small number of movements and executed by a limited number of muscles and tendons.
Workers maintain unchanging body postures and perform repetitive

motions for long periods of time, often over the entire workday. This overuse of a limited number of body parts can lead to injury.

CTDs have a variety of symptoms, and these symptoms may be difficult to detect, especially in the early stages. The following is not intended to be an exhaustive list, but rather an indication of the types of symptoms that commonly occur. *A person experiencing any of the following symptoms should consult with a medical professional:*

- ▶ burning pain during noncomputer time, particularly during sleeping hours
- ▶ localized pain or dull ache, with or without movement
- ▶ radiating pain that travels up and down the arm or shoulder
- ▶ numbness and tingling
- ▶ weakness or stiffness
- ▶ loss of muscle coordination or control
- ▶ hands or arms that tire easily[2]

Carpal Tunnel Syndrome

Carpal tunnel syndrome is one form of RSI. (*Carpal* comes from the Greek word *karpos,* meaning wrist.) The carpel tunnel is the passageway, composed of bone and ligament, through which a major nerve system of the forearm passes into the hand. The carpal tunnel is like a cable for the median nerve and nine tendons. The nerve supplies sensation and controls the muscles in part of the hand, and the tendons allow the fingers to flex. The wear and tear of repeated movement may thicken the lubricating membrane of the tendons, increasing pressure inside the carpal tunnel and pressing the nerve up against the bone. This process, called "nerve entrapment," can be caused not only by repetitive strain but also by bone dislocation or fracture, arthritis, diabetes, or fluid retention (as may occur in pregnancy)—in short, by anything that narrows the tunnel and compresses the nerve and tendons. People who work with their hands are at risk of developing carpal tunnel syndrome. Other activities such as piano playing, knitting, and racket sports can contribute to the onset of CTDs. Some typical symptoms of carpel tunnel syndrome include

- ▶ numbness, tingling, pain in the wrist and hand (often felt at night)
- ▶ lack of strength in the hand
- ▶ inability to make a fist, hold objects, or perform other manual tasks
- ▶ loss of sensation in the hands[3]

Tendinitis

Although carpal tunnel syndrome receives the major share of media attention, tendinitis is actually the CTD that most often affects computer users. A tendon is the cord that ties the muscle to the bone, and tendinitis is an irritation of a tendon. Overuse of the muscle and tendon can irritate the tendon and cause swelling, and the chemicals that cause the swelling may further irritate the tendon. Tendinitis is especially common at the wrist, elbow, and shoulder. Tendinitis of the wrist can contribute to carpal tunnel syndrome.[4] Some typical symptoms of tendinitis include

- ► dull ache over the tendon
- ► discomfort with specific movements
- ► tenderness to the touch[5]

Ergonomic Design Criteria

There are a number of steps that can be taken to reduce the likelihood of developing repetitive strain injuries. These may be grouped into the following six categories.

Proper Work Habits. Prevention of RSIs includes good posture, which means balanced use of muscles, ease of movement, and freedom from pain rather than the tension that comes from holding a stiff posture. Preventative exercises that are designed for the purpose of stretching muscles and gaining strength are also helpful. Proper positioning is another means of prevention. In the case of keyboarding, this refers to both the correct configuration of the chair and desk and the correct angling of the body relative to the computer monitor and keyboard. It also means learning how to position one's hands correctly at the keyboard. Lastly, pacing is important in prevention. Those who work at a keyboard should take brief rest pauses from typing after every hour of work. An hourly break could include stretching and nonkeyboard activities. Working in the cold on a regular basis should be avoided because, when hands are cold, blood flow to the wrists is reduced, and that can promote RSIs.

Job Design. Jobs should be designed to allow the maximum amount of variation of tasks possible. Job sharing may also be considered as a way to introduce a greater variety of tasks into the workday.

Workstation Design. Many factors have to be taken into consideration when evaluating proper workstation design, and more-detailed sources should be consulted before undertaking this task. In general, take into account both the site and equipment. The site should have adequate lighting, and sources of glare should be minimized. It should also be roomy enough that adequate distance can be interposed between monitors and operators. Desks should include adjustable keyboard trays and, if intensive mouse work is performed, the mouse should be located at the same height as the keyboard. Chairs should be fully adjustable and provide adequate support for the back and legs. Manufacturers are beginning to offer various keyboard designs to lessen the risks associated with intensive keying; one of these models may be considered, especially if the operator is experiencing symptoms of repetitive stress. Task lighting and copy holders (bookholders in the case of catalogers) are also useful in preventing eyestrain. Other accessories such as wrist and foot rests should also be considered.

Health Habits. A person's susceptibility to RSIs may be increased if his or her overall health declines. Attention to proper diet, adequate sleep, and stress reduction play a role here as in so many other health concerns. In addition, workers should be aware of the types of free-time activities that can contribute to the development of CTDs. Activities such as playing tennis, knitting, or playing a musical instrument, along with additional computer work done at home or playing computer games, all have the potential to cause or aggravate an injury.

Medical Advice. Early intervention by medical professionals can check a developing RSI. If symptoms develop, workers should consult a physician. *Since these injuries are cumulative, do not use pain-killing medications to alleviate or mask the symptoms as an alternative to seeking the advice necessary to effect a long-term correction of the problem.*

Education. Libraries should offer programs that instruct staff in the proper use of computer equipment, especially as part of orientation programs for new employees. Since the causes and treatment of RSIs are the subject of controversy even among professionals in the field, it is important to be aware of the various sources of information that are useful in making sound decisions concerning both prevention and treatment.

Eyestrain

Eyestrain is another common complaint among computer operators. Routine eyestrain is both normal and temporary, but the risk may be increased by intensive use, inadequate or detrimental lighting, poor monitor adjustment, or preexisting eye conditions. A number of preventive measures may be taken to deal with the following problematic conditions.

Intensive Use. Refocus the eyes approximately every ten minutes. In addition, observe normal pauses for breaks and lunch. Variation in job design allowing for some less-eye-intensive tasks during the course of the workday can also alleviate eyestrain.

Inadequate or Detrimental Lighting. Workstations and lighting should be arranged to avoid reflection on the screen or surrounding surfaces. Light should be directed so that it does not shine into the operator's eyes when the operator is looking at the screen. Further, lighting should be adequate to enable the operator to see the text and the screen but not bright enough to cause glare. Normal office lighting can be supplemented by individual task lighting at a workstation if necessary. Task lighting is particularly helpful for computer work since it enables operators to adjust lighting to their individual preferences. Steps should also be taken to reduce the amount of glare present. Glare may emanate from sources of natural light such as windows as well as from artificial lighting. Care should be taken to position the monitor to reduce glare from windows. In addition, glare screens can be used to reduce glare from all sources.

Poor Monitor Adjustment. Computer monitors are equipped with brightness and contrast controls. Research is currently being conducted into the relationship between monitor colors and eyestrain and may provide more guidance in the not-too-distant future. *In general, soft, soothing colors should be preferred over more garish combinations.* Finally, the monitor should be positioned an adequate distance away from the operator. The rule of thumb is that the screen should be an arm's length away from the operator and the first line of text should be at or slightly below eye level. The screen and document holder should be the same distance from the eye (to avoid constant changes of focus) and close enough together so the operator can look from one to the other without excessive movement of the neck or back. The incline of the document holder should be adjustable.

Preexisting Eye Conditions. The intensity of computer work may reveal preexisting eye problems that were not apparent under less-demanding conditions. A computer operator should seek medical advice in the event of persistent symptoms, and regular eye examinations are recommended even in the absence of symptoms.

Extremely Low Frequency Electromagnetic Radiation. Computer monitors emit extremely low frequency (ELF) electromagnetic radiation, as do televisions and other appliances. The potential danger of exposure to this type of radiation is a matter of some dispute. The issue is further complicated by the fact that manufacturers make differing claims as to the amount of radiation their monitors emit. To minimize risk of exposure, consider upgrading older monitors to models that meet the Swedish National Board of Testing's MPRII guidelines or the more stringent guidelines of the Tjänstemännens Centralorganisation (TCO), the Swedish white-collar labor union. In addition, operators should be seated an arm's length from the front of the monitor and four feet from the back and sides of the monitor where fields may be stronger.[6]

Designing an Ergonomics Program

This section provides a description of the preparation and contents of an ergonomics program. The basis for this description is the *Harvard College Library Ergonomics Program and Policies* prepared by the Harvard College Library Standing Committee on Ergonomic Issues and Policy and completed in January 1996.

Rights and Responsibilities

The first section of the policy lists the rights and responsibilities of the three groups to whom the policy is addressed: administrators, supervisors, and individual staff members.

The elimination of ergonomic hazards is a joint task involving all members of the library community both in terms of responsibilities and rights. The growing and soon-to-be-ubiquitous presence of computers in the library system means that no individuals are spared potential risk, and the identification and elimination of risks need to be an ongoing concern at all levels. To implement an effective ergonomics program, the concept of the psychology of a safe and healthy work environment must be introduced. The steps that managers take in terms of job design and equipment purchases will not suffice; issues of stress, especially those surrounding the process of automation, must be addressed, and the awareness and cooperation of staff must be ensured. Supervisors cannot constantly monitor staff to ensure proper ergonomic practices. Individuals must be aware of their own best interests and act accordingly, and it is the role of supervisors and administrators to provide the staff with the means to work in an ergonomically sound way. This interaction is a function of the ergonomic environment of the workplace.

The goal of the rights and responsibilities section of the program is to create an awareness of ergonomics in general and the role that each member of the community must play to ensure the success of the program. Without this awareness and cooperation, mere policies and procedures will be inadequate. Staff must realize that all members of the community have a role to play. These roles should be listed and explained before introducing specific procedures.

The Administration

It is the responsibility of the administration to set the tone for the development and implementation of an ergonomics program. Many administrators have had to respond to a sharp increase in ergonomic injuries as a result of a piecemeal approach to the introduction of computers in the workplace. Over time it has become clear that, when a library automates its technical services operations, the entire workstation must be planned with consideration given to such factors as room lighting, furniture and equipment, location of computers, etc. Much of the sudden rise in ergonomic complaints is due to locating computers on old, existing furniture, resulting in totally inappropriate operator posture and practices. An important goal of the ergonomic policy maker should be to move from *reacting to complaints* to taking a *proactive approach,* and this can be accomplished only by the introduction and coordination of a program that takes a comprehensive view of the problems. This, in turn, will require that the administration provide both leadership and resources.

The administration can provide leadership in a number of important ways. It is up to the administration to form committees to design ergonomic policies and to give them complete support to do so. The committees will act as a liaison between administration and staff and review the ergonomic programs on a regular basis to ensure that they continue to address current conditions. The administration must also coordinate communication between heads of libraries or departments to ensure cooperation in all aspects of the program. It is especially important to include ergonomic considerations in the planning stage whenever remodeling is proposed.

Another important area for the administration is to plan and implement training programs for all staff members and to provide informational updates as technologies change and new automated systems are introduced. At Harvard, an outside consultant developed and implemented an ergonomics training program. This program was initially offered to all staff members and has subsequently been given annually to new employees.

It is imperative that the library's top administrators also participate in the training programs that are introduced to underline the fact that staff at all levels are exposed to risk and to emphasize the importance that is attached to the success of the ergonomics program.

Finally, the administration must provide the funds necessary for effective workstation design and operation. This includes not only equipment and furniture but also items such as wrist rests, copy stands, and glare screens. To summarize, it is the library's administration that sets the wheels in motion and ensures both adequate funding and monitoring for an ongoing ergonomics program.

The Supervisor

The library technical services supervisor plays an especially important role in the ergonomics process, and defining the rights and responsibilities of this position were key elements in the formation of Harvard's ergonomics program. The supervisor occupies an intermediate position between the administration and the individual staff member. Supervisors both translate policy into everyday procedures and often actively work according to these same procedures. To the greatest extent possible, design jobs to integrate varied tasks into staff members' daily routine so that strains produced by repetitive motions are minimized. In today's technical services environment where every effort is being made to automate tasks, this is a challenging assignment. It is not unusual to encounter supervisors who are at a loss to identify tasks not linked to the computer. Observing what happens when a computer system goes down will confirm the degree to which technical services staff members are dependent on their computers.

In addition to the increasingly difficult task of devising noncomputer-related activities, there are other ways supervisors can minimize repetitive strain hazards. Staff members should be aware of allotted break periods and lunch times and should be required to take them. In addition, they should be encouraged to take brief rest pauses after extended periods of keyboarding. These can be as simple as stretching or standing. Ironically, repetitive strain injuries often strike the staff members who seem to be the most dedicated and productive. Staff members must realize that their long-term performance depends on the proper pacing of their daily work.

It is also incumbent on supervisors to ensure that appropriate ergonomic practices are observed, including the correct use of equipment and proper posture. Supervisors should be aware of the work habits of their staff members, and a feel for the ergonomic soundness of the work area is also important. Supervisors should ensure that the work area is properly lighted and that each individual has the appropriate equipment. Since planning is the key in this area, a thorough acquaintance with procedures relating to purchasing equipment and supplies is necessary, whether the supervisor is responsible for the budget or simply makes recommendations. It is little consolation to a staff member with an incipient repetitive strain injury to hear that corrective equipment will be ordered in the *next* budget cycle. To assist the supervisor in this area, a purchasing policy should be in place that allows for off-cycle purchasing in urgent situations. But it is ultimately the supervisor's responsibility to order equipment in a timely fashion.

The supervisor plays an indispensable role in education. For prospective employees, ergonomics should be stressed beginning with the initial interview. A prospective employee should be apprised of the nature of the tasks to be performed and the degree to which repetitive tasks such as keyboarding will be required. Any potential problems should be identified at this stage, if possible. When a new staff member begins work, the supervisor must be certain that explanations of the proper use of equipment and the important role of rest periods or breaks are given and that the new staff member has an active awareness of ergonomic considerations from the outset. The supervisor must also ensure that the staff member is aware of the ergonomic training offered by the library and participates in it. A copy of the library's ergonomic program and policies should be a part of each new employee's orientation package.

Supervisors should take ergonomic considerations into account in designing the jobs of students and other temporary employees. Unfortunately, supervisors often feel that only full-time employees need to have properly designed workstations, while part-time employees can always "make do." Although a part-time employee may work only a few hours a day, if those hours are all spent at a keyboard, repetitive strain injury is still a possibility. The same awareness of ergonomically correct work procedures is always mandatory. Moreover, students often spend a great deal of time at the keyboard meeting course requirements, so their total amount of time keyboarding may equal or even exceed that of full-time employees.

Finally, the supervisor must take a leadership role in remedying situations where ergonomic injuries have occurred or potential risks have been identified. The supervisor then acts as the intermediary between the staff member and the various offices that must be consulted such as Human Resources, Workers' Compensation, etc. (See the problem-resolution section for more on this topic.)

Staff

The third group identified in the Harvard program are the individual staff members. As with administrators and supervisors, individual employees have both rights and responsibilities in the ergonomics process. It is the responsibility of staff members to avail themselves of all the educational and material resources that the library puts at their disposal and to develop an attitude toward their work that makes awareness of ergonomics an ongoing concern. Although the supervisor is assigned the task of overseeing the day-to-day operations of the unit to ensure correct ergonomic practices, it is ultimately up to individual staff to engage in the kind of personal monitoring that only he or she can do. This includes routinely taking breaks and lunch periods and developing a concern for the proper use of equipment. It is important to emphasize that break periods are for time *away* from the keyboard and should not be used to check E-mail or play computer games.

To the extent that a staff member is free to arrange tasks independently, he or she should integrate online and offline activities in such a manner as to avoid repetitive strain. The staff member also should not treat his or her work area passively. When staff feel that there are deficiencies in either the design or furnishing of a workstation, that should be brought to the attention of the supervisor. Staff members should also be aware that outside activities can contribute to their risk of injury. Many activities ranging from sports such as tennis to knitting or playing a musical instrument are potential sources of risk and should be approached with the same awareness of sound ergonomic practices.

It cannot be emphasized strongly enough that staff members should not ignore pain. Whenever discomfort arises and there is any possibility that the tasks being performed or the equipment being used contribute to it, the staff member should report the situation to the appropriate supervisor. Often simple remedial actions can rectify the situation before any serious injury occurs. Repetitive strain injuries occur over time. Early diagnosis and treatment are the best means of prevention.

Problem-Resolution Procedures

The second major section of the Harvard ergonomics program deals with problem-resolution procedures. Despite the emphasis placed on prevention in the sections dealing with the rights and responsibilities of staff members at all levels, there is still a need to address the various problems that will inevitably arise. These will normally take the form of complaints about workstation design or reports of injury. In either case a well-defined set of procedures will ensure that problems are dealt with appropriately and that all parties are satisfied that all possible steps are being taken to deal with the situation.

In the Harvard College Library ergonomic problems that cannot be easily remedied within a unit are referred to Harvard College Library Human Resources for resolution. Human Resources, in turn, avails itself of the resources of the Harvard University Office of Environmental Health and Safety, which has industrial hygienists who evaluate work sites, equipment purchases, and work routines. The office serves as a conduit for information about university ergonomics policies and the standards promulgated by agencies such as OSHA (Occupational Safety and Health Administration) and ANSI (American National Standards Institute). Human

Resources also acts as the intermediary when an ergonomic injury is so serious that it must be referred to the university's Disabilities Claims Unit. After receiving and approving a claim for disability, the Disabilities Claims Unit assumes responsibility for the management of the case until such time as the staff member is cleared for a return to normal work assignments by the appropriate medical personnel.

Site Visits

The problem-resolution process is used whenever a situation cannot be remedied locally. The complaint may refer to a worksite situation that a staff member feels may lead to undue exposure to ergonomic hazards or when a staff member may be experiencing pain and may suspect that an injury may already have occurred. In the former case, Human Resources puts in motion the procedures for a site visit. The Office of Environmental Health and Safety is contacted, and an appointment for a site visit is made. The staff member making the complaint, the staff member's supervisor, a representative from Human Resources, and the industrial hygienist must attend.

The site visit consists of a detailed examination of both the staff member's work habits and the conditions under which the work is performed. The hygienist begins by asking the staff member for a description of the nature of the problem and then for a detailed description of the work performed and the staff member's perceptions relative to the potential problems in the work environment. In addition, the hygienist questions the staff member about existing health complaints and any treatment he or she may be receiving. The evaluation of the workstation includes an assessment of the illumination available to the workstation and an estimation of both direct and reflected glare. Screen and copy height are noted as well as the operator's distance from the computer screen and the position of the keyboard and mouse. Chair height, backrest height and position, and the height and depth of the chair pan are other important factors. When the evaluation has been completed, the hygienist will make some initial recommendations. In addition, a written report is made, and copies are sent to the staff member, the supervisor, Human Resources, and Harvard College Library facilities in the event that the purchase of equipment is recommended.

Recommendations

Although there is no requirement that the Harvard College Library follow the recommendations of the industrial hygienists, in practice the rate of compliance is virtually 100 percent. Typical recommendations are for equipment such as glare screens, copy holders, new chairs, or improved lighting. If the staff member complains of eye irritation, an eye exam is recommended, and if in the judgment of the hygienist the eye problems could have been caused by a deficiency in the workstation design, the library will pay for an eye exam at the University Health Services plus a specified amount toward corrective lenses. The industrial hygienist also follows up with the staff member to see if there is any improvement and recommends further action if necessary. The industrial hygienist may also recommend changes in the staff member's job routine, such as the integration of noncomputer tasks, and makes clear the importance of observing proper rest pauses. If for some reason the staff member does not agree with the results of the site visit, he or she may request additional steps, including a second site visit. After the implementation of the industrial hygienist's recommendations, it is the responsibility of the staff member and his or her supervisor to continue to monitor the situation.

After an Injury

In the event that the staff member indicates an injury has occurred, there are additional routines to follow. The first is to fill out an accident report. At Harvard, the accident report is a university form. (One unfortunate aspect of typical university accident forms is that they are tailored to sudden accidents, such as falling off a ladder, rather than to conditions that develop over time, as is the case with repetitive strain injuries. Changing the accident report to reflect the nature of this new type of injury is one of the future goals at Harvard.)

The accident report is forwarded to the Disabilities Claims Unit so it may begin to document the staff member's case in anticipation of workers' compensation being necessary. Any injury involving five or more days of absence from work must be reported to the state.

The Massachusetts State Department of Industrial Accidents has established deadlines for notification and penalties for noncompliance. In Massachusetts, the university is fined if it does not file state forms within seven days of the fifth day of lost time due to a work-related disability. In addition to the accident report, the staff member is advised to see a physician as soon as possible. After these two steps have been taken, a site visit is arranged according to the procedures described previously. After this has been completed and the written reports received, the parties involved—namely the injured staff member, the staff member's supervisor, and Human Resources—must meet to determine a course of action for the duration of the injury. It should be noted that support staff at Harvard are represented by the Harvard Union of Clerical and Technical Workers, AFSCME (American Federation of State, County, and Municipal Employees), AFL-CIO. Staff members may request that union representatives be present at site visits and meetings dealing with the disposition of their claims.

At Harvard, case management is assigned to a consultant from the Disability Claims Unit for all work-related injuries involving lost time from work and for all repetitive stress injuries regardless of whether work time has been lost or not. The consultant inputs the accident report into the workers' compensation database and thereafter enters additional information as the case proceeds. Next, the consultant contacts the claimant to research the details of the claim, confirm medical treatment, and explain procedures and paperwork. The consultant may seek information concerning the possibility that activities outside work may be causing or contributing factors.

After consulting with the staff member, the consultant contacts Human Resources. Again the details of the claim are reviewed and the information on the accident report is confirmed. The consultant also inquires about any other outstanding personnel issues that may have a bearing on the case to be sure that the accident claim is not part of a larger problem situation that needs to be addressed in conjunction with the injury itself. Finally, the consultant obtains a copy of the staff member's job description and determines whether the staff member was paid for lost time. The consultant also receives copies of all pertinent medical records. On the basis of this accumulated information, the consultant makes a determination of the appropriateness of the claim.

For a workers' compensation claim to be accepted, duties performed on the job must be the major contributor to the documented disability. For disabilities lasting less than five days, a procedure is established with the department to confirm a return to work. In the event of longer absences or the need for a gradual return to a full work schedule, an appropriate plan is arranged in cooperation with the staff member, department head, and Human Resources. If desired, the Disability Claims Unit will assign a job rehabilitation specialist to assist in job redesign to ensure a reasonable and timely resolution.

Return to Work

When an injury is involved, the diagnosis and recommendations of the staff member's physician are the guiding factors. Before steps can be taken to remedy workstation conditions or job design, the physician must first certify that the staff member has indeed suffered a work-related injury and recommend what types of work, if any, the staff member may continue to perform during the course of rehabilitation. In addition, the physician is asked to provide details of the recommended rehabilitation program, including the anticipated return to a normal work schedule. If the staff member cannot return to the job, the management of the case is handled by the consultant from the Disability Claims Unit until a return to work is contemplated or a replacement of the staff member is necessary.

On the other hand, if something less than a total cessation of work is recommended, the involved parties—staff member, supervisor, and Human Resources—must work out an appropriate course of action that is in the interests of both the staff member and the library and that falls within the recommendations of the physician. Staff members are always accorded leave time to attend physical therapy sessions if prescribed by the physician. Any other recommendations of the physician are also followed. In some cases physicians have recommended more frequent or longer breaks and the performance of various types of mild exercises, such as stretching during these breaks. Corrective equipment such as wrist braces is purchased. In one case a staff member was suffering from an eye disorder that was being aggravated by computer work. On the recommendation of a specialist, a 21-inch monitor was ordered. If the Office of Environmental Health and Safety identifies any deficiencies in the work environment, corrective measures are taken.

The supervisor and the staff member should also attempt at this stage to evaluate the current job description to determine if any changes in assignments might introduce a degree of relief from offending activities. However, in the typical technical services department today there exists only a limited number of noncomputer-related activities. The supervisor must avoid shifting all of these activities to the injured staff member. By doing this, the supervisor may shift most or all of the noncomputer work away from healthy staff members, rendering their jobs more hazardous and running the risk of additional injuries in the future. Adjusting the work routine of injured staff members is important, but the supervisor must not lose sight of the needs of the staff as a whole.

Another serious problem for managers is the case of an injured staff member who can perform some kinds of work, but not the duties that were being performed at the time of the injury. Again, the number and variety of noncomputer jobs is limited. In addition, other activities such as wanding, stamping, or shelving may also strain injured body parts. Human Resources has introduced as a part of the current ergonomics policy a new light duty alternative project work statement:

> In the event that a staff member is advised by a physician to significantly limit or refrain totally from the use of a computer, HCL Human Resources will make every attempt to solicit temporary alternative project work from departments within the HCL in accordance with the physician's stated recommendations. Such work will involve noncomputer work and will be deemed temporary until the person is able to return to his or her regular job and/or upon completion of the specific project. Light duty alternative project work may come from a variety of sources and will be reviewed periodically.[7]

Another alternative is job sharing. This can range from simply working on another job for a few hours a week to actually holding two separate part-time jobs that add up to a full-time job. Of course the staff member who has a computer-intensive job should seek a second assignment that has little or no computer work, if possible. One common form of job sharing is between cataloging and the reference desk. Work at the reference desk can be a necessary relief from intensive keyboarding and a way to enhance the cataloger's insight into the context of cataloging.

Once an alternative schedule has been arranged and a return date to normal duties determined, the problem-resolution procedure has run its course. All that remains is to implement the kind of ongoing follow-up and monitoring that help to ensure that there will be no recurrence of the injury. Placing staff members in noncomputer-intensive positions, even for relatively short periods of time, is not an easy task and will only grow more difficult as the move toward increased automation continues. Nevertheless, it is necessary to make every attempt to identify such opportunities and to integrate them into the work routine, not only for injured staff but also to provide variation for healthy staff members.

Ergonomics Policy Statements

The final section of the Harvard College Library ergonomics program consists of appendixes covering policy statements from units within the library and in other parts of the university that are involved in the ergonomics process. Gathering this type of material would seem to be a fairly straightforward matter, but in fact it was one of the more difficult and time-consuming aspects of putting together a program. Representatives from each unit were invited to meetings of the ergonomics committee and questioned about their procedures. In some cases units did not have written policy documents or their documents were obsolete, and so they were asked to prepare something for the committee to include in its own program. A more difficult situation arose when there proved to be contradictions among different units. These differences had to be worked out with the committee acting as intermediary. In addition, when the program was actually being written, any changes in these sections had to be reported back to the unit in question for approval.

In its final form the program document contained the following appendixes:

1. Computer-Related Injuries
2. Workstation Design
3. Eye Exam and Glasses Policy
4. Guidelines for Purchasing Ergonomic Items
5. Environmental Health and Safety Workstation Evaluation Program
6. Workers' Compensation Procedures
7. Standing Committee on Ergonomic Issues and Policy (a description of the committee's structure and function)

When the ergonomics program was complete, printed copies were distributed to all staff members, and a copy is included in the orientation package given to new employees. In addition, there are plans to make it available online on the Harvard College Library's home page at a later date.

Preparing an ergonomics program of this sort is a difficult and time-consuming process, but the benefits are numerous. To begin with, it is essential that all members of the community speak the same language in terms of ergonomic issues. Staff members should not receive different treatment in similar situations, and assuring the staff that this is indeed the case will make it easier to obtain the cooperation necessary to establish an environment of awareness and trust for the avoidance of ergonomic hazards. Although mistakes in the early stages of automation brought into focus the need for a detailed problem-resolution procedure, in the long run the focus has to be on the implementation and monitoring of the types of proactive measures that minimize the incidence of injury. At the same time, some people are naturally prone to this type of injury and will have difficulties under even the best of circumstances, thus necessitating the maintenance of a sound problem-resolution procedure. In the majority of cases, however, sound design principles and reasonable job design should minimize problems.

The work of the library's ergonomics committee did not end when the program document was complete. Procedures for updating the document have to be devised and implemented. Changes in the field have to be monitored as well. Equipment is constantly being redesigned to achieve better ergonomic functioning. Health programs designed to either prevent or treat ergonomic injuries continue to be developed, and new software products that advise the computer user when to take breaks and, in many cases, furnish ergonomic advice, continue to appear. All of these developments need to be monitored, evaluated, and made known to the library community.

The field of computer ergonomics is in its early stages. Much remains to be done, and library ergonomics committees should play important roles in making known to ergonomists and health care professionals what their needs are and in introducing the work of these professionals to the library community.

Finally, it should be noted that ergonomic concerns in libraries extend beyond the computer workstation to the areas of the library where staff are performing other types of physical tasks entailing the risk of injury. Computer ergonomics has been the hot media item for some time now, but these other jobs can also result in injury. Both the personal suffering and the costs to the operation can be equally serious.

Notes

1. Nancy Barbour, *Computer Science Newsletter* 5, no. 3 (Nov. 1994): 2.

2. Don Sellers, *Zap!: How Your Computer Can Hurt You—And What You Can Do about It.* Ed. by Stephen F. Roth (Berkeley, Calif.: Peachpit, 1994), 71–2.

3. Barbour, *Computer Science Newsletter,* 2.

4. Lauren Andrew Hebert, *The Neck-Arm-Hand Book: The Master Guide for Eliminating Cumulative Trauma Disorders from the Work Place* (Bangor, Maine: IMPACC, 1989), 9.

5. Barbour, *Computer Science Newsletter,* 2.

6. Sellers, *Zap!,* 71–2.

7. Harvard College Library Standing Committee on Ergonomic Issues and Policy, *Harvard College Library Ergonomics Program and Policies* (Cambridge, Mass.: Harvard College Library, 1996), 10.

APPENDIX
▼
Resources for Ergonomics Research

Web Sites

CTD News Online
  http://ctdnews.com/

ErgoWeb
  http://www.ergoweb.com

NIOSH
  http://www.cdc.gov/niosh/homepage.html

A Patient's Guide to Carpal Tunnel Syndrome
  http://www.sechrest.com/mmg/cts/ctsintro.html

Typing Injuries Index
  http://alumni.caltech.edu/~dank/typing-archive.html

Wallach, Dan S. (1995) "Typing Injury FAQ: General Information"
  http://www.cs.princeton.edu/~dwallach/tifaq/general.html

Mailing List Subscription Requests

Computers & Health
  listserv@iubvm.ucs.indiana.edu

ErgoWeb-list
  http://www.ergoweb.com

RSI-East
  listserv@maelstrom.stjohns.edu

RSI-UK
  listserver@tictac.demon.co.uk

Safety-L
  safety-l@safnet.com

Sorehand
  listserv@ltssrv1.ucsf.edu

US Consumer Product Safety Commission
  listproc@cpsc.gov

Usenet Newsgroups

misc.health.injuries.rsi.misc

misc.health.injuries.rsi.moderated

Monographs

Dul, Jan. *Ergonomics for Beginners: A Quick Reference Guide*. Washington, D.C.: Taylor & Francis, 1993.

Food and Allied Service Trades Dept., AFL-CIO. *Ergonomics: Human Engineering in the Workplace: A Sourcebook*. Washington, D.C.: The Department, 1993.

Godnig, Edward C., and John S. Hacunda. *Computers & Visual Stress: Staying Healthy*. Grand Rapids, Mich.: Abacus, 1991.

Grandjean, Etienne. *Ergonomics in Computerized Offices*. New York: Taylor & Francis, 1987.

Hebert, Lauren Andrew. *The Neck-Arm-Hand Book: The Master Guide for Eliminating Cumulative Trauma Disorders from the Work Place*. Bangor, Maine: IMPACC, 1989.

Imrhan, Sheik N. *Help! My Computer Is Killing Me!: Your Complete Guide to Preventing Aches and Pains in the Computer Workplace*. Dallas: Taylor, 1996.

Moore, Deborah J. *Manager's Guide to Workplace Ergonomics*. Madison, Conn.: Business & Legal Reports, 1991.

National Safety Council. *Ergonomics: A Practical Guide*. Chicago: The Council, 1993.

Noro, K., and A. S. Imada, eds. *Participatory Ergonomics*. New York: Taylor & Francis, 1991.

Oborne, David J., ed. *Person-Centered Ergonomics: A Brantonian View of Human Factors*. Washington, D.C.: Taylor & Francis, 1993.

Ostrom, Lee T. *Creating the Ergonomically Sound Workplace: From Training to Performance in the Twenty-First Century. Set 1, Designing the Work Environment for Optimum Performance*. San Francisco: Jossey-Bass, 1993.

Pascarelli, Emil, and Deborah Quilter. *Repetitive Strain Injury: A Computer User's Guide*. New York: John Wiley & Sons, 1994.

Peterson, Baird, and Richard Patten. *The Ergonomic PC: Creating a Healthy Computing Environment*. New York: McGraw-Hill, 1995.

Roughton, James E. *Ergonomic Problems in the Workplace: A Guide to Effective Management*. Rockville, Md.: Government Institutes, 1995.

Sellers, Don. *Zap!: How Your Computer Can Hurt You—And What You Can Do about It*. Ed. by Stephen F. Roth. Berkeley, Calif.: Peachpit, 1994.

Stramler, James H. *The Dictionary for Human Factors/Ergonomics*. Boca Raton, Fla.: CRC, 1993.

Veer, Gerrit C. van der, Sebastiano Bagnara, and Gerard A. M. Kempen, eds. *Cognitive Ergonomics: Contributions from Experimental Psychology*. New York: North-Holland, 1992.

Journals

Applied Ergonomics. Guildford, Surrey, Eng.: IPC Science and Technology, 1969– .

Computers in Libraries. Westport, Conn.: Meckler, 1989– .

Ergonomics: The Official Publication of the Ergonomics Research Society. London: Taylor & Francis, 1957– .

Human Factors. Baltimore, Md.: Johns Hopkins University, 1958– .

Industrial Ergonomics. Amsterdam, New York: Elsevier, 1986– .

Safety & Health. Chicago: National Safety Council, 1987– .

CHAPTER 11

Training

Julia C. Blixrud
Association of Research Libraries

▼ The successful deployment of technical services workstations (TSWs) will depend on the effective use of those workstations by library staff. Training must be an integral part of the planning for development and implementation of TSWs in libraries. Robin Guy, of the National Library of Scotland, writing about the development of in-house training programs for automated systems, notes that hardware and software are capable of nothing without trained personnel. Moreover, he cautions us that obtaining a true level of expertise requires not just planning and organization but also human and financial resources. Investing vast sums in hardware and software only to forgo appropriate sums for trainers and training equipment is short-sighted and negligent. Offering proper training for all staff ensures that the capital investment in equipment is well used, ensures that staff have a complete understanding of the role of the computer in the organization, and helps ensure job satisfaction and commitment to the organization and its goals.[1]

What Constitutes Training?

There are as many definitions of training as there are trainers and articles about training. An American Society for Training and Development (ASTD) publication on technical and skills training quotes Douglas Barney, a trainer who wrote in the *Handbook of Human Resource Development* that technical human resources development consists of precisely those learning systems that provide job-related knowledge and the specific skills required to design, operate, and maintain modern technology.[2] Training can include providing information; it can assist workers through instruction to perform a specific task effectively and efficiently; or it can teach workers how to perform a particular job.

Training can take many forms. Professional training includes the generally accepted practice of instructional systems design (ISD) originally developed by and for the military. It is based on the belief that training is most effective when it provides learners with a clear statement of what they must be able to do as a result of training and how their performance will be evaluated. The classic ISD training model consists of the components of analysis, design, development, implementation, and evaluation.[3] The model encompasses a thorough understanding of adult learning styles, training methods, and presentation skills.

Why Train?

While training is probably no substitute for experience, the rapid pace of technological change requires that organizations constantly retool themselves. Libraries are no exception.

As part of an extensive strategic planning process, the Task Force on Staff and Organizational Development for Harvard College Library assumed that the library had as part of its mission the task of preparing staff to function both effectively and proactively in a rapidly changing environment. Harvard's task force recommended a strategy to acknowledge the value of staff to the library and to encourage learning at all levels. Cross-training and retraining for new responsibilities as responses to new priorities and developing new skills was to be encouraged.[4]

Training is considered a key ingredient for organizational success. Business writers who survey managers in all types of organizations report that respondents describe their staff as organizational resources that must be developed and trained. Organizations use training to

- ▶ respond to new technologies
- ▶ react to changes in technology
- ▶ change behavior or attitudes
- ▶ reduce fear of change
- ▶ solve problems
- ▶ improve organizational effectiveness
- ▶ adjust to organizational changes
- ▶ improve productivity
- ▶ improve quality
- ▶ increase accountability
- ▶ develop skills of individual workers
- ▶ increase staff skills to a new level for present or future work assignments

For training to be effective, it must relate to the organization's vision, mission, and values. Changing organizational missions are strong motivations for training. The mission statement for Harvard College Library states,

> More members of the library's staff will carry multiple responsibilities that cut across the lines separating traditional functions. Both technological competence and solid traditional skills will be required. There will be an emphasis on collaboration and developing shared understandings and shared strategies. The College Library's growing dynamism, broadening concerns, and new initiatives will require a major investment in ongoing training and staff development at all levels.[5]

Trends in Training

As organizations move to embrace the concept of learning organizations, popularized by Peter Senge in *The Fifth Discipline,* there has been a parallel movement from training as an input activity to performance as an output measure. Training is no longer seen as an isolated event or series of activities, but it is considered an important component in overall organizational performance. Organizational learning is the only sustainable competitive advantage in existence today.

Management support for training helps generate organizational loyalty, builds morale, and leads to more-productive workers. That direct investment in staff development is tangible evidence that management is interested in its workers as individuals. In some institutions, technologically empowered jobs will enable employees to assume greater responsibility and add more value to the organization.

These training trends, important for workers, are also leading to an increase in employer expectations. When training is touted as a means to improve an organization's effectiveness, administrators look to tangible evidence that training has "paid off." It behooves training managers to identify some means to calculate the benefits accrued from substantial training investments. (The American Society for Training and Development's flagship journal, *Training & Development,* routinely carries articles that either address the need to calculate return-on-investment or provide new or tested techniques on how to measure training results.)

Training Investments

Much of the positive writing about the importance of training has been contradicted by evidence of the lack of support for training in actual practice. Tom Peters stated it most fervently in the 1980s when he said that our (lack of) investment in training was a national disgrace—but not surprising. "People-as-our-most-important-asset," in his view (and Dilbert's, too, we might add), is not something that management has always really and sincerely believed.[6]

U.S. corporations have, however, responded to Peters's challenge to train. *Investor's Business Daily* reported in April 11, 1995, that the global market for information technology training and education was rising by 13 percent a year and would double by the year 2000. The American Society for Training and Development Web site notes that it is difficult to report confidently the precise amount of money spent annually on "formal" training. Reports range from $30 billion to $66 billion. Using 1980 census data and data from the Bureau of Labor Statistics, ASTD estimated in its most recent comprehensive study that $180 billion was spent on informal (at the workstation) training and an additional $30 billion spent for formal classes. ASTD notes that companies spend an average of 1.5 percent of payroll budgets on formal training. More significantly, companies that place a high priority on training tend to spend 2 percent or more. ASTD's recommendation: Companies should invest a minimum of 2 percent of their payroll in training.[7]

Corporate America is leading the trend to provide continuous training, professional development, and employee skill certification. Motorola, Intel, and Disney are well-known examples of corporations that have highly developed training programs. Don Tapscott reports that the knowledge economy requires lifelong learning. He maintains that the thesis articulated in *The Monster under the Bed,* by Stan Davis and Jim Botkin, says it best, arguing that education, once the responsibility of the church and then of government, now is increasingly the responsibility of business "because it is business that ends up having to train knowledge workers." Davis and Botkin calculate that the increase in formal, budgeted training grew by 126 million additional hours in 1992.[8]

The library picture is not as bright. Comparable data on library expenditures for staff training is not collected, and the library literature reveals no corollary for increased development of technical training programs. In a 1987 article about developing a staff training program for the implementation of an integrated library system (ILS), Stuart Glogoff and James Flynn reported that a literature search for articles on training for an ILS turned up few citations. What little discussion they found was mostly superficial treatments of planning, procuring, and implementing automated systems, but not training as such. Moreover, few authors did more than admit the need for training did exist.[9] A review of the literature since then reveals a paucity of information on staff training. Anecdotal evidence (for example, conversations on Internet lists) suggests training is conducted in libraries, but it is not formal, comprehensive, well-conceived, well-designed, outcome-based, or evaluated. Rather, it is conducted in an ad hoc manner to address a specific system implementation or a staffing situation.

Roy Tennant says that staff is a library's single most expensive resource and deserves appropriate treatment: "Any investment made in retooling staff skills to meet the challenges and opportunities of the electronic age will be repaid many times over in better service to clientele and a vital and engaged workforce."[10] But additional funds for training of this sort are scarce and make it necessary to develop these programs by cannibalizing existing resources. Nevertheless, training is more important than ever and crucial if we are to become more effective. Peters argues passionately that, if libraries expect to meet future technological changes, they should not cut the training budget in time of crisis, but rather increase it![11]

Current Sources for Library Technical Training

Libraries have devised a variety of means to handle training. Terry Smith explored how libraries were approaching training for new staff and compiled a list of training aids for OCLC users. Included in the list were one-on-one training, OCLC documentation, computer-based training modules (CBTs), regional network training, guides, reference cards, online help, workbooks, local guides, professional literature, meetings, informal contact, Internet lists, and library schools.[12] There are several sources of technical training for library staff in the United States. Certainly the major portion of staff training is done in-house by supervisors or colleagues. Much of that training is one-on-one. This process involves two individuals sitting next to each other at a computer and working through a series of steps to complete a task.

Some libraries have established key trainers, usually a staff expert (de facto or named) who has developed the expertise in either a system or an application and is a resource person for other staff. It is quite common to have technically competent individuals serve as trainers in libraries. Unfortunately, library managers and others often assume (sometimes incorrectly) that individuals with technical skills have training and presentation skills as well. Librarians should be cautious when asking a technical expert to serve as a trainer unless that expert either has a demonstrated capability for training or has had requisite training experience in how to be a trainer. *Technical expertise does not guarantee training expertise.*

To solve the problem of lack of trainer expertise, "train the trainer" programs have become quite popular. Many are led by management consultants (including former professional trainers) or training firms. Library networks, consortia, and professional associations also have sponsored programs to enhance trainer skills. The state of Maryland has had a model program for several years. The programs focus on helping potential trainers learn such things as how to analyze user needs, develop learning objectives, and acquire group facilitation skills. These trainer skills, added to their technical knowledge, increase the level of quality in staff trainers.

Many libraries have set up training committees to address technical training needs. Most research libraries have established staff committees or task forces to coordinate training in the use of the library's local integrated library system. An ARL SPEC Kit on technical services staff training noted that 90 percent of respondents to the Association of Research Libraries survey "planned, prepared and provided technical services staff training" when adopting an online catalog.[13] Harvard College Library is an example of a library that has expanded its staff training and development program to be part of an overall organizational change agenda.[14]

Formal training departments are available in some organizations. The Technical Processing and Automation Instruction Office (TPAIO) at the Library of Congress is responsible for providing training in the areas of technical processing, automated technical processing, and microcomputer software packages. The office trains about 3,000 staff per year. An extensive course catalog has been developed and is provided to staff regularly. The schedule also is available online through the Library's Web site. TPAIO also conducts "train the trainer" courses for both group and one-on-one trainers.

Regional library networks on the whole conduct much of the technical training for library staff in the United States. In fiscal year 1994–1995 OCLC regional networks trained 13,500 attendees in 1,025 training sessions.[15] These training sessions cover everything from personal computer training (for example, DOS, Windows, and UNIX) to OCLC services (cataloging, interlibrary loan, etc.) and Internet use (for example, navigation, HTML). Regional networks also work with other groups to present technical courses addressing topics currently of interest in their member libraries.

Vendors can provide training for new system installations. Often this training is bundled into the costs of providing the new system (or the training is provided free with purchase of the system). (The ARL SPEC Kit respondents indicated that vendor training did not generally meet the needs of the library.) With the advent of second generation systems or implementation of subsequent systems, libraries use each other and vendor user groups to augment their vendor and local training.

Schools of library or information science also may include technical training in some of their courses. Many schools, indeed many academic institutions, are now requiring some level of computer expertise for all students.

Professional library associations at the local, state, regional, or national level hold programs and conduct institutes on technical topics of current interest to their members. Some of these events include training, and event leaders may be either professional trainers or volunteers with a strong interest in the topic.

Online sources of training information are becoming more popular. Two general sites for training information are the American Society for Training and Development (http://www.astd.org) and the Bureau of National Affairs (http://www.bna.com/bnac). The University of California at San Diego has a Web site, Technical Processing Online Tools (TPOT), that includes online information for all of its technical services operations (http://tpot.ucsd.edu). It provides documentation for its internal policies and procedures and links to external sources and technical documentation that include items of interest to any technical services department. The "Top 200 Technical Services Benefits of Home Page Development" by Barbara Stewart is included at that site. Stewart's recommended sites for technical services use would be useful additions to any library's set of online documentation.

Development of a Technical Services Workstation Training Program

How, then, should library managers design training for TSWs? It is important that they begin to plan and develop their staff training programs in conjunction with their decision to implement TSWs. Since these workstations will be, in most cases, a significant new technology, a careful program development plan should be established. These training programs should follow standard instructional systems design procedures and specifically address adult learning concepts.

Analysis

A thorough needs analysis is the first step in the development of a training program. Include information about the functional capabilities of the workstation (what it can do), who will have any use for the equipment (how they will use it), and who will expect to receive output from the equipment (what they will get from it). Gather information from all sources about what specific training is needed. Identify and describe the skills to be learned and any problems to be solved. Include identification of differences between what is required and what is already known. Investments in training are costly, and a proper needs assessment can help a library focus its attention on those areas that are most likely to contribute to enhancing the skills of its staff.

Design

Develop a set of learning objectives for each training session. These objectives should address the following questions:

- ▶ Who are the learners?
- ▶ What skills need to be learned?
- ▶ Who will do the training?
- ▶ What instruction methods will be used?
- ▶ Where will the training take place?
- ▶ When will the training be conducted?
- ▶ How will the training be evaluated?

Answers to the questions should be specific, quantifiable, and documented. Some answers will be derived from the needs assessment; others will require additional investigation.

Although the training in TSWs is likely to be specific to the equipment and software purchased, there are common functions that all organizations have to consider. Following is a preliminary list of topics to include in TSW training. They include functions related to the general use of personal computers and networks, and to workstation technology specifically. The order of training topics and the depth of coverage for each topic should be made part of the design component for the training program.

Conceptual Framework

Before beginning any training for a TSW, staff should be introduced to the conceptual framework underlying the workstation. These concepts may include

- ▶ graphical user interface
- ▶ multitasking
- ▶ simultaneous search sessions
- ▶ record transfer
- ▶ record editing
- ▶ cutting and pasting
- ▶ communications software

Many of these concepts may be familiar to staff who work with personal computers. The important training issue is how they are used within the TSW environment.

Hardware

Staff will need to be introduced to new hardware such as personal computers, printers, and local area networks. If familiarity with personal computers is needed, training on the equipment can be conducted by nonlibrary staff from the computing center or outside training firms.

Software

Much of the time spent in training for TSWs will be devoted to the software: operating systems (for example, DOS or Windows), terminal emulation, use of macros, scripting, managing multiple sessions, and E-mail. Trainers well versed in the operations of the library and the workstation are needed most here.

Internet-Specific Software

The close connection between TSWs and the use of the Internet will require some training in software specific to use of the Internet, particularly Web browsers and file transfer protocol (FTP) clients.

Word Processing

Word processing features such as spell checking may be part of workstations, and training should include overviews of word processing software for staff who have not previously used such software.

Spreadsheets

Workstations will gather new and different data that can be incorporated into spreadsheet programs. Staff may need training in the use of spreadsheets and statistical manipulation.

Database Software

Bibliographic databases are the prominent databases used by technical services staff, but workstations will provide opportunities for the development of other types of databases. These databases may contain management data, or data from bibliographic systems may need to be exported or imported to them. Training in database concepts as well as the specific software may be needed.

External Products

Workstations will come equipped with or be linked to new cataloger tools, and training should be provided for staff who will use these products or programs (for example, Cataloger's Desktop).

OPAC Applications

Each workstation will include connections to a library's online catalog and may offer new means to search and retrieve data from the local catalog. Training in OPAC functionality and use of the workstation to access the OPAC will be required.

Documentation

New documentation in new forms will be made available with TSWs. Training for use and development of documentation, especially the online tools, should be a major training topic. Integration of electronic documentation with paper tools and the workstation itself are conceptual training issues.

Help Sources

Workstation help will be available from many sources such as expert users (in person or online), tutorials, context-based help from software, etc. Staff should be trained in locating and using help features.

Troubleshooting Guides

Diagnostics and troubleshooting guides are often overlooked topics for training sessions. Many adult learners, however, appreciate knowing how to determine what kind of help they need, and an overview of basic diagnostic techniques will ensure their comfort in using a new workstation.

Development

As part of the learning objectives, each session should have an identified set of training methods. There are a myriad of methods available to instructors today, and choices can be made based on the needs assessment, knowledge of the learners, funds available, and training environment considerations. There is a fuzzy line between teaching technology and technology as a teaching tool. Hands-on learning will only make this fuzzy line fuzzier still.[16]

New forms of technology have resulted in many new training tools as well as new forms of training, particularly for technical training on new technologies. The key to an effective program is matching learners with the most appropriate methods, such as student-directed or teacher-directed methods.

Following are some commonly used methods and how they might be applied to a TSW training session.

Formal Group Training

A common method within formal group training is the familiar class-room instruction model, often in a lecture or modified lecture format. Training tools include demonstrations, facilitated group discussions, student practice, or role-playing. The training can be classroom-based, computer-based, or conducted through distance education. Group hands-on training is often the first, and sometimes the only, method for technical training used both by in-house and external trainers. This type of training can take advantage of many technologies: projected demonstrations, video, high-definition television, and even virtual reality.

One-on-One Training

Often used for on-the-job instruction, one-on-one training can be a formal set of exercises monitored by an instructor or just one-on-one coaching by a knowledgeable colleague. It is conducted in a hands-on mode and is the most popular form of training for library staff using automated systems. Tools include practice exercises and scripts. One-on-one training is particularly effective when combined with on-the-job skill practicing.

Team Training

Learning organizations emphasize teamwork. A new form of training is team training, which is a combination of group and one-on-one training. Team members work together collectively to learn new procedures and techniques. Training plans are developed by the group, and group members may take turns training each other, functioning as key trainers or expert trainers for a specific function. This is a particularly effective technique when implementing new technologies since the training experience is shared.

Self-Study

Computer-based training is considered one cost-effective way to reach large numbers of workers without imposing schedules or training times on them. These methods work best with individual staff members who are self-directed and prefer a programmed instruction or a desktop training approach. Additional training tools include software tutorials and audio and video tapes. Self-study allows individuals to work at their own pace, but through a guided experience, and may be augmented with hands-on instructor-led training. Staff with high-end workstations may take advantage of desktop video and conferencing systems where instructors can be contacted when needed.

Mentoring

Mentoring, or pairing an experienced staff member with a new learner in an informal arrangement, may work for those individuals who do not want a full hands-on training session but are not completely comfortable with self-directed learning. Tools used here are similar to those used for self-study.

Documentation

Documentation is one of the most important tools for any method of training. For TSW training, documentation should include user manuals, examples, and quick guides. All documentation requires regular updating to remain a useful tool. Documentation can be printed or online; a significant advantage to online documentation is that it can be tailored individually for specific jobs or types of users.

Implementation

Effective technical training involves an understanding of adult learning. Adult learners differ from other learners with different motivations and require different curricula designs and instructional settings.[17] Preparation is essential when training the adult learner. There are several key concepts for adult learning that will be useful when training for TSWs.

Learning takes place in a variety of ways: through the spoken word, from written text, from visual images, and from motor action. Adults learn best when they have a need to know. They can be willing learners but are just as likely to be resistant learners, especially if they have to unlearn previous practices. Dennis Reynolds describes problem trainees as falling into four categories: those afraid of the system, those resentful of having to learn it, those who approach it with abandon, and those with such a mental block they cannot learn to use it effectively.[18] Willing learners and not-so-willing learners will benefit from the application of the following principles:

Learning must be appropriate.

Adult learners need to know the *why* before they are willing to learn the *how*. Training must be relevant to their work. TSW training should begin with a focus on the larger picture of how the workstations will provide staff with a better work experience and how the workstations add value to the organization. This training can be conducted during the planning phase for workstations. Since things learned at the time of need are better learned and retained than things taught before or after the need, actual workstation functions should be conducted in training sessions at the time of workstation installation.

Learners must be motivated.

Positive, nonthreatening management support for training and enthusiastic trainers will help overcome resistant learners. Training sessions should end with real-world implementation plans so learners feel the time spent in training is worthwhile.

Learning must use multiple senses.

Much of the information humans process is visual and, in training for TSWs, learners will best learn though visual means: looking at screen displays, conducting actions by use of a keyboard or mouse, and watching the resulting screen changes. Hands-on experiences should be coupled with classroom lectures, demonstrations, and group discussions to bring information to learners through different sensory experiences.

Learning must be active.

Training for TSWs must be hands-on. Learners should have the opportunity to practice exercises, obtain feedback, and reinforce their new skills by repeating the exercises.

Learning time must be kept short and simple (KISS principle).

Adult learners are particularly sensitive to training information overload. Often a new system has an abundance of features, and trainers and learners expect that all features will have to be learned right away. This leads to frustration for the trainer who never has enough time to provide the necessary instruction and to frustration for the learner who feels overwhelmed with information about functions that may only be used infrequently. Break the training into components, and make each component relevant to a specific training event.

Learning must feature repetition.

Repeat, recap, and *review* are essential watchwords for technical training. Since there is so much to learn, information must be presented in small chunks, repeated at intervals throughout the training session, and reviewed until it becomes very familiar to the learner. Things learned first and last are best remembered. Technical training should be conducted close to the time when the system will be used because recall is an important component of adult learning.

Learning must include retraining.

Retraining is a must and constant skill broadening should be a basic goal. A subset perhaps of repetition, but retraining in a technical setting is critical. No matter how much training is conducted when a workstation is implemented, retraining will be necessary to remind staff of features used infrequently, to update staff on new features added, or to provide opportunities for staff to share new insights into the use of the workstation.

Evaluation

No training program is complete without an evaluation component. Evaluations identify what works and what does not work from both the instructor and trainee perspective. Surveying trainees immediately after completing a training session is the most common evaluation method. While useful to gauge the immediate reaction of the trainees to the training experience, an evaluation form is not the most appropriate tool to determine if learning was accomplished. A better evaluation technique would be to conduct a test of the various functions taught to see that they are performed correctly.

Interviews, surveys, or tests can be conducted immediately after a training experience or after some interval has provided time for the instruction to become assimilated into the trainees' day-to-day work experience. Observation is another technique often used to determine if the objectives of a specific training exercise or program have been met. The instructor may watch work being performed to see if new techniques or instructions conveyed during training are now being followed. Supervisors and trainers may also monitor job performance to determine if instruction has led to improvements in quality or productivity.

There is little evidence that formal assessment processes are conducted for library staff training programs. Slightly over 90 percent of the ARL SPEC Kit respondents indicated they had not evaluated the effectiveness of their training.[19] It is noteworthy that the library literature for bibliographic instruction programs often contains information about an evaluation or assessment component, but those training programs are being conducted for library users, not staff.

If assessment for an individual learner takes place, it is usually done as part of a staff evaluation or performance appraisal program. Assessments of overall training programs are generally done by institutions when they are undergoing either technical system or organizational changes, not as part of a library's general strategic plan. These assessments are often conducted using survey questionnaire techniques.

Assessment can be carried out in several additional ways. The training literature is replete with examples of tools, formal courses, consultants, books, and even advice about conducting formal training program assessment. The American Society for Training and Development is a rich resource for information on training program evaluation.

Training Obstacles

Training programs face a set of obstacles and common mistakes. Recognizing the existence of potential barriers and devising strategies to overcome them are a part of training program development. Justifiable impediments must and can be addressed and problems avoided with good planning.

The employer's concern that training is time consuming is legitimate. The process of developing staff training programs does take time. Most effective programs cannot be developed overnight and may require pretesting and revision before their deployment. Underestimating the time it takes to develop and implement a training program is a common obstacle.

Training also takes time away from "real work." Employees often resist attending training sessions because they feel that training either implies they do not know how to do their current job or that the organization does not value the contribution they make to their current job. Libraries need to assure staff that training and retraining are important components of their jobs.

Training programs can be expensive. They can take up significant library resources in the form of program expenditures and staff time. Libraries should identify cost-effective ways to train their staff. This can be accomplished by breaking training into component parts and then partnering or working with local groups, outsourcing some of the training, and negotiating good contracts for provision of training services.

Organizations sometimes try to use training to solve a problem, but the problem cannot be solved by training. There is no doubt that training can easily become the "flavor of the month" solution for any organization. Training does not always work. There are times when the problem is better addressed by policy or procedural changes. Before thinking that training is an answer, be sure to ask the right questions.

Training may be dehumanizing. If adult learning styles are not taken into consideration, staff may feel that the training was too elementary or too advanced. Good needs analysis and use of appropriate training methods should overcome many negative staff reactions to training.

Training may not have any impact on the bottom line and management may decide that it has been oversold. TSWs do have the potential to provide better data and accountability for technical services operations. Libraries must also consider workflow changes before embarking on a training program. Using technology to do the same old things will not necessarily lead to greater efficiencies or increased productivity, and training in that context will not provide any value to the library. Be sure that training expectations are clearly articulated before beginning the program.

Organizations may use the latest, most advanced technology for training but overlook the basics. Waiting for the perfect training technology or forcing a training method onto an inappropriate technology are mistakes that good planning can avoid.

Staff training needs will not be met if the training program is deployed without a needs analysis and some testing. This obstacle can be easily overcome by early contact with staff and pretesting of some training events.

Not budgeting for maintenance or support is a common mistake organizations make when planning new technologies. Libraries should budget for changes and upgrades to the training program as they budget for new technologies.

Elements for Successful Training Programs

As organizations move to acquire the new technologies to make the technical services functions of the library operate more efficiently, training should be on the top of the list of points to consider. No amount of cutting-edge technology will perform adequately unless it is efficiently and effectively used by an enthusiastic worker. Dennis Reynolds noted that preparation and training of staff is the one stage of implementation that may well prove to be the final determinant of success—but it is frequently the stage most likely to be sacrificed. It is precisely staff training, however, that should begin early and be guaranteed continued emphasis and effort.[20]

Staff from the Rutgers University Libraries developed a list of tips for training staff in automated systems. They identified ten elements that are critical to the success of a training program:

1. relevance as perceived by the trainee
2. agreement between the trainer and trainee about objectives
3. agreement between the trainer and trainee about expectations
4. supervisor or high-level manager attendance at training sessions
5. follow-up programs planned jointly by supervisor and trainee
6. blame-free environment for trainees during practice
7. trainee plan for applying newly learned skills
8. trainee practice with another trainee or coach
9. scheduled progress reports from trainees
10. institutional commitment to train a critical mass of staff[21]

The Rutgers authors created a set of pointers for success divided into concept areas of trainers, trainees, program content and design, training environment and schedule, and follow-up. These concept areas are similar to the key areas in instructional design and reinforce the importance of comprehensive planning for effective training.

Successful training depends on three components: organizational commitment, willing learners, and effective trainers. Implementation of TSWs will benefit significantly from a properly designed training program. If library managers encourage technical training as part of the responsibility of a learning organization, staff will more enthusiastically embrace the technology.

Notes

1. Robin Frederick Guy, "Inhouse Training for Information Technology," *Education for Information 7*, no. 1 (Mar. 1989): 23.

2. *First-Rate Technical and Skills Training,* INFO-LINE 706 (Alexandria, Va.: American Society for Training and Development, 1987), 1.

3. *Basic Training for Trainers,* INFO-LINE 808 (Alexandria, Va.: American Society for Training and Development, 1988), 1.

4. Mary Elizabeth Clack, "The Role of Training in the Reorganization of Cataloging Services," *Library Acquisitions: Practice and Theory* 19 (winter 1995): 440.

5. Clack, "The Role of Training," 444.

6. Tom Peters, "Train and Retrain," in *Thriving on Chaos* (New York: HarperPerennial, 1991), 388.

7. See the ASTD Web site at http://www.astd.org.

8. Don Tapscott, *Digital Economy* (New York: McGraw-Hill, 1995), 199–200.

9. Stuart Glogoff and James P. Flynn, "Developing a Systematic In-House Training Program for Integrated Library Systems," *College & Research Libraries* 48 (Nov. 1987): 528.

10. Roy Tennant, "The Virtual Library Foundation: Staff Training and Support," *Information Technology and Libraries* 14, no. 1 (Mar. 1995): 46.

11. Peters, "Train and Retrain," 393.

12. Terry Smith, "Training Technical Services OCLC Users," *OCLC Systems and Services* 10, nos. 2–3 (summer/fall 1994): 50–3.

13. Assocation of Research Libraries, *Training of Technical Services Staff in the Automated Environment,* ARL SPEC Kit 171 (Washington, D.C.: The Association, 1991), 1.

14. Clack, "Role of Training," 439.

15. Susan Olson, "U.S. Regional Networks: an Introduction," *OCLC Newsletter* 218 (Nov./Dec. 1995): 21.

16. Donna L. Kizzier, "Teaching Technology vs. Technology as a Teaching Tool," in *Technology in the Classroom,* National Business Education Yearbook 33 (Reston, Va.: National Business Education Association, 1995), 11.

17. Margie Epple, Judy Gardner, and Robert T. Warwick, "Staff Training and Automated Systems: 20 Tips for Success," *Journal of Academic Librarianship* 18, no. 2 (May 1992): 87.

18. Dennis Reynolds, *Library Automation: Issues and Applications* (New York: Bowker, 1985), 275–6.

19. *Training of Technical Services Staff,* 5.

20. Reynolds, *Library Automation,* 270–1.

21. Epple, "Staff Training," 87–8.

PART

V

The Symbiotic Future
Technical Services Workstations, the Internet, and the World Wide Web

CHAPTER 12

The TSW and Emerging Technologies

A Researcher's Perspective

Diane Vizine-Goetz
OCLC Online Computer Library Center, Inc.

▼ Technical services professionals have shown great skill in automating the routine and not-so-routine tasks they perform by merging powerful hardware platforms with general and library-specific software packages. Their efforts have motivated bibliographic utilities, national libraries, and library automation vendors to step up their efforts to offer cataloging standards and tools in electronic form. The inventiveness and technical savvy of technical services staff is evident in such programs as Gary Strawn's Cataloger's Toolkit, the Electronic Cataloging-in-Publication data-capture facilities, and Harvard College Library's cataloging services department macro-based cataloging routines.

Technical services staff were also among the early adopters of the World Wide Web and now offer an array of resources ranging from interactive training tools to Web-to-Z39.50 accessible databases. The combination of technical services workstations (TSWs), the Internet, and Z39.50 represents an emerging symbiosis for the technical services profession; together they represent more than the sum of their parts. Furthermore, the emerging combinations of Z39.50 and Web interfaces, the so-called WebZ picture, may well be the window through which our patrons will become accustomed to viewing library catalogs.[1] This is all the more amazing in that the Web and Web browsers were virtually unheard of in the library community before the early 1990s, and now they have taken library-land—and much of the rest of the Internet community as well—completely by storm.

Powerful microcomputers, complete with Internet connectivity, are quickly becoming the norm in retooled technical services (and public services) departments. The Internet, particularly the World Wide Web, has become the new means for delivering traditional library services as well as exploring the new approaches to performing technical services functions that have been demonstrated in this book. Until now, most library-oriented Internet offerings have extended the TSW to familiar realms. That is, they provide access to cataloging guidelines and documentation, to reference tools, to selection databases and tools, and to catalog databases. Some of these network-accessible resources provide technical services professionals with a variety of relevant data and services that are not appropriate for mounting locally, not even on a LAN. In contrast, there are some Internet-centered experimental cataloging tools designed for organizing documents that originate or are available in electronic form that require closer examination by the technical services community to determine their place in the TSW environment. What should their role be in relation to the TSW platform, to cataloging workflows, and to cataloging in general?

Ironically, the next challenge for technical services professionals may not be advanced TSW tool development as such but careful evaluation of these types of emerging technologies that have the potential to significantly enhance or even transform current technical-services functions. Early scrutiny and testing in the TSW environment will help to direct technology-driven efforts into practical, usable tools that promote effective access and control of library resources.

This chapter briefly describes an OCLC research project directed at automatically recognizing the subject content of electronic documents. This project is an example of the kind of technology that could benefit from ongoing testing and evaluation by staff involved in the development of TSWs. This is a researcher's call for action and cooperation between the research community and the technical services community to help develop the next generation of tools that will extend further these emerging technologies.

Scorpion

The practical and theoretical difficulties associated with cataloging Internet resources were first investigated in a systematic way as part of the OCLC Internet Resources Project. One outcome of that project was the development of the USMARC field 856 (Electronic Location and Access). The original study and the follow-up project, Building a Catalog of Internet Accessible Materials (also known as the Intercat Project), have resulted in ongoing improvements in the USMARC formats and in creating guidelines for cataloging networked electronic resources.

In addition to testing the efficacy of current cataloging practices for describing, locating, and accessing networked electronic resources, a major component of the Intercat project is to create a database of all catalog records produced within the project's scope and to provide general Internet access to that catalog. The adaptation of the USMARC format to accommodate Internet resources, and the subsequent creation of a catalog based on these findings, represents the transformation of what was originally a research project into what is now a well-accepted part of the technical services world. But as we are wrestling with issues surrounding possible classification of these resources—and in particular, as those involved with the Dewey Decimal Classification have struggled to use the DDC to categorize these resources—new research areas are emerging. The general applicability of the approaches we are investigating need not be limited to the DDC and to the Internet, however; entire new vistas of machine-assisted classification may well emerge from these experiments.

Scorpion is a research project focused on building tools for automatically recognizing the subject content of electronic documents.[2] In its current form Scorpion consists of a series of ranked retrieval databases generated from the machine-readable version of the twenty-first edition of the Dewey Decimal Classification. These databases can be accessed via a Web interface capable of retrieving an electronic document and generating a database query from its content (figure 12.1). The system returns a ranked list of Dewey numbers as retrieval results.

To explore Scorpion's potential for performing subject analysis from electronic texts in a user-friendly mode, the Internet-accessible electronic table of contents for a document cataloged through the Electronic Cataloging-in-Publication pilot project (OCLC number 31901448) was issued as a query.[3] The table of contents is shown in figure 12.2.

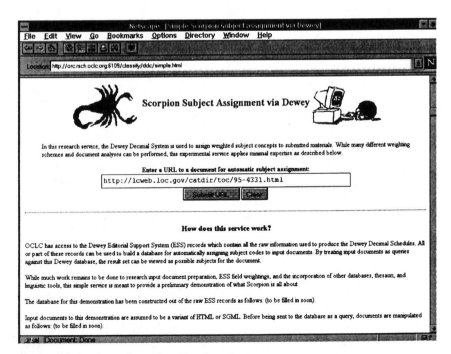

Figure 12.1 Scorpion Classification Page

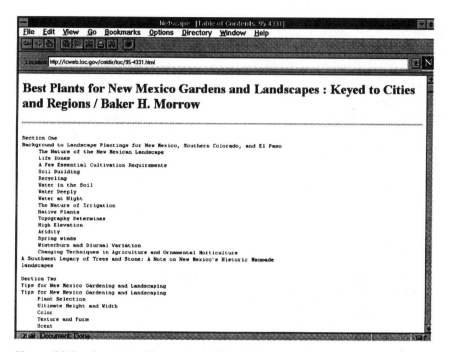

Figure 12.2 Scorpion Electronic Table of Contents

Although Scorpion did not produce an exact match of the Dewey class number assigned to the bibliographic record by the cataloger (635.909789), the results in figure 12.3 represent possible subjects for the document. These numbers could be presented to a cataloger as a starting point for manually assigning class numbers, especially if Scorpion were linked to the online version of the Dewey Decimal Classification (Dewey for Windows).

The Challenge

As a researcher I can imagine many possible directions and system refinements. For example, suppose we were to add synthesized numbers, enhance entry vocabulary, or link Dewey numbers to other subject thesauri? Could Scorpion be used to reclassify from obsolete to current numbers? Could the system provide useful subjects for journal articles? Could it be used as a postretrieval filtering tool? It is not clear which, if any, of these courses will serve catalogers best.

This type of automated work should not be limited just to electronic resources, but it should move also into the world of mainstream cataloging of printed materials. Its potential use extends to the Library of Congress Classification, as well, as it emerges from the shadows of development and becomes a full-blown product. Whether developed as an integral part of the commercial versions of the Library of Congress Classification or possibly as an "add-on," there definitely exists a need

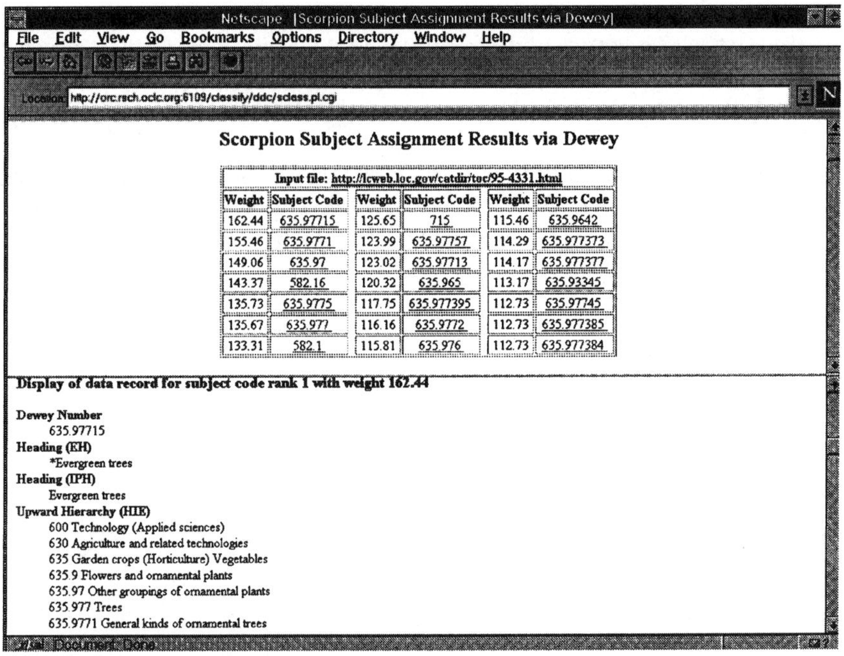

Netscape [Scorpion Subject Assignment Results via Dewey]

File   Edit   View   Go   Bookmarks   Options   Directory   Window   Help

Location: http://orc.rsch.oclc.org:6109/classify/ddc/sclass.pl.cgi

Scorpion Subject Assignment Results via Dewey

Input file: http://lcweb.loc.gov/catdir/toc/95-4331.html

Weight	Subject Code	Weight	Subject Code	Weight	Subject Code
162.44	635.97715	125.65	715	115.46	635.9642
155.46	635.9771	123.99	635.97757	114.29	635.977373
149.06	635.97	123.02	635.97713	114.17	635.977377
143.37	582.16	120.32	635.965	113.17	635.93345
135.73	635.9775	117.75	635.977395	112.73	635.97745
135.67	635.977	116.16	635.9772	112.73	635.977385
133.31	582.1	115.81	635.976	112.73	635.977384

Display of data record for subject code rank 1 with weight 162.44

Dewey Number
  635.97715
Heading (KH)
  *Evergreen trees
Heading (IPH)
  Evergreen trees
Upward Hierarchy (HIE)
  600 Technology (Applied sciences)
  630 Agriculture and related technologies
  635 Garden crops (Horticulture) Vegetables
  635.9 Flowers and ornamental plants
  635.97 Other groupings of ornamental plants
  635.977 Trees
  635.9771 General kinds of ornamental trees

Figure 12.3   Scorpion Proposed Classification

to investigate the application of these techniques to all classification schemes.

Although extensive testing and evaluation by research staff will likely answer many unresolved questions, they may not answer where such technologies fit into library practices and operations. By seeking out, evaluating, and offering useful feedback on emerging technologies, even when practical applications are years away, technical services professionals can help ensure that their concerns will be factored into the research and development process and even hasten development of future TSW components.

In his Introduction to this book, Michael Kaplan compared the TSW configuration to a stereo system and observed that the CDs of the stereo world correspond to the TSW's software or its local bibliographic resources. As a researcher, what I find interesting historically in this analogy is that at one time the software/local resources would have been 33⅓ LP vinyl records. How many among us still collect and listen to them? Times and technology change, and so too does library technology. Our challenge as researchers, as developers, and as members of the technical services profession is to ensure that we have a role in defining and developing the standards that will guide our future. The TSW is the ideal platform for such development. We have had a major role in its development to this point at a grassroots level. As the TSW moves into a larger, more mainstream position, we must be the guarantors of its future so that it does indeed become the ideal technical services platform that we all envision it to be.

Notes

1. Michael Kaplan in a talk to the Manitoba Library Association in Winnipeg, Man., on May 10, 1996.

2. A complete description of Scorpion is available at http://purl.oclc.org/scorpion.

3. See Joyce Owens and Chuck Gialloreto, "Electronic CIP Functions and Features Document," Mar. 17, 1995, Information Technology Services, Library of Congress, and ECIP flyer "Table of Contents Information."

Bibliography

Anderson, Douglas. "Automatically Generated References in Minimal-Level Authority Records." *Information Technology and Libraries* 10, no. 4 (Dec. 1991): 251–62.

Association of Research Libraries. *Microcomputers in ARL Libraries*. ARL SPEC Kit 104. Washington, D.C.: The Association, 1984.

———. *Technical Services Workstations*. ARL SPEC Kit 213. Washington, D.C.: The Association, 1996.

———. *Training of Technical Services Staff in the Automated Environment*. ARL SPEC Kit 171. Washington, D.C.: The Association, 1991.

Basic Training for Trainers. INFO-LINE 808. Alexandria, Va.: American Society for Training and Development, 1988.

Black, Kirsten. "The Development of IWS—An Integrated Workstation for Librarians." *Program* 24, no. 1 (Jan. 1990): 49–58.

Bonner, Paul. "Cross-Application Macro Languages." *PC Magazine* (Feb. 8, 1994): 203–42.

Breeding, Marshall. "Multipurpose Technical Services Workstations: Access to NOTIS/OCLC/GTO with a Single Microcomputer." *Library Hi Tech* 35 (1991): 69–81.

Brisson, Roger. "The Cataloger's Workstation and the Continuing Transformation of Cataloging." *Cataloging and Classification Quarterly* 20, no. 1 (1995): 3–23; 20, no. 2 (1995): 89–104.

Brisson, Roger, and Janet McCue. "Retooling Technical Services: The Development of Technical Services Workstations." In *Encyclopedia of Library and Information Science*. Vol. 58. New York: Dekker, 1996. Also published simultaneously as "Technical Workstations in a Library Environment." In *Encyclopedia of Microcomputers*. Vol. 18. New York: Dekker, 1996.

Chiang, Belinda. "Expediting NOTIS Operations with Programmed Function Keys: A Comprehensive Guide." *Library Software Review* 13, no. 3 (fall 1994): 212–23.

Clack, Mary Elizabeth. "The Role of Training in the Reorganization of Cataloging Services." *Library Acquisitions: Practice and Theory* 19 (winter 1995): 439–44.

Cooperative Cataloging Council Automation Task Group. "Report of the Cooperative Cataloging Council Automation Task Group, Dec. 9, 1994." Available on gopher://marvel.loc.gov:70/00/services/cataloging/coop/coop_cncl/tgauto.

Council on Library Resources Bibliographic Services Study Committee. *The National Coordinated Cataloging Program: An Assessment of the Pilot Project.* Washington, D.C.: The Council, 1990.

Davis-Brown, Beth, and David Williamson. "Cataloging in the Digital Age at the Library of Congress." *Cataloging and Classification Quarterly* 22, no. 3/4 (1996): 171–95.

Entlich, Richard, William Fenwick, and Dongming Zhang. "Enhancing the Processing Environment: The Development of a Technical Services Workstation." *Information Technology and Libraries* 11, no. 4 (Dec. 1992): 324–38.

Epple, Margie, Judy Gardner, and Robert T. Warwick, "Staff Training and Automated Systems: 20 Tips for Success." *Journal of Academic Librarianship* 18, no. 2 (May 1992): 87–9.

Fenley, Charles. *Expert Systems, Concepts and Applications*. Washington, D.C.: Cataloging Distribution Service, Library of Congress, 1988.

Finni, John J., and Peter J. Paulson. "The Dewey Decimal Classification Enters the Computer Age: Developing the DDC Database and Editorial Support System." *International Cataloging* 16, no. 4 (Oct./Dec. 1987): 46–8.

First-Rate Technical and Skills Training. INFO-LINE 706. Alexandria, Va.: American Society for Training and Development, 1987.

Glogoff, Stuart, and James P. Flynn. "Developing a Systematic In-House Training Program for Integrated Library Systems." *College & Research Libraries* 48 (Nov. 1987): 528–36.

Gorman, Michael. "The Corruption of Cataloging." *Library Journal* 120, no. 20 (Sept. 15, 1995): 32–3.

———. "Innocent Pleasures." In *The Future Is Now: The Changing Face of Technical Services. Proceedings of the OCLC Symposium, ALA Midwinter Conference* [Los Angeles], *February 4, 1994.* Dublin, Ohio: OCLC Online Computer Library Center, 1994.

Gregor, Dorothy, and Carol A. Mandel. "Cataloging Must Change!" *Library Journal* 116, no. 6 (Apr. 1, 1991): 42–7.

Guenther, Rebecca S. "The Development and Implementation of the *USMARC Format for Classification Data*." *Information Technology and Libraries* 11, no. 2 (June 1992): 120–31.

Guy, Robin Frederick. "Inhouse Training for Information Technology." *Education for Information* 7, no. 1 (Mar. 1989): 17–27.

Harvard College Library Standing Committee on Ergonomic Issues and Policy. *Harvard College Library Ergonomics Program and Policies*. Cambridge, Mass.: The Library, 1996.

Hebert, Lauren Andrew. *The Neck-Arm-Hand Book: The Master Guide for Eliminating Cumulative Trauma Disorders from the Work Place.* Bangor, Maine: IMPACC, 1989.

Hine, Betsy N. "Automated Workstations for Professional Catalogers: A Survey of 100 non-ARL Academic Libraries." *Library Resources & Technical Services* 36, no. 1 (Jan. 1992): 96–104.

Hirshon, Arnold. "The Lobster Quadrille: The Future of Technical Services in a Re-engineering World." In *The Future Is Now: The Changing Face of Technical Services: Proceedings of the OCLC Symposium, ALA Midwinter Conference* [Los Angeles], *February 4, 1994.* Dublin, Ohio: OCLC Online Computer Library Center, 1994.

Kaplan, Michael. "From Worksheet to Workstation: Technical Services Workstations in Harvard College Library's Cataloging Services Department." *Harvard Library Bulletin* n.s. 6, no. 1 (spring 1995): 8–12.

———. "Technical Services Workstations: A Review of the State of the Art." *Library Resources & Technical Services* 40, no. 2 (Apr. 1996): 171–83.

Kiegel, Joe. "Analysis of the Technical Services Workstation Survey." Available online: gopher://marvel.loc.gov:70/00/services/cataloging/coop/coop_cncl/tswanaly.

———. "Summary of the Technical Services Workstation Survey." Available online: gopher://marvel.loc.gov:70/00/services/cataloging/coop/coop_cncl/tswsurv.

Kizzier, Donna L. "Teaching Technology vs. Technology as a Teaching Tool." In *Technology in the Classroom.* National Business Education Yearbook, no. 33. Reston, Va.: National Business Education Association, 1995.

Knorr, Eric. "Big Screens." *PC World* (Apr. 1995): 103–18.

Lange, Holley R. "Catalogers and Workstations: A Retrospective and Future View." *Cataloging and Classification Quarterly* 16, no. 1 (1993): 39–52.

Mandel, Carol A. "Cooperative Cataloging: Models, Issues, Prospects." *Advances in Librarianship* 16 (1992): 33–82.

Markey, Karen, and Anh Demeyer. *Dewey Decimal Classification Online Project: Evaluation of a Library Schedule and Index Integrated into the Subject Searching Capabilities of an Online Catalog: Final Report to the Council on Library Resources.* OCLC Research Report Series, OCLC/OPR/RR-86/1. Dublin, Ohio: OCLC, 1986.

Marmion, Dan. "State-of-the-Art Library Workstations: A Guided Tour." *Wilson Library Bulletin* 63, no. 2 (Oct. 1988): 28–33.

Martin, Ron G. "Design Considerations for an OPAC Workstation: An Introduction to Specifications and a Model Configuration." *Library Hi Tech* 28 (1989): 19–27.

Matthews, Joseph R. "Using Computers to Enhance Cataloging Productivity." In *Recruiting, Educating and Training Cataloging Librarians: Solving the Problems.* Ed. by Sheila S. Intner and Janet Swan Hill. New Directions in Library Information Management no. 19. New York: Greenwood Press, 1989.

Nordgren, Layne. "The Macintosh as a Library Workstation: Some Significant Advantages." *Wilson Library Bulletin* 63, no. 2 (Oct. 1988): 35–41.

OCLC Online Computer Library Center. *The Future Is Now: The Changing Face of Technical Services: Proceedings of the OCLC Symposium, ALA Midwinter Conference* [Los Angeles], *February 4, 1994.* Dublin, Ohio: OCLC Online Computer Library Center, 1994.

Olson, Susan. "U.S. Regional Networks: An Introduction." *OCLC Newsletter* 218 (Nov./Dec. 1995): 21.

Peters, Tom. "Train and Retrain." In *Thriving on Chaos*. New York: Harper-Perennial, 1991.

Ramsborg, Glen. "Lifelong Learning: The Adult Learner." *Convene* 10, no. 10 (Dec. 1995): 89–96.

Rankin, Katherine L., and Lamont Downs. "FastCat: A Tool for Cataloging." *Wilson Library Bulletin* 69, no. 8 (Apr. 1995): 41–3.

Reser, David W. *Towards a New Beginning in Cooperative Cataloging: The History, Progress, and Future of the Cooperative Cataloging Council*. Washington, D.C.: Library of Congress Cataloging Distribution Service, 1994.

Reynolds, Dennis. *Library Automation: Issues and Applications*. New York: Bowker, 1985.

Rogers, Sally A. "Automated Workstations for Professional Catalogers: A Survey of ARL Libraries." In *Building on the First Century: Proceedings of the Fifth National Conference of the Association of College and Research Libraries, Cincinnati, Ohio, April 5–8, 1989*. Ed. by Janice C. Fennell. Chicago: Association of Research Libraries, 1989.

Rosow, Jerome M., and Robert Zager. *Training, the Competitive Edge: Introducing New Technology into the Workplace*. San Francisco: Jossey-Bass, 1988.

Sellers, Don. *Zap!: How Your Computer Can Hurt You—And What You Can Do about It*. Ed. by Stephen F. Roth. Berkeley, Calif.: Peachpit, 1994.

Senge, Peter M. *The Fifth Discipline*. New York: Doubleday, 1990.

Sievert, Mary Ellen. "Investigating Computer Anxiety in an Academic Library." *Information Technology and Libraries* 7, no. 3 (Sept. 1988): 243–52.

Smith, Terry. "Training Technical Services OCLC Users." *OCLC Systems and Services* 10, no. 2–3 (summer/fall 1994): 49–53.

"Staff Perception of Incentives and Hurdles to the Use of Technology." *Computers in Libraries* 15, no. 2 (Feb. 1995): 28–31.

Stewart, Barbara. "Top 200 Technical Services Benefits of Home Page Development." Rev. ed. 11/21/95. Available online: http://tpot.ucsd.edu/Cataloging/Misc/top200.html.

Tapscott, Don. *The Digital Economy*. New York: McGraw-Hill, 1995.

Tennant, Roy. "The Virtual Library Foundation: Staff Training and Support." *Information Technology and Libraries* 14, no. 1 (Mar. 1995): 46–9.

Tillotson, Martha, and Jeffrey A. Trimble. "Managing MARC Records: Using Lance's Transfer Manager with the University of Alabama's NOTIS System." *Library Software Review* 12 (summer 1993): 38–42.

Urey, Gwen. "Linking Library Workstations: Getting Them Up and Running." *Wilson Library Bulletin* 63, no. 2 (Oct. 1988): 42–51.

Valuskas, Ed. "The Apple Macintosh in Libraries: A Personal View of Current Roles and Future Prospects." *Computers in Libraries* 13, no. 7 (July/Aug. 1993): 8–13.

Waite, Ellen J. "Reinvent Catalogers." *Library Journal* 120, no. 18 (Nov. 1, 1995): 36–7.

Williamson, David. "NLM CIP Productivity Enhancements." *LC Cataloging Newsline* 4, no. 4 (Mar. 1996).

———. "Toward the Intelligent Workstation." *LC Cataloging Newsline* 3, no. 12 (Nov. 1, 1995).

Index

A

AACR2R. See *Anglo-American Cataloguing Rules,* 2nd edition, Revised
Accident reports, 185
Accuracy, 22, 23
ACRL. *See* Association of College and Research Libraries
ActiveX, Microsoft, 119
Administration, 11–12, 173
AFL-CIO, 185
AFSCME. *See* American Federation of State, County, and Municipal Employees
ALA. *See* American Library Association
ALCTS. *See* Association for Library Collections & Technical Services
Allen, George, 15
Alpha testing, 52
American Federation of State, County, and Municipal Employees (AFSCME), 185
American Library Association (ALA), 12, 56, 92, 127
American Library Association (ALA) character set, 21–2, 59

for Cataloger's Desktop, 70
and ClipSearch, 162
and Library of Congress custom keycaps, 153
and Windows, 18, 35
American National Standards Institute (ANSI), 183
American Society for Training and Development (ASTD), 193, 195, 205
Web site, 196, 198
Ameritech Library Services, 127
Analytic Concepts, GameCop, 15
Anglo-American Cataloguing Rules, 2nd edition, Revised, *(AACR2R),* 18, 68, 69, 70, 78–9, 92
Annotation features. *See* Note features
Annotation Manager, SuperLCCS CD, 91
ANSI. *See* American National Standards Institute
API. *See* Application programmer's interface
APIF. *See* Automated Process Information File
Apple, 43. *See also* Macintosh
Application issues, 46–7

Application programmer's interface (API), 18
ARL. *See* Association of Research Libraries; *see also* Program for Cooperative Cataloging, Standing Committee on Automation
ARL SPEC Kit, xvii, 4, 5, 11, 60
    training, 197, 198, 205
Artificial intelligence, 68
ASCII files, 31, 130, 137, 141, 158
Assembler language, 45
Association for Library Collections & Technical Services (ALCTS), ix–x, 69
Association of College and Research Libraries (ACRL), x
Association of Research Libraries (ARL), xvi, 4, 54, 197
Authority records, 22, 54, 59, 60–1, 97
    automating, 126, 127, 135–6
    in Cataloger's Toolkit, 128–9, 130–4, 146–52
Autocat discussion list, 126
Automated Process Information File (APIF), 158
Automated searching, 156–8

B

Backlog reduction, xvi, 30–2
Backward compatibility, 48
Bar code insertion, 23
Barney, Douglas, 193
BASIC, 45
Beacom, Matthew, x
Beall, Julianne, x
Bendig, Mark, x, 81, 103–20
Beta testing, 52, 127
BIBCO, 54, 60
BiblioFile Cataloging MS-DOS, 39–52, 68
Bibliographic records, 59, 60–1, 128–9, 130–4
Bibliographic Workstations (BWS), 153–4, 162, 170
Blixrud, Julia C., 193–208
Bookholders, 173, 184
Bookmark feature, 75–6, 91
BookWhere?, Z39.50, 13, 18, 20
Boolean searching, 69, 70, 74, 90, 94
Borland, Delphi, 32
Botkin, Jim, and Stan Davis, *The Monster under the Bed*, 196

Bremer, Robert, 60, 61
Brisson, Roger, 58
Budgets, 174. *See also* Costs
Building a Catalog of Internet Accessible Materials (Intercat Project), 212
Built numbers, 109–10
Bureau of National Affairs Web site, 198
Business practices, x, xvi, 4
BWS. *See* Bibliographic Workstations

C

C++ language, 45–6
C languages, 45, 125
Call numbers, 136–41, 143
CAPCON, OCLC regional network, x, 12
Card printing, 48
Carpal tunnel syndrome, 175, 176
Cataloger's Desktop (LC), 53, 59, 60, 67–80
    and Cataloger's Toolkit, 134
    customization of, 74–6
    FolioViews Web version, 20
    future of, 78–9
    and LAN compatibility, 12
    machine requirements for, 77–8
    and Macintosh, 58
    origins of, 68–71
    software for, 71
    in TSW applications, x, 173
    working with, 71–8
Cataloger's Toolkit, 33, 59, 60, 123–52, 211
    automating authority records, 126
    call numbers, 136–41
    conflict resolution in, 141–2
    development and distribution, 125–34
    features, 128–30
    and machine-generated authority records, 146–52
Cataloger's workstations, xv. *See also* Bibliographic Workstations; TSWs; Workstations
Cataloging. *See* Copy cataloging; Descriptive cataloging; Original cataloging
Cataloging departments, 12
Cataloging Distribution Service (CDS), 68–9
Cataloging from text, 154–6

Cataloging-in-publication (CIP), 59, 154, 159, 211

Cataloging MicroEnhancer Plus (CatME+), OCLC, 17, 30, 31, 123

Cataloging Rules for the Description of Looseleaf Publications, 69

CatME+. *See* Cataloging MicroEnhancer Plus

CBTs. *See* Computer-based training modules

CCC. *See* Cooperative Cataloging Council

CD Descriptive Cataloging Expert System, 68

CDMARC Bibliographic products, 68

CD-ROM, 41, 48, 49, 82
  and Classification Plus, 92
  and DDC database, 104
  and LANs, 11

CDS. *See* Cataloging Distribution Service

CE Software, ProKey, 32

Central processing units (CPUs), 58

CGA. *See* Color Graphics Adapter

Chairs, 177, 184

CIP. *See* Cataloging-in-publication

CJK catalogers, 35

CLAR, 125–34. *See also* Cataloger's Toolkit

CLARR, 127–8. *See also* Cataloger's Toolkit

Classification Plus (LC), 59, 92–100, 108
  bookmarks and notes in, 98–9
  on CD-ROM disks, 82
  contents of, 93–4
  copying text, 99
  installation of, 93
  journal functions in, 97–8
  and LAN compatibility, 12
  and Macintosh, 58
  manual for, 93
  searching in, 94–7
  system and network requirements for, 102
  in TSW applications, x

Classification record enhancements, 104, 105, 107

Client-server computers, xvii, 16–17

ClipSearch, 162–70
  codes feature, 167–8
  copying headings, 166–7
  generating NARs, 166–7
  lists feature, 168–9

online help, 169
  searching in, 164–6

CLR. *See* Council on Library Resources

Color blindness, 11

Color Graphics Adapter (CGA), 8, 21

Color schemes of monitors, 10–11

Columbia University Library and LANs, 11

Compaq, 5

Component software, 41

Computer-based training modules (CBTs), 197

Computers
  breaks from, 15
  client-server, xvii
  costs of, 4
  games on, 15, 183
  mainframe, xvii
  obsolete, 5
  personal (PCs), 4
  purchasing of, 5

ComTerm terminals, 55–6

Conceptual links, 77

Configuration, threshold, 5

CONSER. *See* Cooperative Online Serials Program

Cooperative Cataloging Council (CCC), ix, 53–64
  Automation Appendix, 4
  Automation Task Group, ix, 20, 58–61
  meeting with library service vendors, 59–60
  "More, Better, Faster, Cheaper," 58
  Strategic Plan Automation Recommendations, 63–4
  task groups of, 56–8
  TSW survey (1994), xv, xvii, 4, 13, 23, 58–9

Cooperative Online Serials Program (CONSER), 35, 54, 56, 71, 72, 73

Copy cataloging, 23, 49, 54, 127, 169
  with NewKey, 26–9

Copy holders, 173, 184

Cornell University Mann Library, x, xv. *See also* TN3270

Cornell University TN 3270, 6, 17, 20, 21–2, 35

Corporate America, 196

Costs
  Bibliographic Workstations, 56
  cataloging programs, 53
  Classification Plus, 99
  computers, 4, 43

Costs (cont.)
  monitors, 7, 8
  personnel, 4
  personnel versus computer, xvi
  software development, 40
  SuperLCCS CD, 92, 99
  threshold, 5
  See also Budgets
Council on Library Resources (CLR),
  54
CPUs. *See* Central processing units
Cross-training, 194. *See also*
  Retraining; Training
Cumulative trauma disorders
  (CTDs), 175–7
Custom applications, 153–70
Custom keycaps, 153
Customization of Cataloger's
  Desktop (LC), 74–6
Customization of keyboards, 6–7
Cut-and-paste, 20, 49, 90, 173, 200
Cutter tables, 136–7, 141

D

Data Connections, 153
Data validation, 19
Database management, 30
Database programs, 59, 200
Databases. *See* Local databases;
  MARC, databases; other specific
  databases
Davis, Stan, and Jim Botkin, *The
  Monster under the Bed,* 196
DDC. *See* Dewey Decimal
  Classification
DDE. *See* Dynamic data exchange
Dell, 5
Delphi, Borland, 32
Descriptive cataloging, 68
Design, ergonomic, 173–92
Desktop metaphor, 46–7
Development of software, 39–52.
  See also TSWs, planning and
  development of
Dewey Decimal Classification
  (DDC), 81, 103, 136, 142, 213
  database, 104, 110
  database indexes, 110–11
  hierarchies, 107
Dewey for Windows (DFW), x,
  103–20, 143, 214
  fixed display views, 113–15
  LAN operations in, 117–19
  system design, 111–19

Diacritics, 6, 19, 21, 50, 70, 74
Dialog boxes, 25, 35, 90
Disabilities, 184
Disability claims, 185–6
Disney, 196
DLL. *See* Dynamic link library
Documentation, 201, 203
DOS, 17, 18, 23, 44
  and Cataloger's Desktop, 71
  interfaces, x, 26
  and monitors, 8
  terminate and stay resident
    programs (TSRs), 25
  training for, 198, 200
  See also TN3270
Dot pitch, 9
Drag-and-drop interaction, 116
Duke, John, 78
Dumb terminals, 4, 10, 16, 26
Dynamic data exchange (DDE), 119
Dynamic link library (DLL), 111–12
DynaText, 83

E

Editing data, 49–51
Editorial support system (ESS), 103–5
Education. *See* Learning; Training
EGA. *See* Enhanced graphics adapter
EHLLAPI. *See* Emulator High-Level
  Language Application
  Programming Interface
Eisenhower Library, Johns Hopkins
  University, 8
Electronic Cataloging-in-Publication,
  211
Electronic CIP Experiment, 154
Electronic Dewey, x, 103–4
Electronic documentation, x
ELF. *See* Extremely low frequency
  electromagnetic radiation
E-mail, 12, 15, 16, 59, 183
Emulator High-Level Language
  Application Programming
  Interface (EHLLAPI), 124–5
Engelbart, Douglas, 3
English language terms, 25, 78. *See
  also* Programming languages
Enhanced graphics adapter (EGA), 8,
  21
Ergonomic Issues in the Workplace,
  Harvard College Library, 175
Ergonomics, 173–92
  breaks from computer, 15, 181,
    183, 186

design criteria, 177–8
and keyboards, 6, 7
policy statements, 188–9
program for, 174–5, 179–87
resources for, 190–2
training for, 181
See also Safety issues of monitors
Error rates, 23, 29
ESS. *See* Editorial support system
Ethernet, 58
EtherTerm, Research Libraries Group
(RLG), 13, 57
Evans, Anaclare Frost, 81–102
Excel, 22
Exercises, 186
Expert systems, 68
*Expert Systems, Concepts and
Applications* (Fenly), 68
Explicit links, 76
Extremely low frequency (ELF)
electromagnetic radiation, 7, 179
Eyestrain, 10–11, 178–9, 184, 186

F

F1 key, 19, 23
Fenly, Charles, *Expert Systems,
Concepts and Applications,* 68
Fifth Discipline, The (Senge), 195
File transfer protocol (FTP), 16, 56,
59, 159, 200
Fixed display views, Dewey for
Windows, 113–15
Flickering, 9
Flynn, James, 196
Folio Site Director, 78
FolioViews, 20, 71, 74, 75, 92, 98
Font cartridges, 21, 22
Foreign language needs, 6
Forest Press, OCLC, 103, 142
Formal group training, 202
*Free-floating Subdivisions: An
Alphabetical Index* (LC), 69
FTP. *See* File transfer protocol
Function keys, 22, 23, 35
Functional extensibility, 44–5
Functionality, 47–51
Future Is Now: The Changing Face
of Technical Services, The
(symposium), x

G

Gale Research, 12, 82, 83, 92, 99
GameCop, Analytic Concepts, 15

Games on the computer, 15, 183
GEAC GeoCat, 20
Generic Transfer and Overlay (GTO),
49
Glare, 11, 177–9, 184
Glogoff, Stuart, 196
Gopher, 16
*Graphic Materials: Rules for Describing
Original Items and Historical
Collections,* 69
Graphical user interfaces (GUIs), 4,
7, 8, 59, 116, 200
Graphics adapters, 8–9
Graphics printers, 22
GTO. *See* Generic Transfer and
Overlay
GUIs. *See* Graphical user interfaces
Guy, Robin, 193

H

*Handbook of Human Resource
Development,* 193
Hard drives, 58, 83
Hardware, 4–6, 42–3
for Dewey for Windows, 117–18
support for, 4
training for, 200
for TSWs, xvi
Harvard College Library
Automation Office, 175
Ergonomic Issues in the Workplace,
175
Human Resources, 175, 183–4
LANs administration at, 11–12
macros usage by, 23
mission statement, 195
NewKey macro package, 25–32
productivity in the Cataloging
Services Department, xv, 23
Standing Committee on
Ergonomic Issues and Policy,
174–5
Task Force on Staff and Organizational Development, 194
TN3270 emulator, 17
*Harvard College Library Ergonomics
Program and Policies,* 179–87
administration, 180–1
problem-resolution procedures,
183–8
rights and responsibilities, 180
staff, 182–3
supervisors, 181–2
Harvard depository (HD), 30

Harvard Union of Clerical and
Technical Workers, 185
Harvard University Office of
Environmental Health, 183
HD. *See* Harvard depository
Health habits, 178
Hertz (Hz), 9
Highlight feature, 75–6
HOLLIS (Harvard's online catalog),
30, 31, 35, 36
HostExplorer, Hummingbird
Communications, Ltd., 33
Hotkeys, 19, 24, 25, 26, 163. *See also*
Macros
HTML. *See* HyperText Markup
Language
Hummingbird Communications,
Ltd., HostExplorer, 33
Hypertext, 69, 75, 76–7, 83, 94, 97,
169
HyperText Markup Language
(HTML), 128, 198

I

IBM, 5, 21, 23, 26, 35
compatible computers, 13, 58, 69
OS/2, 4, 33, 44, 69, 154, 162, 170
Visual REXX, 32, 33, 154
ILS. *See* Integrated library system
Implicit links, 76–7
Indexes to DDC database, 110–11
Indiana University, 127
Information age, 174
Information retrieval, 68
Inforonics, 103
Injuries, 174, 183, 185–6
Instructional systems design (ISD), 194
Integrated library system (ILS), 196
Integrated Technical Services for
Windows. *See* ITS for Windows
Intel, 196
Intel-based PCs, 43, 58
Intercat Project (Building a Catalog
of Internet Accessible Materials),
212
Interlaced versus noninterlaced
monitors, 9
International Standard Bibliographic
Description (ISBD), 59, 154–5,
158
International Standards
Organization (ISO), 48
Internet, 12–13, 153, 212
and bibliographic control, 42

training for, 198, 200
training sites, 198
TSW applications of, 57, 61
See also E-mail; File transfer
protocol; Listservs; Telnet;
World Wide Web
Internet Resources Project, OCLC,
212
Inventory control, 23
Investor's Business Daily, 196
ISBD. *See* International Standard
Bibliographic Description
ISBNs, 27, 30, 31
ISD. *See* Instructional systems design
ISO. *See* International Standards
Organization
ITS (Integrated Technical Services)
for Windows, 20, 40–52

J

Job
description, 187
design, 177, 189
sharing, 177, 187
Johns Hopkins University Eisenhower
Library, monitors at, 8
Johnson, Bruce Chr., x, 67–80

K

Kaplan, Michael, x, 3–15, 16–38,
53–64, 215
Keyboard mapping files, 7
Keyboard trays, 177
Keyboards, 6–7
customization of, 6–7
macro programs for, 7
Keycaps, custom, 153
Keystrokes, 22, 50. *See also* Macros;
Manual keying
Keyword indexes, 110
Keyword retrieval, 69, 70, 90, 143
KISS principle, 204
Knitting, 178, 183
Krauthammer, Charles, 15

L

Label printing, 48
Labor intensive tasks, 50–1
LAMA. *See* Library Administration
and Management Association
Languages. *See* Programming
languages

LANs. *See* Local area networks
Lantastic, 118
LC. *See* Library of Congress
LCCNs. *See* Library of Congress
　　control numbers
LCRIs. See *Library of Congress Rule
　　Interpretations (LCRIs)*
LCSH. See *Library of Congress Subject
　　Headings (LCSH)*
Learning, 203–4. *See also* Training
Learning objectives, 199. *See also*
　　Training
Librarian–developer link, 51–2
Libraries Unlimited, 137
Library Administration and
　　Management Association
　　(LAMA), x
Library and Information Technology
　　Association (LITA), x
Library Corporation, The, 20, 39–52,
　　68
Library of Congress (LC), x, 54–5
　　Bibliographic Workstation. *See*
　　　　Bibliographic Workstations
　　Cataloger's Desktop. *See*
　　　　Cataloger's Desktop
　　*MARC Format for Classification
　　　　Data,* 59
　　Name Authority File, 125, 141
　　productivity at, xv
　　resource files, 26–7
　　Technical Processing and
　　　　Automation Instruction Office
　　　　(TPAIO), 198
Library of Congress Classification,
　　81–102, 214
Library of Congress Classification
　　numbers, 90
Library of Congress control number,
　　27, 30, 31
*Library of Congress Rule Interpretations
　　(LCRIs),* 18, 67–71, 74, 173
*Library of Congress Subject Headings
　　(LCSH),* 81–2, 93, 97, 108, 125,
　　142
Library schools, 198
Lighting, 177, 178
Linked Systems Project (LSP), 55
Listservs, 4, 13, 15, 16, 52
LITA. *See* Library and Information
　　Technology Association
LOC (holdings field), 28
Local area networks (LANs), 11–12,
　　13, 58, 82
　　and Cataloger's Desktop, 70

　　and Dewey for Windows, 117–19
　　at Northwestern University, 124
　　and request for information
　　　　documents, 42
　　See also Networks
Local databases, 48–9
Lotus 1–2–3, 22
Low-frequency emissions, 7, 179
LSP. *See* Linked Systems Project

M

McCue, Janet, x, 3
McGill University, TCP3270. *See*
　　TCP3270
Machine readable cataloging. *See*
　　MARC
Macintosh, 43, 70, 116
　　as TSW platform, xvii, 4, 58
Macros, 22–37, 57, 59
　　in Cataloger's Toolkit, 129
　　elements of, 24–5
　　future of, 36–7
　　at Harvard College Library, 59, 211
　　and keyboard customization, 7, 19
　　at Library of Congress, 153
　　NewKey program, 17
　　and productivity, 23–4, 173
　　in Windows, 32–6
　　See also Hotkeys; Keystrokes;
　　　　Manual keying
Macro-Scripting language, 50–1
Mainframe computers, xvii, 16, 60,
　　125, 153
Maintenance contracts, 4
Management. *See* Administration
Mann Library. *See* Cornell University
　　Mann Library
Manual keying, 22, 23, 29, 36, 59.
　　See also Keystrokes; Macros
Manuals, 127–8, 203
　　online, 19
　　printed, 19
MARC
　　databases, 41, 48–9
　　Format for Classification Data,
　　　　Library of Congress, 59
　　formats, 18, 170. *See also* USMARC
Massachusetts State Department of
　　Industrial Accidents, 185
Medical advice, 178
Medical professionals, 174
Medical Subject Headings (MeSH), 125,
　　142
Memory, 4, 5, 13, 18, 23, 58

Mentoring, 202
Menu metaphor, 46
Menus, 19
MeSH. See Medical Subject Headings
Metaphors, 46, 49
Mice (mouse), 7, 15, 69, 70, 177
Microsoft, 44. *See also* Windows
Microsoft ActiveX, 119
Microsoft Visual Basic (VB), 32, 33,
    111, 125
Minaret format, 59
Minesweeper (computer game), 15
Miniprograms, 22
Mission statement for Harvard
    College Library, 195
Monitors, 7–11, 13, 58, 59
    adjustment of, 179
    color schemes, 10–11, 179
    size and resolution, 7–9
Monolithic systems, 41
Monster under the Bed, The (Davis and
    Botkin), 196
"More, Better, Faster, Cheaper," 58
Mosaic, 18
Motorola, 196
Mouse. *See* Mice
MS-DOS. *See* DOS
MS-DOS BiblioFile Cataloging,
    39–52
Multiple applications, 17, 18, 59
    and Dewey for Windows, 119
    and monitors, 8, 9–10
    at Northwestern University, 124
    training for, 200
Multiple-Use MARC System
    (MUMS), 55, 153
Multitasking. *See* Multiple
    applications
Multithreaded program, 156
MUMS. *See* Multiple-Use MARC
    System
Musical instruments, 178, 183

N

Name Authorities Cooperative Project
    (NACO), 22, 35, 36, 54, 55, 60
Name authority generation, 156–8,
    163, 166–7
Name authority record (NAR),
    156–7, 158
NASA's Goddard Space Flight Center,
    79
National bibliographics utilities, 13
National cooperative programs, 53–64

*National Coordinated Cataloging
    Program: An Assessment of the
    Pilot Project,* 54–5
National Coordinated Cataloging
    Program (NCCP), 54–6
National Library of Medicine (NLM),
    159–62
NCCP. *See* National Coordinated
    Cataloging Program
NELINET, OCLC regional network,
    x, 12
Netscape, 18
Netware, 118
Networks, 212
    importance of, xvii
    and TSWs, 4
    See also Local area networks
New York Public Library, productivity
    at, xv
NewKey macro program, 17, 25–32, 36
Newton search engine, OCLC, 111–12
NLM. *See* National Library of
    Medicine
Northwestern University Cataloger's
    Toolkit. *See* Cataloger's Toolkit
Note features, in Cataloger's
    Desktop, 75–6, 116–17
NOTIS, 21, 23, 26, 33, 36
    at Northwestern University, 123,
        125–7, 133, 141
NOTIS Users' Group Meeting
    (NUGM), 33, 127
Novell LANs, 11
NUGM. *See* NOTIS Users' Group
    Meeting

O

Object Linking and Embedding
    (OLE), 119
Object-Oriented Programming
    (OOP), 45
Obsolete computers, 5
Occupational Safety and Health
    Administration (OSHA), 183
OCLC, 36, 50, 54, 55
    CAPCON and NELINET (regional
        networks), x, 12
    Cataloging MicroEnhancer Plus
        (CatME+), 17, 30, 31, 123
    Forest Press, 103, 142
    Internet Resources Project, 212
    M300 and M310, 21
    Macro Language (OML), 33, 35,
        60, 61

Newton search engine, 111–12
Office of Research, 103, 104
Scorpion, 212–16
Telecommunications Linking
 Project (TLP), 13, 57
and terminal emulators, 19–20
training for services, 198
and winsock compatibility, 18
WorldCat, 29, 108, 123, 133
See also Passport for Windows
OCLC Micro (journal), 23
OCR. *See* Optical character
 recognition
O'Donnell, Pat, 15
OLE. *See* Object Linking and
 Embedding
OML. *See* OCLC, Macro Language
On the MARC, 154–9
and table of contents, 156
One-on-one training, 197, 202
Online Computer Library Center,
 Inc. *See* OCLC
Online editorial support, 103–4
Online manual, 19
Online training sources, 198
OOP. *See* Object-Oriented
 Programming
OPACs, 21, 27, 59, 61, 158, 201
Open versus proprietary systems, 20
Operating systems, 43–6, 70, 71,
 118, 200
Optical character recognition (OCR),
 130
Original cataloging, 67
OS/2. *See* IBM, OS/2
OSHA. *See* Occupational Safety and
 Health Administration
Outsourcing technical services, x

P

Paradox database, 31
Part-time employees, 182
PASCAL, 45–6
Passport for Windows, 17, 142
and Dewey for Windows, 119
keyboard customization in, 6
LAN compatibility of, 12
and macros, 32, 33, 35
and monitor colors, 10
Pay-by-the-search sessions, 20
PC UNIX. *See* UNIX
PCC. *See* Program for Cooperative
 Cataloging
PCs. *See* Personal computers

Pennsylvania State University
 library, productivity at, xv
Pentium processors, 4–5, 13, 43
Personal computers (PCs), 4, 23,
 42–3, 198
Peters, Tom, 195–7
Phrase indexes, 110
Phrase searching, 74
Physical therapy sessions, 186
Policy statements for ergonomics,
 188–9
Prevention of injuries, 174, 183
Printed documentation, 67–8, 128
Printers, graphics, 22
Problem domain, 41, 42
Problem-resolution procedures,
 183–8
Product design, 52
Product maintenance, 44–5
Product reliability, 52
Productivity, xv–xvi, 22, 23–4, 173
Professional Collection CD-ROM,
 137
Professional library associations, 198
Program for Cooperative Cataloging
 (PCC), ix, xvii, 53–64
 Standing Committee on
 Automation, ix, 21
 TSW Survey (1995), xvii, 4
 See also ARL SPEC Kit
Programming languages, 43–6. *See
 also* English language terms
ProKey, CE Software, 32
Proximity searching, 74
Publicity, 52

Q

Query templates, 74, 75, 78
Quick-Keys, 33, 34

R

Reflection, WRQ, 35
Refresh rate, 9
Regional library networks, 198
Rehabilitation, 186
Repetitive strain injuries (RSIs), 7,
 22, 23, 36, 59, 173–4
Request for information (RFI)
 documents, 41–2, 43, 51
Research community, 212
Research Libraries Group (RLG), 54,
 55
 EtherTerm, 13, 57

Research Libraries Information Network (RLIN), 12, 13, 17, 18, 21, 162
Resolution of monitors, 7–9
Resource allocation, 42
Retraining, 194, 204. *See also* Cross-training; Training
REXX, 154. *See also* VX-REXX
Reynolds, Dennis, 203, 206
RFIs. *See* Request for information documents
RLG. *See* Research Libraries Group
RLIN. *See* Research Libraries Information Network
Robocat '94, ix–x
RSIs. *See* Repetitive strain injuries
Rutgers University Libraries, 207

S

SACO. *See* Subject Authorities Cooperative Project
Safety issues of monitors, 7. *See also* Ergonomics
Sales representatives, 51–2
Scanned text, 158
Scanners, 130
Scholar's Workstation, 41
Scorpion, OCLC, 212–16
Sea Change, 20
Search algorithms, 55
Search engines, 82, 92, 100, 111
Searching, automated, 156–8
Segmentation marks, 109
Self-study, 202
Senge, Peter, *The Fifth Discipline*, 195
Shadow files, 75, 78, 98, 99
"Shelflisting" the number, 136, 137, 141
Shneiderman, Ben, 79
Single-threaded program, 156
Site visits, 184
Size and resolution of monitors, 7–9
SmartPad, Softblox, 32, 33
Smith, Terry, 197
Softblox, SmartPad, 32, 33
Software, 16–38
    for Cataloger's Desktop, 71
    development of, 39–52
    for Dewey for Windows, 118–19
    importance of, xvii
    and LANs, 11
    loading of, 5
    training for, 200

for TSWs, xvi, 215
Solitaire (computer game), 15
Special characters, 19, 21
Spell checking, 200
Spreadsheet programs, 59, 200
Stand-alone commercial programs, 32
Standard Generalized Markup Language (SGML), 78–9
Standing Committee on Automation. *See* Program for Cooperative Cataloging, Standing Committee on Automation
Standing Committee on Ergonomic Issues and Policy, Harvard College Library, 174–5
Stateless entity, 20
Stem searching, 74
Stewart, Barbara, "Top 200 Technical Services Benefits of Home Page Development," 198
Storage, 23
Strategic Plan Automation Recommendations, CCC, 63–4
Strawn, Gary, 33, 59, 60, 123–52, 211
Stress reduction, 178
Student employees, 182
Subject Authorities Cooperative Project (SACO), 54
Subject Cataloging Manual: Shelflisting (LC), 69, 94
Subject Cataloging Manual: Subject Headings (LC), 69, 71, 74, 77, 94, 124
Sun Workstations, 43
Super Video Graphics Adapter (SVGA), 8, 9
SuperLCCS CD, 12, 82, 83–92
    bookmarks and notes in, 91
    copying text in, 92
    installation of, 83
    journal functions in, 91–2
    manual for, 83
    searching in, 83–91
    system and network requirements for, 101–2
Surface metaphors, 46, 49
SVGA. *See* Super Video Graphics Adapter
Swedish National Board of Testing's MPRII guidelines, 179
Systems. *See* Operating systems

T

Tapscott, Don, 196
Target user group, 40–2
Task Force on Staff and
    Organizational Development,
    Harvard College Library, 194
TCEC project. *See* Text Capture and
    Electronic Conversion (TCEC)
    project
TCP3270, McGill University,
    18
  and Cataloger's Toolkit, 124
  keyboard customization in, 6
  LAN compatibility of, 12
  and macros, 32, 33, 35
  and monitor colors, 10
  terminal emulators, 20
TCP/IP. *See* Transmission Control
    Protocol/Internet Protocol Team
    training, 202
Technical Processing Online Tools
    (TPOT), 198
Technical services automation, 12
Technical services client (TSC), 20
Technical services workstations. *See*
    TSWs
Technical Services Workstations, ARL
    SPEC Kit. *See* ARL SPEC Kit
Telecommunications Linking Project
    (TLP), OCLC, 13, 57
Telnet, xvi, 16, 59, 61
Templates, 19, 50
Temporary employees, 182
Tendinitis, 175, 176–7
Tennant, Roy, 196
Tennis, 178, 183
Terminal emulators, 16–7, 19–20,
    170
Terminal environments, 23
Terminal Software, Research
    Libraries Information Network
    (RLIN), 12, 17, 21
Terminate and stay resident
    programs (TSRs), 25
Testing, 52
Text Capture and Electronic
    Conversion (TCEC) project, 154,
    159, 170
Text retrieval, 68, 69
Thesaurus searching, 74
Time, 15
TLP. *See* Telecommunications
    Linking Project

TLSH. *See Transportation Library*
    Subject Headings
TN3270, Cornell University, 6, 17,
    20, 21–2, 35
Toolkit. *See* Cataloger's Toolkit
"Top 200 Technical Services Benefits
    of Home Page Development"
    (Stewart), 198
TPAIO. *See* Library of Congress,
    Technical Processing and
    Automation Instruction Office
TPOT. *See* Technical Processing
    Online Tools
Training, 18, 193–208
  for catalogers, 12
  definition of, 193–4
  development of program, 199–205
  in ergonomics program, 178, 181,
    182
  evaluation, 204–5
  implementation of, 203–4
  investments in, 195–7
  learning objectives, 199
  methods of, 201–3
  money spent on, 196
  obstacles to, 205–6
  online sources, 198
  reasons for, 194–5
  sources for, 197–8
  successful programs, 206–7
  and SuperLCCS CD, 92
  tips for, 207
  topics for, 199–201
  "train the trainer" programs, 197,
    198
  trends in, 195
  for TSWs, x, 12
Training and Development (journal),
    195
Transmission Control
    Protocol/Internet Protocol
    (TCP/IP), 11, 18
Transportation Library Subject
    Headings (TLSH), 125
Treatment of injuries. *See* Injuries
TrueType fonts, 22, 50
Trumble, Bruce, 173–92
Trumpet Software International, 18
Trumpet Winsock, 18
TSC. *See* Technical services client
TSRs. *See* Terminate and stay resident
    programs
TSW survey (1994), xv, xvii, 4, 13,
    23, 58–9

TSW survey (1995), xvii, 4
TSWs
    definition of, xvi, 3–4, 173
    and emerging technologies,
        211–16
    future of, xvii
    hardware for, xvi
    installation of, x
    planning and development of,
        ix–x, 18–20, 39–54
    and productivity, xv–xvi
    purchasing of, xvi–xvii
    software for, xvi, 215
    training program for, 199–205
    See also Bibliographic
        Workstations; Cataloger's
        workstations; TSW survey;
        Workstations

U

University of California at Los
    Angeles, productivity at, xv
University of California at San Diego
    Web site, 198
University of Nevada at Las Vegas,
    productivity at, xvi
University of New Mexico Press, 154
University of North Texas library,
    productivity at, xvi
UNIX, 44, 198
Upgrade curve, 5
User interface in Dewey for
    Windows, 111, 112–13
User-defined function keys, 22
User's manuals. *See* Manuals
USMARC
    code lists, 69, 71, 134, 167. *See also*
        MARC
    field 856 (Electronic Location and
        Access), 212–13
USMARC Concise Formats, 71
USMARC Format for Authority Data,
    71
*USMARC Format for Bibliographic
    Data,* 49, 50, 67, 69
*USMARC Format for Classification
    Data,* 81, 82, 104, 105
Utility records, 60

V

Validation and codes, 50
VB. *See* Visual Basic, Microsoft
Vendors, ix, xvi–xvii, 5, 127

local systems, 13
meeting with Automation Task
    Group, 59–60
open versus proprietary systems,
    20
and software development, 39–40
and training, 198
Vertical functionality, 41–2
Video Graphics Adapter (VGA), 8, 9
Visual Basic (VB), Microsoft, 32, 33,
    111, 125
Visual REXX, IBM, 32, 33
Vizine-Goetz, Diane, 81, 103–20,
    211–16
VX-REXX, Watcom, 154, 170

W

Wall Street Journal, 15
WANs. *See* Wide area networks
Watcom Software, 154
Web. *See* World Wide Web
Web browsers, 13, 16, 20, 200, 211
Wide area networks (WANs), 42
Wildcard searching, 74, 90
Williamson, David, 153–70
Wilson, Mark, 39–52
Windows, 4, 5, 23, 44–6, 59, 69
    advantages of, 18–20
    and Cataloger's Desktop, 71
    Dewey for Windows, 103–20
    interfaces, x
    ITS for, 20, 40–52
    macros in, 32–6
    and monitors, 8, 9, 10
    and multiple applications, 17
    at Northwestern University, 124
    Solitaire (game), 15
    training for, 198, 200
    See also Dewey for Windows;
        Microsoft; Passport for
        Windows; TCP3270
Winsock compatibility, 18
Word processing, 49–50, 57, 59, 153,
    200
WordPerfect, 22
Work habits, 177, 182, 184
Workers' compensation, 185–6
Workflow demonstrations, 51–2
Workflow patterns, 47
Workplace ergonomics program,
    174–5
Workstations, 3, 18–20, 173, 177–8.
    See also Bibliographic
        Workstations; Cataloger's

workstations; TSW survey;
TSWs
World Wide Web (WWW), 4, 13, 61,
170, 211
and Cataloger's Desktop, 78
training sites, 198
See also Internet; Web browsers
WorldCat, OCLC, 108, 123, 133
Wright State, x
Wrist braces, 186
"Writing to the metal," 45
WRQ, Reflection, 35
WWW. *See* World Wide Web

Y

Yale University, x, 8, 21–2
YTerm, Yale University library, 21–2

Z

Z39.50, xvii, 19, 20, 57
and BookWhere?, 13, 18, 20
and ITS for Windows, 41, 49
and Library of Congress, 59
and WebZ picture, 211

Contributors

Michael Kaplan is head of database management and coordinator for OCLC/RLIN operations in the Harvard College Library, Harvard University, where he has been a member of the professional staff since 1977. From 1981 through 1991 he was head of the cataloging support service, an internal processing center for many of Harvard's departmental libraries. From 1986 through 1992 he was a member of OCLC's Cataloging and Database Services Advisory Committee. Since 1992 he has been active in developing the technical services workstation in use in the cataloging services department in Harvard's Widener Library. He was a participant in the seminar on copy cataloging at the Library of Congress in 1992, and he was involved in LC's Cooperative Cataloging Council as chair of both its task group on availability and distribution of records and its task group on automation. At present he is chair of the Program for Cooperative Cataloging's standing committee on automation. He is a frequent speaker on topics related to technical services workstations and technical services in an online world.

Mark Bendig is consulting systems analyst, Office of Research, OCLC Online Computer Library Center, Inc., in Dublin, Ohio. On the staff of OCLC since 1978, he created the first version of the ILL MicroEnhancer and was responsible for designing and coding the user interface for Search CD450 and the Dewey for Windows. He holds a degree in electronics engineering from the Ohio State University.

Julia C. Blixrud is senior program officer at the Association of Research Libraries, Washington, D.C. She was previously director of training and education, CAPCON Library Network, Washington, D.C., where she had primary responsibility for the coordination and expansion of the network's training and educational programs. In that position she was responsible for more than 200 training sessions and continuing education opportunities annually.

Anaclare Frost Evans is systems librarian, systems and technical services, Wayne State University Libraries in Detroit, Michigan. She has held a variety of positions at Wayne State University in both the medical library and in technical services. Previously she was head of the database management and the authority control sections within technical services. She is also a part-time faculty member of the Wayne State University library and information science program. She is a graduate of the Library School at Western Reserve University (now Case Western Reserve University).

Bruce Chr. Johnson is senior library information systems specialist and team leader of the Cataloger's Desktop development team, Cataloging Distribution Service, Library of Congress, Washington, D.C. Long active in ALA, he edited the *Guidelines for Bibliographic Description of Reproductions* (1995, ALA) for ALCTS and is currently chair of ALCTS's Cataloging and Classification Section (CCS). He received his M.S.L.S. from Case Western Reserve University.

Gary L. Strawn is authorities librarian/cataloger and library systems analyst/programmer, Northwestern University Libraries, Evanston, Illinois. He is the author of dozens of programs for personal computers, including a stand-alone acquisitions system, authority record creation and card-printing programs, and the Cataloger's Toolkit. He is also author of several programs and enhancements for the mainframe NOTIS system. He received his A.M.L.S. from the University of Michigan in 1977.

Bruce Trumble is team leader, German and Scandinavian cataloging team, cataloging services department, Harvard College Library at Harvard University. He currently chairs the standing committee on ergonomic issues and policy for the Harvard College Library. He received his M.S.L.S. from Columbia University in 1978.

Diane Vizine-Goetz is consulting research scientist, Office of Research, OCLC Online Computer Library Center, Inc., Dublin, Ohio. She is a prolific author on issues related to retrieval and access and the Dewey Decimal Classification and has a long-standing interest in cataloging productivity tools. She has her M.L.S. from the State University of New York at Buffalo and a Ph.D. in information and library science from Case Western Reserve University.

David Williamson is senior descriptive cataloger, social sciences cataloging division, and senior cooperative cataloger, regional and cooperative cataloging division, Library of Congress, Washington, D.C. He has been at the Library of Congress since he graduated from the University of Virginia in 1982. He has always been involved in automation at LC, first with office automation and more recently with automating the cataloging process. He received his M.L.S. from the Catholic University of America.

Mark Wilson is director for research and development for the Biblio-File division of The Library Corporation, Inwood, West Virginia. In addition to eight years with The Library Corporation, he spent twenty years as director or dean of learning resources in several academic libraries. He received his M.L.S. from the University of Oregon and has a Ph.D. from the University of Michigan.